NEW DEVELOPMENTS IN CHILD ABUSE RESEARCH

NEW DEVELOPMENTS IN CHILD ABUSE RESEARCH

STANLEY M. STURT

EDITOR

Nova Science Publishers, Inc.
New York

NOTICE TO THE READER

The Publisher has taken reasonable care in the preparation of this book, but makes no expressed or implied warranty of any kind and assumes no responsibility for any errors or omissions. No liability is assumed for incidental or consequential damages in connection with or arising out of information contained in this book. The Publisher shall not be liable for any special, consequential, or exemplary damages resulting, in whole or in part, from the readers' use of, or reliance upon, this material.

This publication is designed to provide accurate and authoritative information with regard to the subject matter covered herein. It is sold with the clear understanding that the Publisher is not engaged in rendering legal or any other professional services. If legal or any other expert assistance is required, the services of a competent person should be sought. FROM A DECLARATION OF PARTICIPANTS JOINTLY ADOPTED BY A COMMITTEE OF THE AMERICAN BAR ASSOCIATION AND A COMMITTEE OF PUBLISHERS.

LIBRARY OF CONGRESS CATALOGING-IN-PUBLICATION DATA

New developments in child abuse research / Stanley M. Sturt (editor).
    p. cm.
Includes index.
ISBN 1-59454-980-X
1. Child abuse. 2. Abused children. 3. Abused children--Mental health. I. Sturt, Stanley M.
HV6626.5.N45   2006
362.76--dc22   006000709

Published by Nova Science Publishers, Inc. ✦New York

CONTENTS

PREFACE

Child abuse and neglect is as, at a minimum any recent act or failure to act on the part of a parent or caretaker which results in death, serious physical or emotional harm, sexual abuse or exploitation; or an act or failure to act which presents an imminent risk of serious harm. Four major types of maltreatment are usually included: neglect, physical abuse, sexual abuse, and emotional abuse. Although any of the forms of child maltreatment may be found separately, they often occur in combination. This book presents issues and research in this field.

Chapter 1 presents five cases of fatal child abuse and highlight the problems associated with social treatment of child abuse cases in Japan. Recently, in Japan, there have been fatal child abuse cases in which neighbors have been aware of the signs of abuse but have not notified the Child Care Authorities. Lack of concern about child welfare in the community is the greatest obstacle to protecting children at risk of abuse. The most effective means of preventing child abuse is to educate the community about how to recognize the signs of abuse and to inform the authorities. The authors emphasize that the community has an obligation to protect children against crime, including child abuse. The role of the Social Services in preventing child abuse has been extended. Forensic pathologists are now required to play key roles in child abuse prevention, and in Japan their activity should be extended to the administrative field.

Clinicians, educators, and researchers of child development have long known that child maltreatment leads to language delays and deficits. Empirical studies have documented some striking differences in how maltreating parents interact with their children. Given that caregiver input plays a central role in language acquisition, one might expect there to be a relationship between specific qualities of parental input, and specific language impairments, in maltreating dyads. However, few controlled studies of language acquisition in maltreated individuals have been carried out; of those studies, most have used gross qualitative rather than specific quantitative measures of language ability. Chapter 2 reviews the literature on language abilities in maltreated children across development, with a particular focus on vocabulary (lexical) skills and grammatical development, where the impact of maltreatment has been shown to be greatest; we report in detail an empirical investigation of syntactic complexity in maltreated children at age five. Drawing on both the specific findings and the literature reviewed, we discuss possible mechanisms that may link differences in parent-child interactions in maltreatment to language delays.

Chapter 3 compared the effects of Dyadic Developmental Psychotherapy on a group of children who met the DSM IV criteria for Reactive Attachment Disorder with a control group of children who also met the DSM-IV criteria for Reactive Attachment Disorder. All children in the study had serious histories of chronic maltreatment and abuse during the first three years of life. The measures were taken four years after children in the treatment group ended therapy. The measures used were the Child Behavior Checklist (CBCL), also called the Achenback, and the Randolph Attachment Disorder Questionnaire (RADQ). This study extends the results of an earlier study that compared these two groups of children one year after therapy ended. That earlier study found clinically and statistically significant changes in the variables measured one year after treatment ended for the children receiving Dyadic Developmental Psychotherapy, but no changes for the children in the control group. This study confirms the findings of that earlier study. The children in the treatment group continued to show clinically and statistically significant improvements in the variable measured four years after treatment ended. The children in the control group, all of whom continued to receive "usual care" from other treatment providers, showed clinically and statistically significant *deteriorations* in their behavior on the variables measured. This study confirms that Dyadic Developmental Psychotherapy is an effective treatment for children with trauma-attachment disorders and that the positive effects of treatment continue for at least four years. Traditional forms of treatment such as play therapies, talk-therapies, behavior-modification, level systems, charts, stickers, and similar treatment methods are ineffective with such children, but Dyadic Developmental Psychotherapy is an effective treatment method.

Reduced autobiographical memory specificity, or overgeneral memory, is an important feature and vulnerability factor of depression and is closely associated with a trauma or abuse history in childhood. Chapter 4 examined the relation between autobiographical memory specificity and trauma in 28 patients with major depression. Trauma-related intrusive memories and efforts to avoid such memories were significantly related to reduced autobiographical memory specificity, whereas trauma itself was not. Moreover, this relationship could not be explained by a reduction in working memory capacity. Results further revealed rumination as a moderator of the relation between trauma and overgeneral memory. The results as a whole suggest that how one copes with trauma or abuse afterwards is of more importance for developing overgeneral memory following trauma, than mere trauma experience itself.

As children have become more involved in the legal system as victims or witnesses, special accommodations for child witnesses have been developed and utilized. One often used accommodation is hearsay testimony in place of, or in conjunction with, the child's in-court testimony. Although hearsay has traditionally been inadmissible, there are numerous exceptions to the hearsay rule that are relevant to child sexual abuse trials. In chapter 5, the legal standards for admitting hearsay testimony and relevant US Supreme Court cases addressing accommodations for child witnesses are discussed in the context of hearsay evidence. Research has only just begun to empirically explore the impact of hearsay testimony on trial results. The following areas of research relating to hearsay testimony are discussed: 1) the accuracy of hearsay witnesses' reports of children's statements and 2) jurors' reactions to hearsay testimony. Finally, the legal implications of this research are analyzed.

In the past year, expert testimony and its role in child abuse trials has received much unwelcome publicity in the United Kingdom. The case of Angela Cannnings, wrongfully convicted on the basis of testimony by Professor Sir Roy Meadow, has not been unique. Rather, it is only one of several instances where the testimony of experts has, directly or indirectly, caused courts to decide cases wrongly. Chapter 6 will first describe the instances where this phenomenon has been seen to occur, then continue by analysing what lessons may be learnt in order to minimise the chances of a recurrence. The chapter will thus consider how the courts should treat medical experts and their evidence in future. In particular, it focuses on a paradox that exists in the UK between the civil and criminal courts. In the former, recent developments have ensured that medical evidence is critically evaluated by the judge - a response to perceived medical dominance and a reassertion of the role of the judiciary as the ultimate arbiters of behaviour. In the criminal courts, in the wake of the successful appeal by Angela Cannings, the opposite has occurred. The courts now hold that, in the criminal sphere, expert evidence for the defence should be taken as demonstrating 'reasonable doubt', and thus requiring acquittal. The chapter argues that the approach taken by the criminal courts is counterproductive, and does not prevent miscarriages of justice. It concludes by suggesting proposals for how courts should treat medical experts and their evidence.

How many are the victims of child sexual abuse? Of course, there is no univocal and certain answer to the question as explained in chapter 7. For a trustworthy assessment of the problem, all victims should in fact disclose what happened to them to the police or, otherwise, describe and register in a special "anonymous notepad" every episode of violence, so that not a single incident would be lost. Anyhow, even if this was the case, the actual number of sexually abused victims would still be obscure. It stands to reason that the obscured rate of child sexual abuse, along with that "hidden number" to it related, are so far quite elevated. In spite of that, many other countries tried to define by means of reliable surveys the true extent of the problem.

Despite its occurrence throughout history, sexual violence within the context of armed conflict has long been dismissed and minimized by historians, scholars, and military and political leaders. While often regarded as a private crime or stemming from the 'unfortunate' behaviour of renegade soldiers, literature over the past decade has revealed the widespread and systematic nature of wartime sexual violence. Drawing on examples from the former Yugoslavia, Rwanda, and Sierra Leone, this paper examines the phenomenon of wartime sexual violence against girls. In particular, it addresses the prevalence and patterns of wartime sexual violence, its meaning, purpose, and importantly, its long-term effects. Also explored are the historical and contemporary international responses to the phenomenon. Chapter 8 highlights the ways in which sexual violence is used as a strategy of conflict, acting as a weapon of war where ultimately, girls continue to be victims of a devastating form of child abuse.

In: New Developments in Child Abuse Research
Editor: Stanley M. Sturt, pp. 1-22

ISBN 1-59454-980-X
© 2006 Nova Science Publishers, Inc.

Chapter 1

PROBLEMS WITH THE SOCIAL TREATMENT OF CHILD ABUSE CASES IN JAPAN: THE FORENSIC PATHOLOGIST'S VIEW

Masataka Nagao and Yoshitaka Maeno

Department of Forensic Medical Science, Nagoya City University, Graduate School of Medical Sciences, Nagoya 467-8601, Japan

ABSTRACT

We present five cases of fatal child abuse and highlight the problems associated with social treatment of child abuse cases in Japan. Recently, in Japan, there have been fatal child abuse cases in which neighbors have been aware of the signs of abuse but have not notified the Child Care Authorities. Lack of concern about child welfare in the community is the greatest obstacle to protecting children at risk of abuse. The most effective means of preventing child abuse is to educate the community about how to recognize the signs of abuse and to inform the authorities. We emphasize that the community has an obligation to protect children against crime, including child abuse.

The role of the Social Services in preventing child abuse has been extended. Forensic pathologists are now required to play key roles in child abuse prevention, and in Japan their activity should be extended to the administrative field.

Keywords: Child abuse; Neglect; Child welfare; Social Service; Education

1. INTRODUCTION

Child abuse has been recognized as a widespread social problem since the early 1960s [1]. It can include physical and sexual violence, neglect, or mental abuse, and has reached epidemic proportions in some industrialized countries [2]. It is a problem of great public concern, and has gained wide attention among pediatricians, psychiatrists, social workers, forensic pathologists, and workers in other fields. In Japan, a new anti-child abuse law came into effect in 2000, giving the government legal powers to challenge the custody rights of abusive parents. This law obliges doctors, nurses, teachers and welfare officials to be on the lookout for early signs of child abuse and to report it to the authorities. Even so, many children still die as a result of abuse. We previously reported a case of severe neglect in a girl aged 3 years and 20 days, who died of starvation [3]. Although several doctors, health visitors, public health practitioners, and welfare workers had expressed concern about this case, they were unable to save the child. Such workers should be recognized as playing key roles in the protection and care of children. Another major problem is failure by the public to notify the Child Care Authorities about child abuse, even when it is recognized.

We present here one case of severe neglect [3]; the fatal physical abuse of a 7-year-old girl who was confined to her home by her mother and stepfather [4]; two fatal cases of child abuse in which neighbors were unaware of the victims' disappearance for long periods [5]; and one fatal case, involving a 4-year-old boy, in which the neighbors had recognized the signs of child abuse [4]. These cases highlight the problems associated with social attitudes toward child abuse in Japan.

2. CASE REPORTS

Case 1 [3]

Case Profile

A girl aged 3 years and 20 days was living with her 21-year-old natural parents and her brother, aged 1 year and 6 months. The parents had not cared for the victim, had not fed her sufficiently, and had finally put her in an open packing case. One day in winter they went out with their son leaving the victim alone at home. When they returned home that night, they found her dead in the packing case.

Autopsy Findings

Autopsy revealed an emaciated girl 89 cm tall and weighing 5 kg. She had well-demarcated ribs and a concave abdomen (Fig.1A). Decubitus ulcers were present on the left temporal and left occipital areas of the head and on the left of the back and pelvis (Fig. 2). Bilateral contracture of the knee joints and bilateral edema of the feet were observed (Fig. 1A). Dried feces and urine adhered to the waist, hip, anus, vulva and the backs of both thighs (Fig. 1B). Recent subcutaneous hemorrhages were observed on the right temporal area and the face, and a few scars were present on the forehead (Fig. 3). The muscles of the head, face, trunk, and lower and upper extremities were flaccid. There was no subcutaneous or omental fat (Fig. 1B,C). The orbital adipose tissue was spent and the eyes were open. Because of drying of the eyes, the choroid could be seen through the dried sclera. The stomach and small intestine were contracted and empty, and the large bowel contained hard pellets of fecal material. The weights of most of the victim's organs were markedly less than the normal averages (Table 1). The thymus was extremely atrophic (1.7 g). In addition, there was almost no glycogen in the liver on PAS (para-amino salicylic acid) staining (Fig. 4).

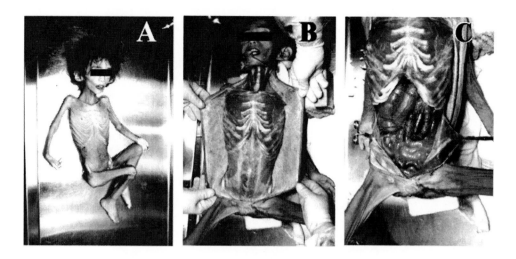

Fig. 1. Case 1: A. View of the victim in the supine position. Bilateral contracture of the knee joints and bilateral edema of the feet can be seen. B. Complete lack of subcutaneous fat. C. Complete lack of omental fat.

Table 1. Weights of organs of Case 1 at autopsy, in comparison with the mean weights in 2-year-old and 3-year-old Japanese girls

Organ	Victim (g)	Average±S.D.[*] 2 y.o.	Average±S.D.[*] 3 y.o.
Brain	980	1180 ± 96	1234 ± 110
Heart	40	62 ±8.1	72 ± 10.2
Left lung	35	95 ± 26.6	114 ± 23.8
Right lung	40	106 ± 30.2	133 ± 33.2
Liver	210	440 ± 85	475 ± 72
Pancreas	6.8	23 ± 6.1	30 ± 9.3
Spleen	10	41 ± 14.1	45 ± 8.8
Left kidney	20	40 ± 6.5	43 ± 6.6
Right kidney	25	37 ± 5.6	42 ± 7.3
Left adrenal gland	1.7	2.2 ± 0.95	2.4 ± 0.87
Right adrenal gland	1.4	1.9 ± 0.89	2.2 ± 0.72
Thymus	1.7	25.1 ± 10.2	30.9 ± 10.9

*Jpn J *Legal Med* 1992; 46: 225-235.

Background

When the victim was 2 years and 8 months old, her mother had taken her to the hospital. At that time, her body weight was 9 kg and the pediatrician diagnosed her as being malnourished. The pediatrician pressed the mother to have the girl admitted, but the mother rejected this recommendation and took her back home. Six days later the mother brought the victim back to the same hospital. Her body weight had increased to 11 kg (Fig. 5), so the doctor's worries about possible child abuse were negated.

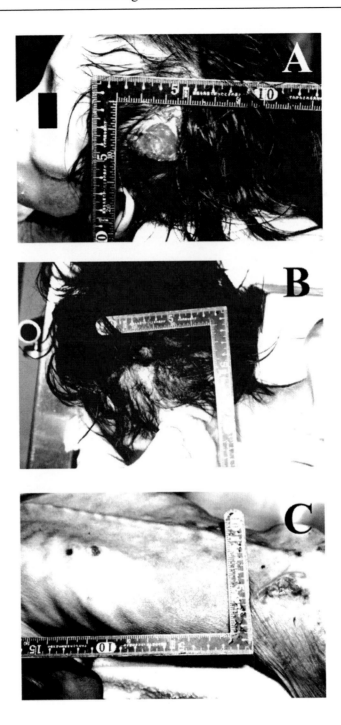

Fig. 2. Case 1: Decubitus ulcers found on victim. A. Left temporal area. B. Left occipital area. C. Left side of the back and pelvis.

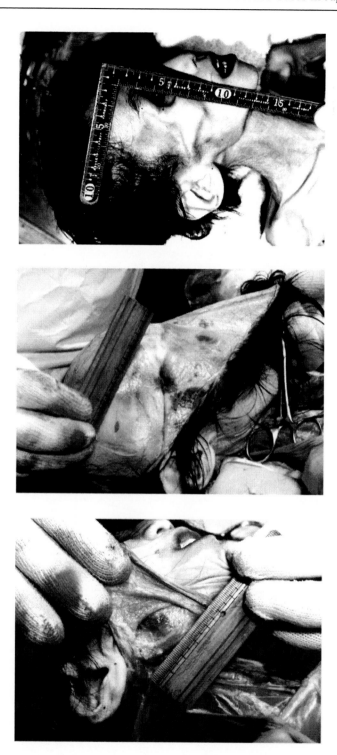

Fig. 3. Case 1: Recent subcutaneous hemorrhages on the right temporal area and the right side of the face.

PAS Stain (Liver)

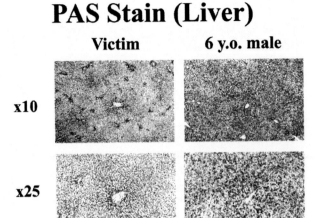

Fig. 4. Case 1: PAS staining of the victim's liver. Corresponding specimens from a 6-year-old boy are included for comparison.

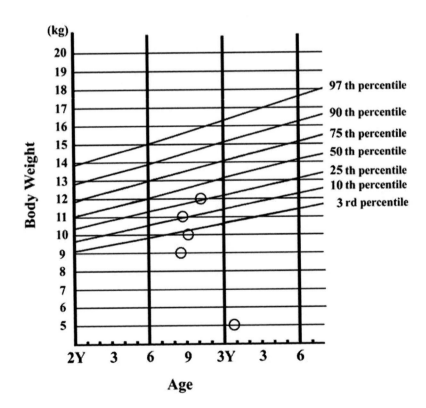

Fig. 5. Case 1: Changes in the victim's body weight (open circles) on a standard growth curve for Japanese girls.

When the victim was 2 years and 9 months old, she entered the care of her grandmother. Her body weight was 10 kg and she could not stand alone. The grandmother cared for her adequately but wondered why her grandchild ate so hungrily. At 2 years, 10 months, and 11 days old, the girl was returned to her parents. Her body weight by this time was 12 kg.

The parents confessed that they kept the victim in a small room for about 30 days, and then in a packing case. The amount of food served to her decreased with time (Fig. 6). When she was 3 years and 20 days old, she was found dead in the packing case. Her body weight was 5 kg at the time of death, having decreased by 7 kg (58.3% of her previous body weight) in 70 days.

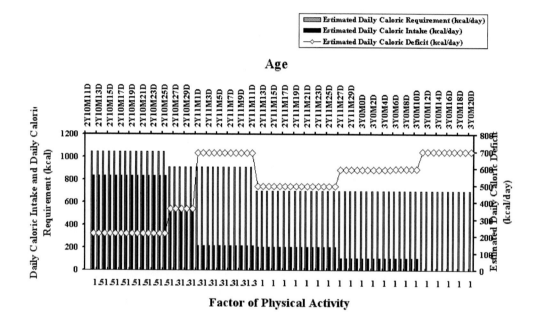

Fig. 6. Case 1: Changes in the estimated daily caloric requirement, intake, and deficit of the victim.

Calculation of Caloric Deficit

The Recommended Dietary Allowance for Japanese, 6th edition (Public Health Council, Ministry of Health and Welfare, Japan), indicates that the requirement for basal metabolism in a 2-year-old Japanese girl is 700 kcal/day [6]. Activity factors are given as 1.3 for low physical activity (I), 1.5 for moderate activity (II), 1.7 for light-heavy activity (III) and 1.9 for heavy activity (IV). Therefore, the daily recommended dietary allowance for a 2-year-old Japanese girl is 700 kcal/day × the appropriate factor for physical activity, plus 16 kcal/day, which is the number of calories needed for weight gain. Because this child had been neglected, and had not been fed enough food, we omitted the caloric allowance for weight gain, as described below.

From statements by the parents, we calculated the daily caloric requirement of the victim as 700 kcal/day (basal metabolism), multiplied by a factor for physical activity (Fig. 6). The victim had stayed inside her house for the first 2 weeks, without playing outside. The parents then locked her in a small room for approximately the next 2 weeks. From this information, we estimated the factors for physical activity as 1.5 and 1.3, respectively. After that, she lay in a packing case until death. The activity factor in this period was taken as 1.0. The daily caloric deficit was calculated from the difference between the calculated daily caloric intake and the estimated daily caloric requirement, based on the estimated activity factor for the victim. The range of percentage body fat at age 1 year is 28%–30%, and that at ages 4–6 years is 22% [7]. We assumed the range at ages 2–3 years to be 24%–26%. As the victim was a thin girl, her percentage body fat was assumed to be 20%, leading to a calculated fat content of 2.4 kg (12kg x 0.2). The internal autopsy findings revealed that the victim had no subcutaneous or omental fat. Therefore, assuming that 2.4 kg of the weight deficit was attributable to loss of fat and the rest to loss of protein, we calculated the caloric deficit. Fat reserves of 2.4 kg would be sufficient to compensate for a caloric deficit of 2,400 g × 7.2 kcal/g body fat [8]. We assumed that, after the fat reserves had been exhausted, protein would have been used to compensate for the caloric deficit (4 kcal/g protein) until death. On the basis of these assumptions, the calculated body weight at the time of death was 4.988 kg (Fig. 7). When we assumed the percentage body fat to be 25%, the calculated body weight was 5.468 kg.

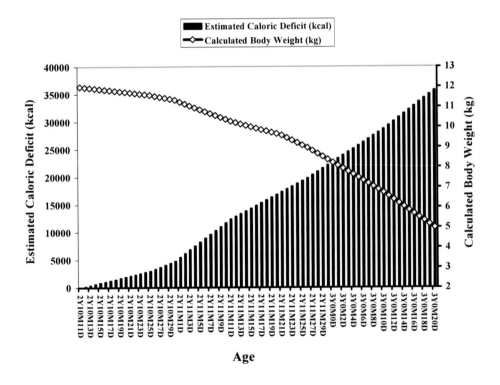

Fig. 7. Case 1: Changes in the calculated body weight of the victim and the estimated caloric deficit.

Case 2. [4]

A 7-year-old girl living with her mother and stepfather was confined to the house and prevented from going to school in the end of May. One month after the girl had first been prevented from attending school, her teacher visited her house, but the parents prohibited the teacher from meeting her. After the teacher's visit, the intensity of physical abuse increased for about 3 weeks. One day in July the stepfather lifted and droped repeatedly her body several times and then found that she was not breathing. The parents called the ambulance immediately, and as soon as the emergency medical technicians arrived they performed emergency treatment for cardiac arrest, then transferred the girl to hospital. Although the doctors attempt resuscitation, they could not save the patient. Because of the presence of bilateral massive swelling and subcutaneous hemorrhage on the face (Fig. 8), as well as many round skin lesions, which were initially suspected of being cigarette burns, on her legs (Fig. 9), a judicial autopsy was performed.

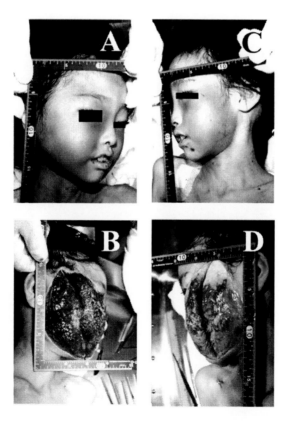

Fig. 8 [4]. Case 2: A 7-year-old girl. Death from traumatic shock. Bilateral massive swelling and subcutaneous hemorrhage of the face can be seen. A. Right lateral view of the face. B. Massive subcutaneous hemorrhage on the right side of the face. C. Left lateral view of the face of Case 2. D. Massive subcutaneous hemorrhage on the left side of the face.

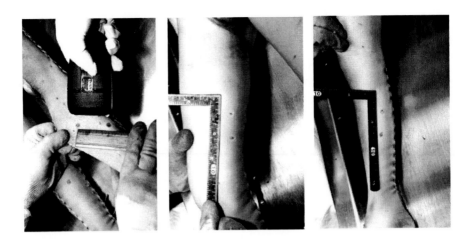

Fig. 9 [4]. Case 2: The distance between the paired skin lesions found on the leg were found to match the distance between the electrodes of the stun gun.

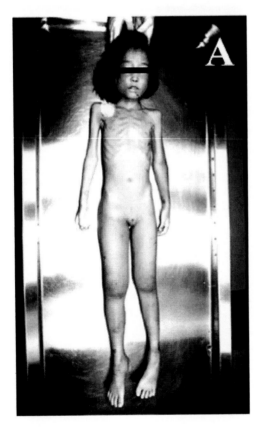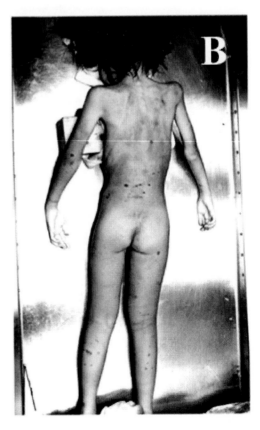

Fig. 10 [4]. Case 2: A. View of the victim in the supine position. The right leg was thicker than the left leg. B. View of the victim in the prone position. Many excoriations and bruises were present on the back.

Table 2. Weights of organs of Case 2 at autopsy, compared with the mean weights in 7-year-old Japanese girls

Organ	Victim (g)	Average ± S.D.[*] 7 y.o.
Brain	1,235	1,290 ± 91
Heart	90	112 ± 18.2
Left lung	110	182 ± 65.2
Right lung	110	218 ± 65.6
Liver	500	648 ± 101
Pancreas	30	41 ± 8.2
Spleen	40	54 ± 10.9
Left kidney	70	63 ± 9.2
Right kidney	60	62 ± 10.3
Left adrenal gland	3	2.5 ± 0.99
Right adrenal gland	2.3	2.4 ± 0.66
Thymus	5.8	28.2 ± 14.4

*Jpn J *Legal Med* 1992; 46: 225-235.

Table 3. Laboratory Data for Case 2 [4]

Item	Volume on admission	Normal range
BUN (mg/dL)	18	7.7 – 19.6
Creatinine (mg/dL)	0.5	0.4 – 0.8
Na (mEq/L)	138	139.9 – 144.7
K (mEq/L)	8.2	4.26 – 5.14
Cl(mEq/L)	104	103.1 – 106.7
CRP (mg/dL)	0.78	0.044 – 1.070
Blood FDP (µg/mL)	400 <	5.6 – 8.0
RBC ($\times 10^4$/µL)	117	400 – 520
Hb (g/dL)	3.7	11.5 – 15.5
Ht (%)	12.1	35 – 45
Plts. ($\times 10^4$/µL)	7.8	15.0 – 35.0
WBC (/µL)	8,400	5.5 – 15.5
AST(GOT)	313	15 – 37
ALT(GPT)	119	4 – 24
LDH (U/L)	1,873	280 – 588
ChE (U/L)	92	249 – 493
Amylase (U/L)	47	62 – 218
CK (U/L)	957	52 – 249
t-Bil (mg/dL)	1.5	0.45 – 0.99
d-Bil (mg/dL)	0.5	0.27 – 0.73
t-Protein (g/dL)	5.1	6.4 – 8.1

Scars from wearing handcuffs were observed on the girl's wrists and ankles, and cigarette lighter burn was present on the right thumb. The right leg was thicker than the left leg, and double linear marks were observed on the lateral side of the right thigh. The distance between the pairs of skin lesions on the leg was found to match that between the electrodes of a stun gun (4–5 cm). Many excoriations, bruises, and massive subcutaneous hemorrhages were found on the body (Fig. 10). The weights of most of the victim's organs were less than the normal averages (Table 2). The thymus was extremely atrophic (5.8 g).

Examination of the victim's laboratory data on admission (Table 3) revealed a low red blood cells (RBC) count and a high level of creatine kinase (CK), which was present in myocytes in the victim's blood. These findings suggest that the girl had suffered chronic anemia and massive muscular damage from repeated violence. From these findings, we diagnosed the cause of death as traumatic shock.

Case 3. [5]

A boy aged 1 year and 6 months was punched by his father because he had consumed snacks and juice without permission. His mother found him dead in bed the following morning. The father did not call the ambulance or the police, and to delay putrefaction, he placed a pile of ice on each side of the victim. One and a half months later, the father committed suicide by hanging. This case surfaced only after the father's death, and we performed a judicial autopsy on the dead child. Old subcutaneous hemorrhages were observed on the trunk, thighs, and chin, and bilaterally in the mandibular and occipital areas (Fig. 11). The left cerebral hemisphere was light reddish, suggesting that the cause of death might have been subdural hemorrhage (Fig. 12).

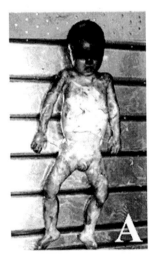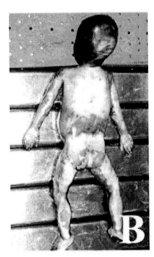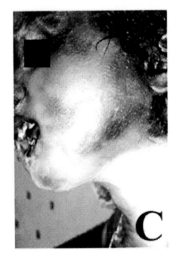

Fig. 11 . Case 3: A. View of the victim in the supine position. B. View of the victim in the prone position. C. Bruising is evident on the chin and the left mandibular area.

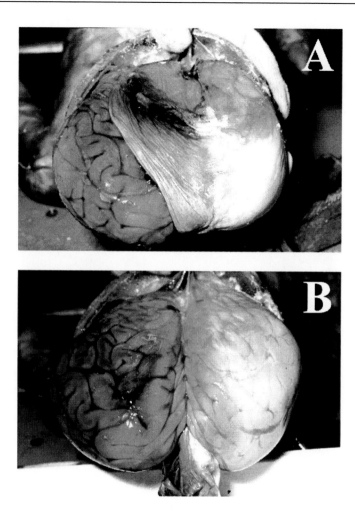

Fig. 12 . Case 3: A. Localized hemoglobin in the dura mater. B. Hemoglobin infiltration on the surface of the left cerebral hemisphere.

Case 4. [5]

A girl aged 3 years and 5 months who had been living with her parents, four brothers, and six sisters was reported to have been missing for more than one year. The police interrogated her mother, and in accordance with the mother's statements the victim was found in a coolerbox on the veranda. About 1 year previously, the mother had found the victim lying dead on the floor, and had wrapped her in a blanket and a plastic bag and hidden the body in a closet. The following summer, in response to complaints from a neighbor about the stench, the victim's body had been transferred to the coolerbox. The body was badly decomposed and adipoceratous (Fig. 13A, B), and the stomach was ruptured (Fig. 13C). These findings suggested that the victim had suffered blunt force to the abdomen. However, because of the severe postmortem changes, the cause of death could not be determined with certainty.

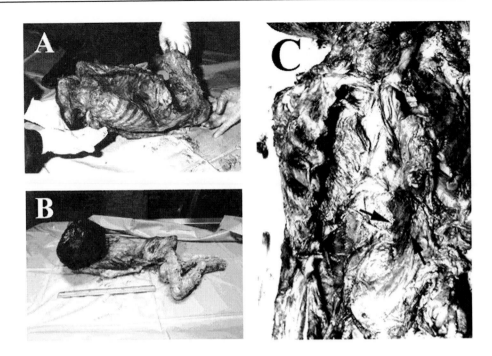

Fig. 13. Case 4: A. View of the victim in the supine position. B. View of the victim in the prone position. C. Internal appearance of the abdominal organs. The stomach is ruptured along the lesser curvature (arrows).

Case 5.[4]

A 4-year-old boy living with his mother and stepfather had broken his left tibia, and his left leg was then placed in a plaster cast (Fig. 14). At mid-night, he had a scratch on his left ankle. Then the father-in-law had the victim's hands tied behind the back, and he had cried bitterly. The father-in-law put a face towel into his mouth and gagged him with gauze. When the victim had stopped roaring, they found him dead.

Several brownish round bruises about 1 cm in diameter on both sides of the mandibular area (Fig. 15) and a spiral fracture of the left tibia (Fig. 16) were observed. Hematomas were present along the fracture lines on the left tibia. Excoriation and hemorrhage were not observed on the surface or in the subcutaneous tissues of the left tibia. These findings suggested that the victim had suffered recurrent physical abuse.

Grooves were observed around both wrists (Fig. 17A). Stomach contents (Fig. 17B) were present in the respiratory tract, and both lungs were congested and edematous (Fig. 17C). Petechial hemorrhages were observed in the eyelids bilaterally and in the palpebral and bulbar conjunctivae (Fig. 18). From these findings, we diagnosed the cause of death as asphyxia by aspiration of the stomach contents.

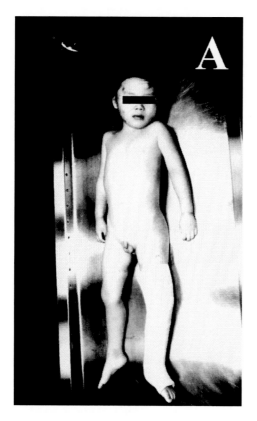
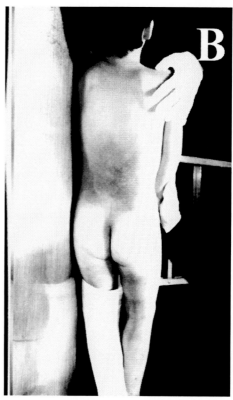

Fig. 14. Case 5: A 4 year-old boy. Death from asphyxia by aspiration of stomach contents. A. View of the victim in the supine position. B. View of the victim in the prone position.

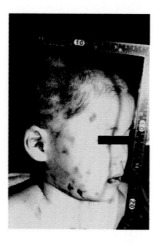
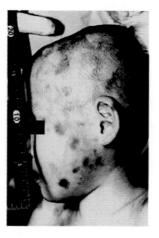

Fig. 15 [4]. Case 5. Several bruises can be seen on the face.

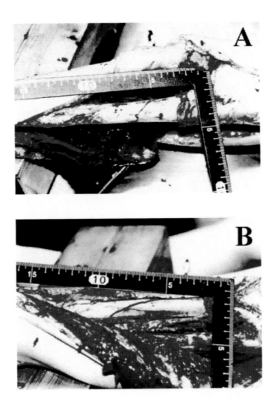

Fig. 16 [4]. Case 5: A. Spiral fracture of the left tibia. B. The fracture was enlarged by supination of the knee joint and pronation of the ankle joint.

Fig 17. Case 5: A. Grooves around both wrists of the victim. B. Stomach contents. C. Stomach contents present in the bronchus.

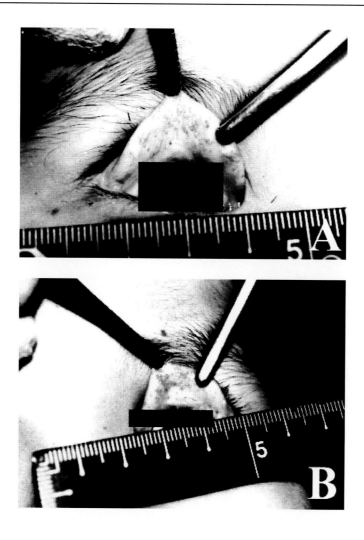

Fig. 18. Case 5: Petechial hemorrhages in the bilateral eyelids and in the palpebral and bulbar conjunctivae in the victim. A. Right. B. Left.

2. DISCUSSION

In Case 1 there was no evidence that the girl's filthy diaper had been changed. The autopsy findings of the victim revealed that muscle and organ proteins had been consumed and the stores of glycogen in the liver had been burned up. These findings suggest that the malnutrition was due to marasmus (the lack of both calories and protein), not kwashiorkor (dietary protein deficiency with a still substantial intake of energy) [9]. The victim had gained 2 kg in 6 days at the age of 2 years and 6 months (Fig. 5). These facts indicate that she had not suffered from an intestinal absorption disorder, but instead had been maltreated by her parents.

The presence of decubitus ulcers on the victim's left side, contracture of both knee joints, and edema of both feet indicates that the victim had been lying on her left side for a long time. Conversely, recent subcutaneous hemorrhages on the right side of her face indicated that her parents had hit her on the head and face several days before her death. Scars on the forehead suggested that the victim had suffered recurrent physical abuse.

Abused or neglected children suffer serious stress. Stressors trigger physiological responses, including activation of the hypothalamic-pituitary-adrenal axis, which releases glucocorticoids. An increase in endogenous glucocorticoid levels induces apoptosis of the thymocytes in the cortex of the thymus, resulting in thymic involution [10,11]. Thymic involution is an important factor in determining child abuse, and has been reported to be an important parameter for estimating the degree and duration of child abuse [12]. The victim's thymus was severely affected, showing that she had been suffering serious stress and severe malnutrition for a long time.

To verify that the parents had maltreated the victim, from the parents' statement we developed a theoretical calculation model of her caloric deficit. Although the victim had no access to water, the parents gave her 100 to 150 mL milk once every few days. The degree of dehydration was unclear. One previous study [13] classified dehydration as mild (5%), moderate (10%), or severe (15%). Thus, we extrapolated the hydrated death weights to be 5.263 kg (5 kg÷0.95) to 5.882 kg (5 kg÷0.85). The model assumed a body fat content of 20% or 25%. It also assumed that protein would be used for energy only after the fat reserves had been exhausted. In reality, both fat and protein are broken down at the same time. However, in this case, almost all the body fat was spent on compensating for the caloric deficit. The calculated body weight of 4.988-5.468kg at death was close to the hydrated actual weight. Therefore, this theoretical model verified the parents' statements.

Madea and Brissie, in reporting on the starvation of a 6-week-old baby, calculated the number of days of total food and liquid deprivation [13]. The rate of daily physical activity is stable in a 6-week-old baby, and the daily caloric requirement can be calculated reliably. However, the daily physical activity of young children varies, so estimating caloric deficit is more difficult in starved young children than in starved infants. Our calculation method is more applicable to cases of nutritional neglect than that described in the previous report [13]. To verify the reliability of the statements of perpetrators, it might be useful to calculate the caloric deficit on the basis of their statements, as described here.

About 4 months before the death of Case 1, her mother had taken her to a hospital. At that time, her body weight was 9 kg and the pediatrician diagnosed her as being malnourished. The pediatrician pressed the mother to have the victim admitted, but the mother rejected this recommendation and took the girl back home. Six days later, the mother brought the victim back to the same hospital. At this time, her body weight had increased to 11 kg, and the doctor's doubts about possible child abuse were negated.

A crucial factor in this case was the inability of the pediatrician to recognize the case as one of child neglect, because of the 2-kg weight gain shown by the victim in 6 days. Although awareness of, and attention to, child abuse has recently improved among Japanese clinicians, it is still inadequate compared with that in the United States. Japanese medical school courses offer only a few hours of lectures on child abuse. To protect Japanese children against abuse, it is important that medical students and interns are educated adequately about child abuse during their undergraduate and postgraduate training. The main aim of receiving training should be to acquire the ability to recognize the signs and symptoms of physical abuse, neglect, and sexual abuse. Physical indicators of child abuse include bruises on uncommonly injured body surfaces; marks made by blunt instruments, burns, human hands or bite;

evidence of poor care or failure to thrive; scalds; and unexplained retinal hemorrhages. Injuries of the genitourinary tract, perineal pain, and sexually transmitted diseases are indicative of sexual abuse. Knowledge of child abuse should be shared among medical practitioners, public health practitioners, and welfare workers [14].

The crucial problem for treatment in Case 2 was that the teacher had not been able to meet with the victim and confirm her safety. The anti-child abuse law in Japan defines child abuse as physical abuse, neglect, sexual abuse, or emotional maltreatment. This girl was confined to her home by her parents, who had prevented her from coming to school. Truancy, which is not defined as child abuse by the law, was the result of the parents' locking the girl in the house, and we should therefore recognize this case as one of neglect and therefore child abuse as defined by the law. If the parents of truanting pupils prohibit teachers from visiting them at home, then schools should recognize these cases as child abuse and cooperate with the Child Abuse Authorities in taking action. However, in Case 2, the school was unable to recognize the signs of abuse and did not move to save the victim. Moreover, two severe abuse cases of confined schoolchildren to their home by their parents, similar to Case 2, have occurred in Japan after 1 year and 2.5 years in Japan [15,16]. These results indicate that educators in Japan have not yet learned their lesson from Case 2. To prevent abuse of schoolchildren, teachers should, at the very least, acquire knowledge of child abuse, as described above.

On the other hand, there have also been some recent fatal cases of child abuse in which neighbors failed to notify the Child Care Authorities, even though they had recognized the signs of abuse [4]. In Case 5, the neighbors recognized bruises on the face of the victim and his crying at midnight 2 weeks before his death. They notified the caretaker of the apartment where the boy lived, but not the Child Care Authorities. In Cases 3 and 4, the victims' disappearance was not been noticed by neighbors for a long period. The victim in Case 1 might have suffered recurrent physical abuse. Lack of concern about child welfare in the community is the greatest obstacle to protecting children at risk of abuse. The most effective means of preventing child abuse is to educate the community about how to recognize the signs of child abuse and to report it to the authorities. We emphasize that the community has an obligation to protect children from crime, including child abuse.

According to one report of forensic autopsies on battered children in Japan (1990–1999), public support for child welfare could prevent more than 100 murder cases over a 10-year period [17]. Kitamura et al. reported that some negative life events experienced during childhood were correlated with poorer quality of life measures in some subgroups [18]. The roles of the Social Services in preventing child abuse have been extended [19]. Aichi Prefectural Child Welfare Centers (Fig. 19), which deal with child abuse cases occurring in Aichi Prefecture (with the exception Nagoya City), commissioned MN to be their medico-legal adviser in 2002. The duty of the medico-legal adviser is to differentiate injuries on a child's body due to abuse from those due to genuine accidents, and to educate child welfare and health care workers about child abuse [20–22]. As shown in Table 4, MN consulted on 44 cases over a period of 3 years and 5 months, and in almost of these cases the children were successfully separated from their parents. On the basis of forensic pathological evidence, the Centers have been able to separate children from abusive parents with certainty. Welfare and health care workers who attend the lectures are gradually becoming aware that they, themselves, play key roles in the protection and care of children, particularly in respect of the identification and detection of child abuse. To obtain Family Court orders for removal of parental power, expert opinions are exhibited in court, and no fatalities have yet been reported in child abuse cases in which the Centers have been involved. Forensic pathologists are also required to play key roles in the prevention of child abuse [20, 22]. The activities of forensic pathologists in Japan should be extended to the administrative field.

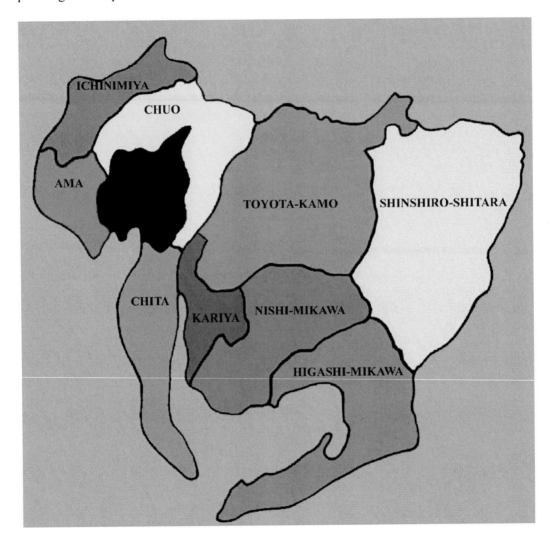

Fig. 19. Aichi Prefectural Child Welfare Centers.

Table.4 Activities of MN as a Medico-legal Adviser for the Aichi Prefectural Child Welfare Centers (April 2002 to August 2005)

Kind of consultation	Number
Consultation on suspected child abuse cases	44
Expert opinion	3
Lecture	8
Total	**55**

REFFERENCES

[1]   Kempe H, Silverman FN, Steele BF, Droegemueller W, Silver HK. The battered child syndrome. *JAMA* 1962; 181:17-24.

[2]   Kobayashi M, Naya Y, Suzuki A, Kato Y, Hirata Y, Gough D. Child abuse viewed through the hot-line in Osaka, Japan. *Acta Pediatr Jpn* 1995; 37: 272-8.

[3]   Nagao M, Maeno Y, Koyama H, Seko-Nakamura Y, Monma-Ohtaki J, Iwasa M, Li XZ, Kawashima N, Yano T. Estimation of caloric deficit in a fatal case of starvation resulting from child abuse. *J Forensic Sci* 2004; 49(5): 1073-6.

[4]   Nagao M. Problems of social treatment for child abuse cases as viewed by a forensic pathologist. *Pediatr Jpn* 2004; 45: 2213-9. (in Japanese)

[5]   Nagao M, Koyama H, Maeno Y, Iwasa M, Kato H, Seko-Nakamura Y, Monma-Ohtaki J, Li XZ, Tsuchimochi T. Two fatal cases of child abuse in which neighbors were unaware of the victims' disappearance for a long period. *Legal Med* 2006:8;48-51.

[6]   Society of informatics for health and nutrition. *Recommended dietary allowance. Dietary reference intakes.*[in Japanese] Tokyo: Dai-Ichi Shuppan Publishing Co. Ltd.,1999.

[7]   Nakamura H, editor. Growth disorders and nutrition of children. [in Japanese] Osaka: Nagai Shoten Co., Ltd., 1998.

[8]   Iwamatsu S, Haccho Y, editors. *Nutrition education.* 3rd ed. Rev. [in Japanese] Tokyo: Ishiyaku Publishers, Inc., 1995.

[9]   Graham GG. Starvation in the modern world. *N Engl J Med* 1993; 328: 1058-1061.

[10]   Gruber J, Sgonc R, Hu YH, Beug H, Wick G. Thymocyte apoptosis inducing by elevated endogeneous corticosterone levels. *Eur J Immunol* 1994; 24: 1115-1121.

[11]   Tarcic N, Ovadia H, Weiss DW, Weidenfeld J. Restraint stress-induced thymic involution. and cell apoptosis are dependent on endogeneous glucocorticoids. *J Neuroimmunol* 1998; 82: 40-46.

[12]   Fukunaga T, Mizoi Y, Yamashita A, Yamada M, Yamamoto Y, Tatsuno Y, Nishi K. Thymus of abused/neglected children. *Forensic Sci Int* 1992; 53: 69-79.

[13]   Meade JL, Brissie M. Infanticide by starvation: calculation of caloric deficit to determine degree of deprivation. *J Forensic Sci* 1985; 30: 1263-1268.

[14]   Henry BM, Ueda R, Shinjo M, Yoshikawa C. Health education for nurses in Japan to combat child abuse. *Nurs Health Sci* 2003; 5: 199-206.

[15]   *Mainichi Shimbun.* 2004. 4. 16.

[16]   *Yomiuri Shimbun.* 2004. 1. 26.

[17]   Planning and Development Committee of Japanese Society of Legal Medicine. Forensic autopsy cases of battered children in Japan (1990-1999). *Nippon Hoigakkai Zasshi* 2002; 56(2/3): 276-86. (in Japanese)

[18]   Kitamura T, Kawakami N, Sakamoto S, Tanigawa T, Ono Y, Fujihara S. Quality of life and its correlates in a community population in a Japanese rural area. *Pshychiatry Clin Neurosci* 2002; 56: 431-41.

[19]   Sakai S, Okuyama M, Inoue N, editors. *Medical Diagnosis and Management of Child Abuse and Neglect.* Tokyo: Nanzando, 2005, (in Japanese)

[20]   *Tokyo Shimbun.* 2005. 2. 28.

[21]   *Shikoku Shimbun.* 2005. 4. 11.

[22] *Chunichi Shimbun*. 2005. 7. 31.

In: New Developments in Child Abuse Research
Editor: Stanley M. Sturt, pp. 23-41

ISBN 1-59454-980-X
© 2006 Nova Science Publishers, Inc.

Chapter 2

CHILD MALTREATMENT: EFFECTS ON GRAMMATICAL AND LEXICAL ASPECTS OF LANGUAGE ACQUISITION

Inge-Marie Eigsti[*]
University of Connecticut

ABSTRACT

Clinicians, educators, and researchers of child development have long known that child maltreatment leads to language delays and deficits. Empirical studies have documented some striking differences in how maltreating parents interact with their children. Given that caregiver input plays a central role in language acquisition, one might expect there to be a relationship between specific qualities of parental input, and specific language impairments, in maltreating dyads. However, few controlled studies of language acquisition in maltreated individuals have been carried out; of those studies, most have used gross qualitative rather than specific quantitative measures of language ability. This chapter reviews the literature on language abilities in maltreated children across development, with a particular focus on vocabulary (lexical) skills and grammatical development, where the impact of maltreatment has been shown to be greatest; we report in detail an empirical investigation of syntactic complexity in maltreated children at age five. Drawing on both the specific findings and the literature reviewed, we discuss possible mechanisms that may link differences in parent-child interactions in maltreatment to language delays.

Key words: Morphosyntax, language acquisition, child abuse, child-directed speech.

---

[*] Correspondence should be addressed to Inge-Marie Eigsti, Department of Psychology, University of Connecticut; 406 Babbidge Road, Unit 1020; Storrs, CT 06269; inge-marie.eigsti@uconn.edu. Part of this work was previously reported in Eigsti and Cicchetti (2004).

INTRODUCTION

Typically-developing children acquire their native language with complete proficiency, within a quite predictable timeframe (Gleitman, 1981), in the face of considerable variability in home environments (e.g., languages, cultures, and child-rearing norms, Lieven, 1994; Pye, 1986) and in internal characteristics of children (e.g., differences in short-term phonological memory, Gathercole *et al.*, 1997). Thus, the process of language acquisition is marked by a striking universality and predictability. However, ever since initial descriptions of the "battered child syndrome" (Kempe *et al.*, 1962), clinicians have observed that child maltreatment has negative impact on language development. Given the highly robust nature of child language acquisition, it might be somewhat surprising that child maltreatment could contribute to quantifiable changes in this process. In this chapter, we review the empirical literature on language acquisition in children who are maltreated, as well as potential mechanisms that may account for the effects.

Origins of Child Language Delays in Maltreatment

The child language acquisition literature provides some clues to the etiology of any differences in language abilities of maltreated children. In one study, the overall syntactic (grammatical) complexity of maternal speech (specifically, the number of clausal units per utterance) was positively correlated with a child's linguistic development (Gleitman *et al.*, 1984). In an observational study, mothers who frequently used yes-no questions (e.g., *is that a blue dog?*) had children who learned the verbal auxiliary system at a faster rate, and that maternal use of verbal deixis (look at that one over there!) was correlated with children's knowledge of inflections and noun phrases (Newport *et al.*, 1979). This study demonstrated negative correlations as well: the children of mothers who frequently used imperatives (go get it!) were typically *slower* to learn the verbal auxiliary system; the same was true for children of mothers who repeated themselves frequently. Thus, there appear to be significant interactions between the syntactic structure of maternal input, and children's acquisition of related syntactic structures.

Other work has focused on acquisition of words (e.g., the lexicon). The rate of child vocabulary learning, and overall vocabulary size, has been shown to correlate with maternal differences in talkativeness (Huttenlocher *et al.*, 1991). A study contrasting children with large vocabularies to those with small ones indicated that mothers of the former group were more talkative during a brief play session in the lab (Smolak and Weinraub, 1983). Similarly, the number of different words (e.g., lexical variety) spoken by toddlers during a laboratory play session has been found to correlate with number of maternal utterances in that same period (Tomasello *et al.*, 1986). This relationship between language development and maternal language input has been demonstrated in at-risk populations as well. Depressed mothers appear to direct fewer utterances to their children (Breznitz and Sherman, 1987), and lower verbal IQs have been reported in the children of such depressed mothers (Cicchetti *et al.*, 2000; Cohler *et al.*, 1977; Murray *et al.*, 1996). More generally, the quality of mother-child interactions has been found to predict cognitive and linguistic outcomes in a sample of high social risk mothers and their preschoolers (Kelly *et al.*, 1996).

Multiple factors, including maternal IQ, impact on child language skills. A study of child vocabulary skills at 20 months in 131 mother-child dyads demonstrated that factors influencing child vocabulary include maternal attitudes toward parenting and maternal vocabulary as well as, indirectly, maternal personality and knowledge of child development (Bornstein *et al.*, 1998). An analysis of 80 mother-child dyads demonstrated that maternal IQ contributed to child IQ scores and receptive vocabulary skills (assessed with the Peabody Picture Vocabulary Test - Revised, or PPVT-R) to a greater extent than home environment ratings (Longstreth, 1981). More generally, Dollaghan (1999) demonstrated a correlation between maternal educational achievement and child language abilities.

Similar relationships between maternal IQ and child language have been found in at-risk samples. In a study of low birth weight infants, child IQ was significantly correlated with maternal IQ, with less variance accounted for by other variables including marital status, family income, and quality of home environment (Bacharach and Baumeister, 1998a, 1998b). In a study of high-school graduates in Chile, maternal IQ (along with child brain volume and nutritional history in the first year of a child's development) contributed the greatest variance to child IQ scores (Ivanovic *et al.*, 2002).

As is suggested by some of the studies described above, another factor that may play a significant role in child language skills is socioeconomic status (SES) variability. This is particularly important for studies of maltreatment, because maltreatment is often confounded with SES; specifically, maltreatment is more frequently documented in low-SES groups. In a longitudinal study of the interaction between linguistic and cognitive development, measurements of SES and home environments accounted for more of the difference in IQ and language skills at 8 years than that captured by developmental measurements in the first 2 years (Moore, 1968). Hoff-Ginsberg (1991, 1998) has demonstrated the huge variability in the types of words produced by children from different backgrounds, in spontaneous speech. She notes that the differences appear to hinge on the quantity of maternal input: mothers from low SES groups appear to talk less overall with their children, and to use a less varied vocabulary, than do mothers from middle SES groups. Similarly, Hart and Risley (1995) found that despite the rich and varied interactions experienced by children from low SES backgrounds, these youngsters reached school age knowing fewer words (although other work has found limited correlations between family background and child language until school entry, when correlations were greatly amplified; Wells, 1985). In several studies, home environment has contributed a unique prediction of children's intelligence when controlling for SES and maternal intelligence (Church and Katigbak, 1991), particularly in younger children (Luster and Dubow, 1992).

Differences may be most prominent in low SES groups; in a four-year longitudinal study, Bee et al. (1982) found that measures of family stress, social support, maternal education, and parent perception of the child, especially when assessed at birth, were strongly related to child IQ and language within a low-education subsample, but not among mothers with more than high school education. It is critical for studies of maltreatment to include appropriate comparison samples experiencing similarly impoverished environments (Augoustinos, 1987; Coster and Cicchetti, 1993).

There is a final factor that must be accounted for when assessing the relationship between caregiver input and language development in maltreatment: cognitive abilities of the child. It is known that maltreatment exerts a negative, rather general, influence on cognitive development. While these cognitive sequelae have received somewhat less attention than emotional and psychological impairments, such as attachment difficulties (Carlson *et al.*, 1989; Lynch and Cicchetti, 1991) or PTSD (Deblinger *et al.*, 1989; McLeer *et al.*, 1988), numerous studies have documented the effects of maltreatment on academic performance or global IQ. In a very severely physically abused sample of 42 children, borderline IQ scores and significant language delay were related to neurological damage incurred in the course of maltreatment (Martin *et al.*, 1974). In a study of 69 children ages 8-16 years with either physical abuse or neglect, the maltreated children exhibited academic delays relative to non-maltreated controls (Wodarski *et al.*, 1990). A study of physically abused children at a variety of ages, compared with their unharmed siblings, found decreases in verbal IQ (Lynch and Roberts, 1982).

A number of studies of large, representative community samples of maltreated children have indicated lower standardized test scores, poorer grades, more grades repeated, and more disciplinary referrals, relative to matched non-maltreated peers (Eckenrode *et al.*, 1993; Kendall-Tackett, 1996; Wodarski et al., 1990). Long-term studies of children who were maltreated in childhood confirm the pervasive nature and severity of impairments. One study reported a 20-year follow up of almost 700 children (413 abused or neglected and 286 controls) and demonstrated a negative impact of maltreatment on IQ, reading ability, and high school completion rates (Perez and Widom, 1994), and, in an even longer-term follow-up, rates of violent crime convictions (Maxfield and Widom, 1996). Any study which hopes to address specific language delays in maltreated children must therefore account for general cognitive delays, which clearly could act as a mediator and completely account for any language differences that are a function of maltreatment, regardless of the effects of caregiver input.

Differences in Caregiver Language Input in Maltreatment

The literature suggests that there are dramatic differences in the child-directed language of maltreating parents. In early research on interactions in maltreating mother-infant dyads, neglecting mothers were found to be unresponsive and abusing mothers were controlling (Crittenden, 1981, 1988). Differences are quantitative: maltreating mothers have been found to produce less language altogether to their children, both young (Christopoulos *et al.*, 1988) and school-age (Egeland and Sroufe, 1981). Differences are also qualitative. For example, maltreating mothers have been shown to be less likely to clarify ambiguous statements (Westerman and Havstad, 1982); in the 1981 Egeland and Sroufe study, maltreating mothers were less likely to verbally instruct their children, and less responsive to children's utterances. Similarly, Allen and Wasserman (1985) studied toddler-mother dyads and found that abusing mothers were more likely to ignore their children and were less likely to label objects, explain aspects of the environment, and ask questions of the child. More generally, maltreating parents are less likely to have developmentally appropriate expectations about their children's skills (Pianta *et al.*, 1989). Evidence is quite consistent in demonstrating that language input from maltreating caregivers differs in both quality and quantity (Rogosch *et al.*, 1995).

Evidence of Language Delays in Child Maltreatment

Given the preponderance of evidence that parental language input has a strong impact on child language development; and furthermore, that maltreating parents talk differently to their children, it follows that children who are maltreated are likely to evince language delays. Furthermore, such a prediction would concur with clinical impressions. However, there have been relatively few studies that have demonstrated specific language delays in maltreatment.

Several studies have demonstrated language delays in a maltreated sample (Culp et al., 1991; Fox et al., 1988); however, maltreatment was confounded with SES or there was no comparison sample. As described above, accounting for the role of socioeconomic status is critical in studies of language development, as it is a known contributor to language variability during development. In a better-controlled correlational study, Allen and Oliver (1982) reported language delays on the Preschool Language Scales in a sample of four-year-old neglected children (n = 7) and abused and neglected children (n = 31) but not for abused-only children (n = 13), relative to non-maltreated controls. More recently, a series of reports has examined maltreatment and its sequelae in a large controlled sample of children from the Harvard Child Maltreatment Project (HCMP; Cicchetti and Rizley, 1981). Participants were carefully matched for SES, age, sex, ethnicity, and a number of family environment variables. One study of this sample reported that, at 31 months, maltreated toddlers exhibited less sophisticated language structure (e.g., shorter mean length of utterance, or MLU) and delays in expressive vocabulary, as well as pragmatic deficits including fewer topic-maintaining utterances and less self-descriptive language (Coster et al., 1989). The authors hypothesized that the pragmatic delays were related to impairments in emotional and self-concept development. This is supported by a subsequent investigation of the same sample, which indicated that maltreated toddlers used fewer words referring to their internal states than their non-maltreated peers (Beeghly and Cicchetti, 1994).

However, studies have not consistently found language delays in this sample of maltreated children. Reporting on the same group of children studied in the Coster et al. (1989) and Beeghly and Cicchetti (1994) papers, Gersten et al. (1986) reported no differences in MLU at 25 months. Findings indicated that the quality of mother-toddler attachment was the best predictor of language skills, rather than maltreatment status or cognitive development. The difference in outcomes across several age points suggests an interaction between age, the cumulative impact of the ongoing experience of maltreatment, and language outcomes.

If language delays in maltreatment are present, their effects appear to be as long-lasting as the cognitive effects. Using a picture narration task, one study of nine-year old maltreated children demonstrated impoverished expressive language skills relative to two groups of non-maltreated controls (Elmer, 1981). In a study of adolescents ages 13-17, McFadyen and Kitson (1996) reported that the maltreated group's language was more repetitive and less self-descriptive than controls.

In general, studies of language acquisition in maltreated children have demonstrated clear effects on lexical development, with mixed findings about syntactic, or grammatical, development. While large-scale longitudinal studies are critical in establishing the impact on child outcomes of different factors such as subtype (e.g., neglect, or physical, sexual, or emotional abuse), severity, patterns of timing, and perpetrators (see Manly, 2005), there is a role as well for smaller, richly-detailed investigations of the impact of maltreatment on child development. The study reported in detail here presents an effort to address limitations of previous work; specifically, it thoroughly evaluates language abilities in a carefully matched sample of maltreated children, where controls are matched for SES, early PPVT (receptive vocabulary) skills, and maternal IQ. The study draws on a detailed measure of spontaneous language complexity, likely to be more sensitive than a general verbal IQ measure or even a measure of MLU. Given the importance of parental input for child language, and the impoverished nature of input in maltreating caregivers, a second goal was to confirm that maternal language differed qualitatively between maltreated and nonmaltreated groups, as shown in previous reports, if so, and whether maternal differences correlated with syntactic abilities in children. Further study details may be found in Eigsti and Cicchetti (2004).

EXPRESSIVE SYNTAX IN MALTREATED CHILDREN AT 60 MONTHS

Methods

Participants

Drawing on the HCMP sample described above (Cicchetti and Rizley, 1981), analyses included 33 mother-child dyads. While the sample as a whole comprises a longitudinal effort, the data described here are cross-sectional in nature. Of the 33 participating children, 19 were maltreated and 14 served as a non-maltreated comparison sample. None of the individual children had been included in previous studies (e.g., the Gersten et al., 1986, Beeghly and Cicchetti, 1994, or Coster et al., 1989 samples).

It is increasingly recognized that cases of child maltreatment are most likely to include multiple subtypes. For example, a report of 492 maltreated children indicated that only 8% (*n* = 38) had experienced physical abuse alone; similarly, of the sexually abused children in the sample, only 5% (*n* = 24) had experienced that form of abuse alone (Manly, 2001). Consistent with this and other findings, participants in this study, who were drawn from the caseloads of Child Protective Service (CPS) social workers in Massachusetts Department of Social Services, experienced multiple forms of abuse, as documented by social workers' ratings on an 87-item interview checklist of maltreatment incidents (Giovannoni and Becerra, 1979). Specifically, of the 19 maltreated children, 16 had experienced emotional abuse, 10 had experienced physical abuse, and 9 had experienced neglect; an additional 9 children had experienced both neglect and physical abuse. Although neglect may have been cited in the social workers' records as secondary to physical abuse, essentially all (18 of 19) of the children had developed in a neglecting environment. None of the cases included sexual abuse, which, in the 1980's, was rarely reported to CPS. (Data suggests that sexual abuse, which is the least well-understood form of maltreatment, is also the least prevalent, accounting for a total of 10% of maltreatment cases; Putnam, 2003).

Importantly, all children had been indicated as maltreated by CPS prior to age two, and all cases were active or open at the time of enrollment into the study. Furthermore, the biological mother was named as a perpetrator or co-perpetrator in all cases. As all participants were engaged in parent skills training and other activities addressed at improving both parenting and the parent-child relationships, none of the children were in foster care. Thus, all the children in the maltreated group were experiencing chronic, early-onset maltreatment.

As noted above, it is important to establish that any language differences that emerge cannot be attributed to SES differences between groups. The participants in the present study were primarily from low-income families, and most were receiving Aid to Families with Dependent Children (AFDC). A comparison sample was identified by recruiting families also receiving AFDC through advertisements placed in welfare offices and stores in low-income neighborhoods. Nonmaltreatment status was verified, with families' permission, through searches of the state registry of maltreatment cases. Maltreating and comparison groups did not differ on the following indices of socioeconomic status: Hollingshead Four-Factor Index (Hollingshead, 1975), maternal education, annual family income, AFDC use, or food stamp use.

Child participants in the maltreated group had a mean age of 57 months (range = 55 to 59 months); mean age in the comparison group was 59 months (range = 58 to 60 months). While group differences in chronological age were not significant, t (31) = 1.72, p < .10, clearly participants' ages spanned a wide range. To address this variability, chronological age was covaried in all analyses. Gender and ethnicity did not differ across groups. Group demographic information is presented in Table 1.

Table 1. Descriptive Data: Language delays in Maltreatment Maltreated and Comparison groups (Eigsti and Cicchetti, 2004)

	Maltreated Participants n = 19	Comparison Participants n = 14	p [a]
Chronological Age, months	57.6 (SD = 3.5)	59.4 (SD = 1.8)	.10
Gender (M: F)	10:9	7:7	.88
Ethnicity [b]	17:2:0	9:4:1	.08
Current use of AFDC [c, d]	17/19	9/13	.15
Lifetime use of AFDC [c, d]	19/19	13/13	n.s.
Current use of Food Stamps [d]	16/19	13/13	.13
Highest grade attended (mother)	11.1	11.9	.14
Annual family income	$6000	$6360	.75

[a] p-value for Chi-square comparisons or for t-test (Chronological Age, Family Income).
[b] Ethnicity = Caucasian: African-American: Hispanic.
[c] AFDC = Aid to Families with Dependent Children.
[d] Data were not available for one participant in the comparison group.

Procedure

Mother-child dyads were invited to the lab for standardized assessments and a 30-minute free-play session. The session took place in a playroom, well-stocked with age-appropriate toys including a furnished dollhouse with family figures, a "Bobo the Clown" punching doll, and make-believe toy sets including cowboy gear and a cooking set with food. A one-way mirror permitted videotaping of sessions. The sessions were structured such that mothers were directed not to initiate interactions with their child during the first and final 10-minute periods; during the intermediate 10 minutes, they were directed to interact as they normally might at home. Intervals were signaled via a knock on the door.

The author transcribed all play sessions from videotape according to standard guidelines (e.g., Brown and Hanlon, 1970; Demuth, 1996). Transcription and coding was completed without knowledge of maltreatment status. Utterances formed the basic unit of analysis, and were jointly defined by intonational contour, by the presence of pauses between utterances, and by sentence structure. All speech that was only partially intelligible or was semantically opaque was given a phonetic gloss which included representations of the intelligible portions. Reliability of transcriptions was calculated on ten percent of all sessions by a second trained independent coder and was calculated at $K = .90$.

Child Measures

Syntactic Complexity

To assess the relative syntactic complexity present in children's spontaneous speech, and its developmental level, play session transcripts were analyzed with the Index of Productive Syntax (IPSyn, Scarborough, 1990). To use the IPSyn, the coder assesses whether a child has produced any of 56 different syntactic and morphological forms; that is, whether the child combines parts of words (such as, in English, -*ing* or -*ed*) and combines words into phrases to produce grammatical structure.. The IPSyn has been applied in longitudinal studies of morphosyntactic development of language-delayed samples (Scarborough *et al.*, 1991; Tager-Flusberg *et al.*, 1990), and its reference norms permit comparisons to a typical age group. Evidence suggests that the IPSyn may be a more sensitive assessment of language complexity than Mean Length of Utterance (MLU) in this age group (3-5 years; Scarborough et al., 1991).

The child's first 100 utterances were scored for the presence of specific syntactic and morphological structures. This procedure presents a built-in control for between-child differences in talkativeness. Each utterance was analyzed in turn. If an utterance met the requirements for a given grammatical structure, the child received one point. Subsequent utterances were also analyzed for each structure, with a maximum of two points per structure. A structure could be scored regardless of whether it was accurate according to adult norms – for example, a child would have received credit for producing a past tense morpheme in the utterance *We wented to the store*, despite the over-regularization error.

Auxiliary Verb Production

As a second assessment of the complexity of a child's syntactic development, the production of auxiliary verbs in obligatory contexts was assessed. This measure was based on the finding from the typical language acquisition literature, reviewed above, that the verbal auxiliary system is particularly sensitive to maternal input differences. In the play session transcripts, it was possible to tally up the number of main verbs which required auxiliary verbs and determine the proportion of those utterances in which the required auxiliary was produced.

Lexical Knowledge

As a measure of lexical ability, children completed the Peabody Picture Vocabulary Test-Revised (PPVT-R). This frequently-used standardized assessment of receptive vocabulary skills requires no reading skills or verbal responses. It was chosen to provide a measure of language ability that was somewhat independent of syntactic skills. The PPVT-R was administered by a research assistant who was naïve to maltreatment status.

Maternal Measures

Maternal Language

As with the child's language, the language of mothers from each dyad was transcribed and coded with respect to several categories that were predicted, based on the literature reviewed above, to be relevant for child language skills. These measures included a) Total number of maternal utterances produced during the period in question (e.g., the time it took for the child to produce 100 codable utterances), with minutes entered as a covariate; b) Wh-questions (e.g., *what do you do with this one?*); c) Yes/No questions with inverted auxiliaries (*Do you want to do the house now?*), d) Complex sentences with multiple propositions (verb plus arguments) falling within a single utterance (*that looks like the bear that I got you for Christmas*); e) Imperatives (*Do it like that*), and f) Negative imperatives (*Don't throw it at me*). Items b-f were calculated as proportions of total utterances (item a).

Maternal IQ

It was critical to assess group differences in maternal verbal skills for three reasons. First, mothers who have strong verbal skills may pass those skills along to children (e.g., via genetic inheritance). Second, mothers with strong verbal skills may be better able to scaffold their children's utterances, helping children to produce more sophisticated structures at an earlier age. Third, because of the substantial correlations between mother and child IQ (Silva and Fergusson, 1980), this measure may serve as a proxy for child cognitive abilities. To control for these possibilities, mothers completed the short form of the Wechsler Adult Intelligence Scales (WAIS, Wechsler, 1955), yielding a Deviation Quotient Score with a mean of 100 and standard deviation of 15. As with other measures, the WAIS was administered by research assistants naïve to maltreatment status.

RESULTS

Child Language Measures

Index of Productive Syntax (IPSyn)

Children's spontaneous utterances were assessed for syntactic complexity and developmental level using the IPSyn. Data were analyzed using MANCOVA with group (Maltreated vs. Comparison) as the independent variable and with child age in months and maternal IQ as covariates. An initial analysis of the maltreated group alone was also performed, contrasting the group who was neglected only ($n = 9$) with the group who was both neglected and physically abused ($n = 10$). As with results from all measures, this group contrast indicated no significant differences (all $F < 1.9$, all $p > .17$). This is unsurprising, as essentially all of the children experienced the same omission of attention to their basic needs and lack of supervision which may be the primary ingredient in language delays. For the IPSyn, the maltreated group scores ($M = 78.1$) were lower than the comparison sample's ($M = 82.7$), a difference which was significant, $F(1, 27) = 5.33$, $p = .03$. Lower scores were indicative of less developmentally advanced syntactic abilities.

An additional MANCOVA analysis was performed on the IPSyn data, with child gender entered as a covariate, to assess for the presence of gender differences in language development over and above maltreatment status. There is a large literature on gender and language acquisition (Bornstein *et al.*, 2000; Bornstein *et al.*, 2004; Huttenlocher et al., 1991; Naigles, 1996), which demonstrates that girls are generally advanced relative to boys on a variety of language domains (lexical and morphosyntactic). Results indicated a significant main effect of gender, $F(1, 27) = 4.29$, $p < .05$, and no significant interaction; surprisingly, findings showed that girls ($M = 76.7$, $SD = 8.7$) had *lower* scores than boys ($M = 82.7$, $SD = 6.3$) across both groups, reflecting a greater delay in syntactic development.

Auxiliary Verbs in Obligatory Contexts

As an additional measure of syntactic abilities likely to be sensitive to maternal input differences, we examined children's production of auxiliary verbs in grammatically obligatory contexts (e.g., *"the dog was going to the park"*)[1]. Results were consistent with findings from the IPSyn, in that the maltreated group ($M = .784$, $SD = .204$) produced fewer such verbs than the comparison group ($M = .854$, $SD = .097$), a result that approached significance with maternal VIQ and child age as covariates, $F(1, 27) = 2.998$, $p < .10$. Results also indicated that the production of obligatory auxiliaries was strongly correlated with IPSyn score, $r = .52$, $p < .001$.

PPVT scores

Receptive vocabulary skills were assessed with the PPVT-R. Findings indicated that the maltreatment group's scores ($M = 87.9$, $SD = 14.2$) were lower than the comparison group's ($M = 102.1$, $SD = 22.8$), a difference that was significant, $t(30) = 2.16$, $p < .04$. The maltreated group scores were in the low average range, indicating that they had less advanced vocabulary skills than would be expected of their age, whereas the comparison group scores were in the average range (and thus were age-appropriate).

Maternal Measures

Maternal Language

To assess for the possibility that the maternal speech characteristics could account for significant variance in child language skills, we examined how much mothers talked to their children, and contrasted this across groups. Findings indicated that the mothers in the maltreating dyads were significantly less talkative ($M = 102.7$, $SD = 52.0$) than the comparison mothers ($M = 151.0$, $SD = 52.4$), a difference which was significant, $F(1, 30) = 5.58$, $p < .04$. Mothers in the maltreatment group also produced significantly fewer Yes/No

---

[1] It should be noted that this measure is not likely to reflect ethnicity-related differences in dialect, as the groups were balanced in terms of race. In fact, the maltreated group included numerically fewer African-Americans, whose dialect would be more likely to reflect omitted auxiliary verbs.

questions (maltreatment $M = 3.3$, $SD = 3.1$, comparison $M = 7.0$, $SD = 5.3$), $F(1, 30) = 4.50$, $p = .04$, and Complex multi-clause utterances (maltreatment $M = 2.2$, $SD = 2.5$, comparison $M = 4.4$, $SD = 3.7$), $F(1, 30) = 4.86$, $p = .04$. There were no group differences in Wh-questions (maltreatment $M = 10.5$, $SD = 8.3$, comparison $M = 14.9$, $SD = 8.1$) or Imperatives (maltreatment $M = 21.2$, $SD = 15.7$, comparison $M = 13.9$, $SD = 13.4$), F's < 1.5, p's $> .23$.

Maternal IQ

The assessment of maternal IQ permitted an analysis of whether child language abilities were strongly influenced by this factor, and furthermore, whether group differences might be mediated by maternal IQ. Findings indicated no significant group differences, with mothers in the maltreatment group ($M = 96.7$) performing similarly to comparison mothers ($M = 102.1$), $t(27) = 1.7$, $p > .10$. Between-group differences in maternal language characteristics did not change when maternal IQ was added as a covariate to analyses, and these variables were all uncorrelated with IQ.

As predicted, maternal IQ across groups did correlate significantly with child lexical abilities (PPVT-R scores), $r(31) = .41$, $p < .02$, and with child syntactic abilities (IPSyn score), $r(31) = .38$, $p < .04$, such that mothers with higher IQs had children with more advanced language skills.

Correlations Between Child and Maternal Language Measures

The results reported above clearly indicate that maltreated children, as a group, tended to have less well-developed morphosyntactic and lexical abilities; similarly, maltreating mothers as a group tended to direct less language towards their children, and were less likely to produce complex sentences and questions with auxiliary movement (yes/no questions). However, these separate findings are most interesting if they are specifically related with each other. Planned correlations between child language and maternal language measures indicated that mothers whose children were more likely to produce auxiliary verbs in obligatory contexts were themselves more likely to produce multi-clause utterances, $r(33) = .35$, $p < .05$, and Wh-questions, $r(33) = .41$, $p < .02$. While cross-sectional data cannot demonstrate causality, this finding is consistent with the notion that children benefit from the presence (or frequency) of certain types of syntactic structures in the language they hear from their primary caregivers, and that they make use of this input in building their own representations of grammatical structure.

One final analysis assessed maternal expansions and repetitions of child utterances (something characteristic of caregiver speech with young children). While there were no group differences, correlations between child age and maternal expansions and repetitions were significant in the comparison group, $r(14) = -.77$, $p < .001$, but not in the maltreated group, $r(19) = .005$, n.s., raising the possibility that non-maltreating mothers may be more responsive to child-specific factors such as age and relative language skill.

CONCLUSION

A consensus is emerging that child language development is specifically impacted by child maltreatment, above and beyond the non-specific effects of cognitive delay. This finding is supported by the study detailed here (previously reported in Eigsti and Cicchetti, 2004) as well as by several other investigations of language in maltreatment. Other, related work has raised questions about the effects of maltreatment on theory of mind skills (Cicchetti *et al.*, 2003) as well as socioemotional development, but the focus of this chapter has been on the domain of language acquisition.

The study presented here indicated a clear negative impact of child maltreatment on language development. Specifically, children who had been maltreated since (at least) age two exhibited language delays even at the age of five years, producing less grammatically complex language and less advanced vocabulary skills. Consistent with a number of other studies, maltreated mothers were significantly less talkative with their children; furthermore, the language they directed to their children contained fewer yes/no questions and fewer complex multi-clausal utterances. Interestingly, these are sentence types that have been shown in the typical language acquisition literature to be particularly important for the process of language learning. Tying together the child and mother findings, there were specific individual correlations between mothers who used fewer of these structures and relative delays in children's morphosyntactic development.

As might be expected, given that the children who participated in this study were living in poverty, both maltreated and non-maltreated comparison children were delayed by more than one year, compared to chronological age expectations, in syntactic abilities (e.g., IPSyn score). The 59-month-old comparison group had scores that would be expected for 46-month-olds; the 57-month-old maltreated group scores were at the 41-month-old level. Thus, over and above the syntactic deficits that appeared related to maltreatment, there were additional delays that were likely due to SES factors. In contrast to this general delay across the entire sample, lexical abilities (measured by the PPVT-R) were at age norms for the comparison group, whereas the maltreated group was in the low average range. Interestingly, these vocabulary differences (at 60 months) were not found in a very similar sample at age 31 months (Coster et al., 1989). While speculations must be tempered by the fact that the investigations did not assess the same children, there is some data that may reflect on this developmental difference. Huttenlocher et al. (1991) found that in a sample of typically developing children, there were significant effects of gender that decreased over time, and that the effect of environment and speech input became more significant over time. The present pattern of findings fits well with this work in suggesting that the effects of a maltreating environment (in which the caregiver's speech may be quantitatively and qualitatively different) on a child's vocabulary will become intensified over time.

The present results also support earlier findings that maltreating mothers were less likely to regulate their interactions in relation to the child's developmental level (Pianta et al., 1989). Specifically, non-maltreating mothers were more likely to expand upon and repeat their child's utterances when their child was of a younger age, whereas the maltreating dyads did not exhibit this sensitivity. Repetitions and expansions, or "recasts," of a child's utterances have been shown to affect a child's acquisition of the recasted elements (Farrar, 1990). This suggests a mechanism for language delay in maltreatment that may reflect similar processes in other aspects of development, such as self-help skills.

There was an interesting and counter-intuitive effect of gender on language abilities in the present study. Specifically, in addition to the main effect of maltreatment, there was a main effect of gender (with no interaction) indicating that girls had lower scores for both the IPSyn and the PPVT. This is the reverse of the typical finding that girls score better than boys on language measures for which there are gender differences (Bornstein et al., 1998; Hopman-Rock *et al.*, 1988; Huttenlocher et al., 1991; Maccoby and Jacklin, 1984; although cf. Hyde and Linn, 1988). In this study, gender differences were present in the maltreatment but not the comparison samples, when these samples were considered separately. Analyses of maternal utterances failed to uncover any gender-related differences; that is, mothers did not appear to be more talkative, or to direct more or less of any category of utterance, towards their male children. Similarly, mothers of boys did not have higher overall verbal IQs, higher social class demographics, or any other characteristics that, in the present study, were related to child outcomes.

While no interpretation for this unexpected finding can be conclusive, hints may be drawn from a study of gender differences in an impoverished at-risk family sample. Findings demonstrated strong correlations between family risk factors and verbal ability for girls but not boys (Morisset *et al.*, 1995), which was interpreted as reflecting the greater psychological distance (and less time spent together) for boy-mother dyads in the sample. Although the present findings must be interpreted with caution due to the relatively small sample size, they suggest that girls may be uniquely vulnerable to aspects of the maltreating environment that may influence language development.

These findings dovetail with previous controlled studies of language delays in maltreated children, reviewed extensively above, which taken together indicate effects on multiple domains of language: the lexicon, syntax and morphology, and pragmatic and discourse functions. The data are consistent with the hypothesis proposed in the typical language acquisition literature that the acquisition of morphosyntactic structure is directly tied to the quantity of input to which the learner is exposed; that the learner can abstract underlying grammatical regularities only when given a sufficient number of examples in the language input.

The work that has been performed to date has several limitations. First, many early studies failed to control for socioeconomic status and gender effects, both of which contribute significant variance to language skills. More germane to the issue of maltreatment's impact on language skills is the lack of control of specific subtypes of maltreatment. For example, in the study reported here, the maltreated sample did not permit the direct comparison of the impact of physical versus neglect on language skills. That said, research samples restricted to "pure" subtypes may be nonrepresentative, and likely oversimplify the phenomena of maltreatment (Barnett *et al.*, 1993).

One major limitation of all studies of child maltreatment and language acquisition to date (including that reported in detail here) is the dependence on single measures collected at a single timepoint and in a single setting. Assessment in multiple contexts has been helpful in fully characterizing relations between maternal style and children's language and, at least, narrative skills (e.g., Haden and Fivush, 1996). Future work will be necessary to elucidate the relationships between maternal input and child language, across a variety of settings (e.g., home vs. lab vs. school), conversational partners (e.g., mother vs. familiar non-maltreating adult), and measures (e.g., spontaneous conversation vs. structured competence-based assessments).

Taking these limitations into account, the findings from all the work reviewed here have several implications. Firstly, while findings do not necessarily support a prediction that adults who were maltreated in childhood will exhibit impairments in language, the significant language delays early on are likely to lead to later emotional, social, and academic difficulties, and may exacerbate existing difficulties in other domains. Thus, socioemotional and other difficulties encountered later in life may be due not just to direct effects of maltreatment, but to mediated effects from language and communicative delays.

In addition, results highlight an urgent clinical need. To date, maltreatment services have not reliably assessed developmental lags and targeted those lags for intervention services (Pears and Fisher, 2005). Given the prevalence of maltreatment (estimated at 906,000 confirmed cases in the US in 2002, according to a Department of Health and Human Services 2003 report), this is a significant number of children who are at risk for significant language delays. "Best practice" guidelines for the future should include a referral for children indicated for maltreatment to a developmental evaluation with a specific assessment of language abilities.

AUTHOR NOTE

I would like to acknowledge the significant support of Dante Cicchetti in carrying out this research, which was also supported by grants from the National Center on Child Abuse and Neglect, the National Institute of Mental Health, and the Spunk Fund, Inc., to Dante Cicchetti.

REFERENCES

Allen, R., and Wasserman, G. A. (1985). Origins of language delay in abused children. *Child Abuse and Neglect, 9*(3), 335-40.

Allen, R. E., and Oliver, J. M. (1982). The effects of child maltreatment on language development. *Child Abuse and Neglect, 6*, 299-305.

Augoustinos, M. (1987). Developmental effects of child abuse: Recent findings. *Child Abuse and Neglect, 11*, 15-27.

Bacharach, V. R., and Baumeister, A. A. (1998a). Direct and indirect effects of maternal intelligence, maternal age, income, and home environment on intelligence of preterm, low-birth-weight children. *Journal of Applied Developmental Psychology, 19*(3), 361-75.

Bacharach, V. R., and Baumeister, A. A. (1998b). Effects of maternal intelligence, marital status, income, and home environment on cognitive development of low birth weight infants. *Journal of Pediatric Psychology, 23*(3), 197-205.

Barnett, D., Manly, J. T., and Cicchetti, D. (1993). Defining child maltreatment: The interface between policy and research. In D. Cicchetti and S. L. Toth (Eds.), *Child Abuse, Child Development, and Social Policy* (pp. 7-74). Norwood, NJ: Ablex.

Bee, H. L., Barnard, K. E., Eyres, S. J., Gray, C. A., Hammond, M. A., Spietz, A. L., et al. (1982). Prediction of IQ and language skill from perinatal status, child performance, family characteristics, and mother-infant interaction. *Child Development, 53*(5), 1134-56.

Beeghly, M., and Cicchetti, D. (1994). Child maltreatment, attachment, and the self system: Emergence of an internal state lexicon in toddlers at high social risk. *Development and Psychopathology, 6*, 5-30.

Bornstein, M., Haynes, O., Painter, K., and Genevro, J. (2000). Child language with mother and with stranger at home and in the laboratory: a methodological study. *Journal of Child Language, 27*(2), 407-20.

Bornstein, M., Leach, D., and Haynes, O. (2004). Vocabulary competence in first- and secondborn siblings of the same chronological age. *Journal of Child Language, 31*(4), 855-73.

Bornstein, M. H., Haynes, M. O., and Painter, K. M. (1998). Sources of child vocabulary competence: A multivariate model. *Journal of Child Language, 25,* 367-93.

Breznitz, Z., and Sherman, T. (1987). Speech patterning of natural discourse of well and depressed mothers and their young children. *Child Development, 58,* 395-400.

Brown, R. (1973). *A first language: The early stages*. Cambridge, MA: Harvard University Press.

Brown, R., and Hanlon, C. (1970). Derivational complexity and the order of acquisition in child speech. In J. R. Hayes (Ed.), *Cognition and the development of language* (pp. 11-53). New York: Wiley.

Carlson, V., Cicchetti, D., and Barnett, D. (1989). Disorganized/ disoriented attachment relationships in maltreated infants. *Developmental Psychology, 25,* 525.

Christopoulos, C., Bonvillian, J. D., and Crittenden, P. M. (1988). Maternal language input and child maltreatment. *Infant Mental Health, 9,* 272-86.

Church, A. T., and Katigbak, M. S. (1991). Home environment, nutritional status, and maternal intelligence as determinants of intellectual development in rural Philippine preschool children. *Intelligence, 15*(1), 49-78.

Cicchetti, D., and Rizley, R. (1981). Developmental perspectives on the etiology, inter-generational transmission, and sequelae of child maltreatment. *New Directions for Child Development, 11,* 31-55.

Cicchetti, D., Rogosch, F., and Toth, S. (2000). The efficacy of toddler-parent psychotherapy for fostering cognitive development in offspring of depressed mothers. *Journal of Abnormal Child Psychology, 28*(2), 135-48.

Cicchetti, D., Rogosch, F. A., Maughan, A., Toth, S. L., and Bruce, J. (2003). False belief understanding in maltreated children. *Development and Psychopathology, 15*(4), 1067-91.

Cohler, B., Gallant, D., Grunebaum, H., Weiss, J., and Gamer, E. (1977). Attention, dysfunction, and child-care attitudes among mentally ill and well mothers and their young children. In J. C. Glidewell (Ed.), *The social context of learning and development* (pp. 133-62). New York: Gardner-Wiley.

Coster, W. J., and Cicchetti, D. (1993). Research on the communicative development of maltreated children: Clinical implications. *Topics in Language Disorders, 13*(4), 25-38.

Coster, W. J., Gersten, M. S., Beeghly, M., and Cicchetti, D. (1989). Communicative functioning in maltreated toddlers. *Developmental Psychology, 25*(6), 1020-9.

Crittenden, P. M. (1981). Abusing, neglecting, problematic, and adequate dyads: Differentiating by patterns of interaction. *Merrill-Palmer Quarterly, 27,* 201-8.

Crittenden, P. M. (1988). Relationships at risk. In J. Belsky and T. Nezwarski (Eds.), *Clinical implications of attachment* (pp. 136-74). Hillsdale, NJ: Erlbaum.

Culp, R. E., Watkins, R. V., Lawrence, H., Letts, D., Kelly, D. J., and Rice, M. L. (1991). Maltreated children's language and speech development: Abused, neglected, and abused and neglected. *First Language, 11*(33), 377-89.

Deblinger, E., McLeer, S., Atkins, M., Ralphe, D., and Foa, E. (1989). Post-traumatic stress in sexually abused, physically abused, and nonabused children. *Child Abuse and Neglect, 13*(3), 403-8.

Demuth, K. (1996). Collecting spontaneous production data. In D. McDaniel, C. McKee and H. Smith Cairns (Eds.), *Methods for assessing children's syntax* (pp. 3-22). Cambridge, MA: MIT Press.

Dollaghan, C., Campbell, T., Paradise, J., Feldman, H., Janosky, J., Pitcairn, D., et al. (1999). Maternal education and measures of early speech and language. *Journal of Speech, Language, and Hearing Research, 42*(6), 1432-43.

Eckenrode, J., Laird, M., and Doris, J. (1993). School performance and disciplinary problems among abused and neglected children. *Developmental Psychology, 29*(1), 53-62.

Eigsti, I. M., and Cicchetti, D. (2004). The impact of child maltreatment on expressive syntax at 60 months. *Developmental Science, 7*(1), 88-102.

Egeland, B., and Sroufe, A. (1981). A: Developmental sequelae of maltreatment in infancy. In R. Rizley and D. Cicchetti (Eds.), *New directions for child development: Developmental perspectives on child maltreatment* (pp. 77-92). San Francisco: Jossey Bass.

Elmer, E. (1981). Traumatized children, chronic illness, and poverty. In L. Pelton (Ed.), *The social context of child abuse and neglect* (pp. 185-219). New York: Human Sciences Press.

Farrar, M. (1990). Discourse and the acquisition of grammatical morphemes. *Journal of Child Language, 17*(3), 607-24.

Fox, L., Long, S. H., and Anglois, A. (1988). Patterns of language comprehension deficit in abused and neglected children. *Journal of Speech and Hearing Disorders, 53*, 239-44.

Gathercole, S. E., Hitch, G. J., Service, E., and Martin, A. J. (1997). Phonological short-term memory and new word learning in children. *Developmental Psychology, 33*(6), 966-79.

Gersten, M., Coster, W., Schneider-Rosen, K., Carlson, V., and Cicchetti, D. (1986). The socio-emotional basis of communicative functioning: Quality of attachment, language development, and early maltreatment. In M. E. Lamb, A. L. Brown and B. Rogoff (Eds.), *Advances in developmental psychology:* (Vol. 4, pp. 105-51). Hillsdale: Erlbaum.

Gleitman, L. R. (1981). Maturational determinants of language growth. *Cognition, 10*, 103-14.

Gleitman, L. R., Newport, E. L., and Gleitman, H. (1984). The current status of the motherese hypothesis. *Journal of Child Language, 11*, 43-79.

Haden, C. A., and Fivush, R. (1996). Contextual variation in maternal conversational styles. *Merrill-Palmer Quarterly, 42*(2), 200-27.

Hart, B., and Risley, T. R. (1995). *Meaningful differences in the everyday experience of young American children.* Baltimore, MD: Paul H. Brookes Publishing Co.

Hoff-Ginsberg, E. (1991). Mother-child conversation in different social classes and communicative settings. *Child Development, 62*(4), 782-96.

Hoff-Ginsberg, E. (1998). The relation of birth order and socioeconomic status to children's language experience and language development. *Applied Psycholinguistics, 19*(4), 603-29.

Hollingshead, A. B. (1975). *Four factor index of social status.* New Haven, CT: Yale University Department of Sociology.

Hopman-Rock, M., Gerritsen, F. M., and Talsma, P. (1988). Socioeconomic status and gender differences in language development of children aged 3 to 6 years. *Pedagogische Studien, 65*(11), 437-50.

Huttenlocher, J., Haight, W., Bryk, A., Selyzer, M., and Lyons, T. (1991). Early vocabulary growth: Relation to language input and gender. *Developmental Psychology, 27*, 236-48.

Hyde, J. S., and Linn, M. C. (1988). Gender differences in verbal ability: A meta-analysis. *Psychological Bulletin, 104*, 53-69.

Ivanovic, D. M., Leiva, B. P., Perez, H. T., Almagia, A. F., Toro, T. D., Urrutia, M., et al. (2002). Nutritional status, brain development and scholastic achievement of Chilean high-school graduates from high and low intellectual quotient and socio-economic status. *British Journal of Nutrition, 87*(1), 81-92.

Kelly, J. F., Morisset, C. E., Barnard, K. E., Hammond, M. A., and Booth, C. L. (1996). The influence of early mother-child interaction on preschool cognitive/linguistic outcomes in a high-social-risk group. *Infant Mental Health Journal, 17*(4), 310-21.

Kempe, C. H., Silverman, F. M., Steele, B. B., Droegemuller, W., and Silver, H. C. (1962). The battered child syndrome. *Journal of the American Medical Association, 181*, 17-24.

Kendall-Tackett, K. (1996). The effects of neglect on academic achievement and disciplinary problems: A developmental perspective. *Child Abuse and Neglect, 20*, 161-9.

Lieven, E. V. M. (1994). Crosslinguistic and crosscultural aspects of language addressed to children. In C. Gallaway and B. J. Richards (Eds.), *Input and interaction in language acquisition* (pp. 56-72). New York: Cambridge University Press.

Longstreth, L. E. (1981). Separation of home intellectual environment and maternal IQ as determinants of child IQ. *Developmental Psychology, 17*(5), 532-41.

Luster, T., and Dubow, E. (1992). Home environment and maternal intelligence as predictors of verbal intelligence: A comparison of preschool and school-age children. *Merrill-Palmer Quarterly, 38*(2), 151-75.

Lynch, M. A., and Cicchetti, D. (1991). Patterns of relatedness in maltreated and non-maltreated children: Connections among multiple representational models. *Development and Psychopathology, 3*, 207-.

Lynch, M. A., and Roberts, J. (1982). *Consequences of child abuse*. London: Academic Press.

Maccoby, E. E., and Jacklin, C. N. (1984). *The psychology of sex differences*. Stanford, CA: Stanford University Press.

Manly, J. T. (2001). Dimensions of child maltreatment and children's adjustment: Contributions of developmental timing and subtype. *Development and Psychopathology, 13*, 759-82.

Manly, J. T. (2005). Advances in research definitions of child maltreatment. *Child Abuse and Neglect, 29*, 425-39.

Martin, H., Beezley, P., Conway, E., and Kempe, C. (1974). The development of abused children. *Advances in Pediatrics, 21*, 25-73.

Maxfield, M. G., and Widom, C. S. (1996). The cycle of violence. Revisited 6 years later. *Archives of Pediatric and Adolescent Medicine, 150*(4), 390-5.

McFadyen, R. G., and Kitson, W. J. H. (1996). Language comprehension and expression among adolescents who have experienced childhood physical abuse. *Journal of Child Psychology, Psychiatry and Allied Disciplines, 37*(5), 551-62.

McLeer, S., Deblinger, E., Atkins, M., Foa, E., and Ralphe, D. (1988). Post-traumatic stress disorder in sexually abused children. *27*(5), 650-4.

Moore, T. (1968). Language and intelligence: A longitudinal study of the first eight years. *Human Development, 11*(1), 88-106.

Morisset, C. E., Barnard, K. E., and Booth, C. L. (1995). Toddlers' language development: Sex differences within social risk. *Developmental Psychology, 31*(5), 851-65.

Murray, L., Fiori-Cowley, A., Hooper, R., and Cooper, P. (1996). The impact of postnatal depression and associated adversity on early mother-infant interactions and later infant outcome. *Child Development, 67*(5), 2512-26.

Naigles, L. (1996). The use of multiple frames in verb learning via syntactic bootstrapping. *Cognition, 58*(2), 221-51.

Newport, E. L., Gleitman, H., and Gleitman, L. R. (1979). Mother, I'd rather do it myself: Some effects and non-effects of maternal speech style. In C. E. Snow and C. A. Ferguson (Eds.), *Talking to children* (pp. 109-49). Great Britain: Cambridge University Press.

Pears, K., and Fisher, P. A. (2005). Developmental, cognitive, and neuropsychological functioning in preschool-aged foster children: associations with prior maltreatment and placement history. *Journal of Developmental and Behavioral Pediatrics, 26*(2), 112-22.

Perez, C. M., and Widom, C. S. (1994). Childhood victimization and long-term intellectual and academic outcomes. *Child Abuse and Neglect, 18*(8), 617-33.

Pianta, R., Egeland, B., and Erickson, M. F. (1989). The antecedents of child maltreatment: Results of the Mother-Child Interaction Research project. In D. Cicchetti and V. Carlson (Eds.), *Child Maltreatment: Theory and research on the causes and consequences of child abuse and neglect* (pp. 203-53). New York: Cambridge University Press.

Putnam, F. W. (2003). Ten-year research update review: child sexual abuse. *Journal of the American Academy of Child and Adolescent Psychiatry, 42*(3), 269-78.

Pye, C. (1986). Quiche Mayan speech to children. *Journal of Child Language, 13*, 85-100.

Rogosch, F., Cicchetti, D., Shields, A., and Toth, S. L. (1995). Parenting dysfunction in child maltreatment. In M. H. Bornstein (Ed.), *Handbook of Parenting* (Vol. 4, pp. 127-59). Hillsdale, NJ: Erlbaum.

Scarborough, H. (1990). Index of Productive Syntax. *Applied Psycholinguistics, 11*, 1-22.

Scarborough, H., Rescorla, Tager-Flusberg, H., Fowler, A., and Sudhalter. (1991). Relation of utterance length to grammatical complexity in normal or language-disordered groups. *Applied Psycholinguistics, 12*, 23-45.

Silva, P. A., and Fergusson, D. (1980). Some factors contributing to language development in three year old children: A report from the Dunedin Multidisciplinary Child Development Study. *British Journal of Disorders of Communication, 15*(3), 205-14.

Smolak, L., and Weinraub, M. (1983). Maternal speech: Strategy or response? *Journal of Child Language, 10*, 369-80.

Tager-Flusberg, H., Calkins, S., Nolin, T., Baumberger, T., Anderson, M., and Chadwick-Dias, A. (1990). A longitudinal study of language acquisition in autistic and Down syndrome children. *Journal of Autism and Developmental Disorders, 20*(1), 1-21.

Tomasello, M., Mannle, S., and Kruger, A. C. (1986). Linguistic environment of 1- to 2-year-old twins. *Developmental Psychology, 22*, 169-76.

Wechsler, D. (1955). *Manual for the Wechsler Adult Intelligence Scale* (1 ed.). New York: Psychological Corporation.

Wells, G. C. (1985). *Language development in the pre-school years*. Cambridge: Cambridge University Press.

Westerman, M. A., and Havstad, L. F. (1982). A pattern-oriented model of caretaker-child interaction, psychopathology and control. In K. Nelson (Ed.), *Children's language* (Vol. 3, pp. 204-46). Hillsdale: Erlbaum.

Wodarski, J., Kurtz, P., Gaudin, J. J., and Howing, P. (1990). Maltreatment and the school-age child: major academic, socioemotional, and adaptive outcomes. *Social Work, 35*(6), 506-13.

In: New Developments in Child Abuse Research
Editor: Stanley M. Sturt, pp. 43-60

ISBN 1-59454-980-X
© 2006 Nova Science Publishers, Inc.

Chapter 3

DYADIC DEVELOPMENTAL PSYCHOTHERAPY: A MULTI-YEAR FOLLOW-UP

Arthur Becker-Weidman
Center For Family Development[*]
5820 Main Street, suite 406,
Williamsville, NY 14221
716-810-0790

ABSTRACT

This study compared the effects of Dyadic Developmental Psychotherapy on a group of children who met the DSM IV criteria for Reactive Attachment Disorder with a control group of children who also met the DSM-IV criteria for Reactive Attachment Disorder. All children in the study had serious histories of chronic maltreatment and abuse during the first three years of life. The measures were taken four years after children in the treatment group ended therapy. The measures used were the Child Behavior Checklist (CBCL), also called the Achenback (Achenback 1991), and the Randolph Attachment Disorder Questionnaire (RADQ) (Randolph 2000). This study extends the results of an earlier study (Becker-Weidman, 2005a) that compared these two groups of children one year after therapy ended. That earlier study found clinically and statistically significant changes in the variables measured one year after treatment ended for the children receiving Dyadic Developmental Psychotherapy, but no changes for the children in the control group. This study confirms the findings of that earlier study. The children in the treatment group continued to show clinically and statistically significant improvements in the variable measured four years after treatment ended. The children in the control group, all of whom continued to receive "usual care" from other treatment providers, showed clinically and statistically significant *deteriorations* in their behavior on the variables measured. This study confirms that Dyadic Developmental Psychotherapy is an effective treatment for children with trauma-attachment disorders and that the positive effects of treatment continue for at least four years. Traditional forms of treatment such as play

---

[*] WWW.Center4FamilyDevelop.com

therapies, talk-therapies, behavior-modification, level systems, charts, stickers, and similar treatment methods are ineffective with such children, but Dyadic Developmental Psychotherapy is an effective treatment method.

INTRODUCTION

In a previous study (Becker-Weidman, 2005a) it was found that Dyadic Developmental Psychotherapy was an effective treatment for children with Reactive Attachment Disorder. That study found clinically and statistically significant reductions in behaviors as measured by the Child Behavior Checklist and the Randolph Attachment Disorder Questionnaire among those receiving Dyadic Developmental Psychotherapy. In that previous study, children in the control group, about 50% of whom received "usual care," such as play therapy, family therapy, individual therapy, and residential treatment, showed no clinically or statistically significant changes in the measured behaviors. The children in the control group who received "usual care," received treatment from other agencies or private practitioners not associated with the Center For Family Development. In the original study, the post-test measures were administered a little over one year after treatment ended for the treatment group

The current study explored the question of whether the positive changes in behavior seen in the treatment group after one year continued beyond this time period. The longer-term effects of Dyadic Developmental Psychotherapy were explored by comparing the initial scores on the Child Behavior Checklist and Randolph Attachment Disorder Questionnaire for the treatment and control groups with the scores for these groups after three to four years.

In this follow-up to that previous study, questionnaires were mailed to the same group of children as in the original study. The average follow-up period is approximately four years for those in the treatment group. About two-thirds of the families could be located and returned the questionnaires (24 of 34 for the treatment group and 20 out of 30 for the control group). Most of the families had moved and we were unable to locate their new addresses. This study is preliminary and exploratory. While the results are intriguing, the small sample size and limited number of families located at this time limit the strength of the findings.

100% of the control group families had sought and continued in treatment, with an average of fifty sessions. As will be shown, despite receiving extensive treatment, the control group actually exhibited an increase in symptoms over the 3.3 years. 42% of the treatment group received treatment after completing Dyadic Developmental Psychotherapy. Most of this continued treatment was for co-morbid conditions, such as Bipolar Disorder and Attention Deficit/Hyperactivity Disorder. The majority of the children in the treatment group who received continued treatment after competing Dyadic Developmental Psychotherapy received medication management treatment. See Table 1 below.

Children with histories of maltreatment, such as physical and psychological neglect, physical abuse, and sexual abuse, are at risk of developing severe psychiatric problems (Gauthier, Stollak, Messe, and Arnoff, 1996; Malinosky-Rummell and Hansen, 1993). These children are likely to develop Reactive Attachment Disorder (Lyons-Ruth and Jacobvitz, 1999; Greenberg, 1999). These children may be described as experiencing trauma-attachment problems. The trauma experienced is the result of abuse or neglect, inflicted by a primary caregiver, which disrupts the normal development of secure attachment. Such children are at risk of developing a disorganized attachment (Lyons-Ruth and Jacobvitz 1999; Solomon and George, 1999; Main and Hesse, 1990). Disorganized attachment is associated with a number of developmental problems, including dissociative symptoms (Carlson, 1988), as well as depressive, anxiety, and acting-out symptoms (Lyons-Ruth, 1996, Lyons-Ruth, Alpern, and Pepacholi, 1993).

Table 1

	TREATMENT GROUP	CONTROL GROUP
NUMBER	24	20
FOLLOW-UP. Time between first assessment and second follow-up	3.9 years; s.d.=0.7	3.3 years s.d.=0.5
% With additional treatment	42% averaging 25 sessions	100% averaging 50 sessions

There has been a substantial amount of confusion and controversary about the diagnosis and treatment of Reactive Attachment Disorder (O'Connor and Zeanah, 2003). Attachment therapy, holding therapy, and other terms are often used interchangeably, as are Reactive Attachment Disorder, Attachment Disorder, and related terms, which only adds to the confusion. Dyadic Developmental Psychotherapy is not a "holding therapy" as defined by O'Connor and Zeanah (2003). They describe "holding therapy" as being based on "rage reduction" techniques and that, "the holding approach would be viewed as intrusive and therefore *non-sensitive* and counter therapeutic." (Italics added) (p. 236). Dyadic Developmental Psychotherapy has as its core, or central therapeutic mechanism and as essential for treatment success, the maintenance of a contingent collaborative and affectively attuned relationship between therapist and child, between caregiver and child, and between therapist and caregiver.

Many children with histories of maltreatment, abuse and neglect are violent (Robins, 1978) and aggressive (Prino and Pyrot, 1994) and as adults are at risk of developing a variety of psychological problems (Schreiber and Lyddon, 1998) and personality disorders, including antisocial personality disorder (Finzi, Cohen, Sapir, and Weizman, 2000), narcissistic personality disorder, borderline personality disorder, and psychopathic personality disorder (Dozier, Stovall, and Albus, 1999). Neglected children are at risk of social withdrawal, social rejection, and pervasive feelings of incompetence (Finzi et al., 2000). Children who have histories of abuse and neglect are at significant risk of developing Post Traumatic Stress Disorder as adults (Allan, 2001; Andrews, Varewin, Rose, and Kirk, 2000). Children who have been sexually abused are at significant risk of developing anxiety disorders (2.0 times the average), major depressive disorders (3.4 times average), alcohol abuse (2.5 times average), drug abuse (3.8 times average), and antisocial behavior (4.3 times average) (MacMillian, 2001). The effective treatment of such children is a public health concern (Walker, Goodwin, and Warren, 1992).

Children with chronic histories of maltreatment, meaning abuse or neglect, have internalized a negative working model of the world, adults, relationships, and themselves. The disorganized attachment pattern describes the etiology and psychology of children with trauma-attachment disorders (Main and Hesse, 1990). Significant early neglect and abuse cause important neurobiological dysfunction (Siegel, 2002), including difficulty regulating affect and an incoherent autobiographical narrative. A child uses the caregiver's state of mind to regulate the child's own mental processes (Siegel, 1999). The child's developing capacity to regulate emotions and develop a coherent sense of self requires sensitive and responsive parenting. The best predictor of a child's attachment classification is the state of mind with respect to attachment of the birth mother (Lyons-Ruth and Jacobvitz, 1999). A birth mother's attachment classification before the birth of her child can predict with 80% accuracy her child's attachment classification at six years of age (Main and Cassidy, 1988). Finally, recent research by Dozier (2001) found that the attachment classification of a foster mother has a profound effect on the attachment classification of the child. She found that the child's attachment classification becomes similar to that of the foster mother after three months in placement. These findings strongly argue for a non-genetic mechanism for the transmission of attachment patterns across generations and for the beneficial impact of a healing and healthy relationship.

Early interpersonal experiences have a profound impact on the brain because the brain pathways responsible for social perception are the same as those that integrate such functions as the creation of meaning, the regulation of body states, the regulation of emotion, the organization of memory, and the capacity for interpersonal communication and empathy (Siegel, 2002). Stressful experiences that are overtly traumatizing or chronic cause chronic elevated levels of neuroendocrine hormones (Siegel, 2002). High levels of these hormones can cause permanent damage to the hippocampus, which is critical for memory (McEwen, 1999). Based on this, we can assume that psychological trauma can impair a person's ability to create and retain memory and can impede trauma resolution.

These findings strongly suggest that effective treatment requires an affectively attuned relationship (Becker-Weidman, 2005b). Siegel (1999, p. 333) stated, "As parents reflect with their securely attached children on the mental states that create their shared subjective experience, they are joining with them in an important co-constructive process of understanding how the mind functions. The inherent feature of secure attachment – contingent, collaborative communication – is also a fundamental component in how interpersonal relationships facilitate internal integration in a child." This has implications for the effective treatment of maltreated children. For example, when in a therapeutic relationship the child is able to reflect upon aspects of traumatic memories and experience the affect associated with those memories without becoming dysregulated, the child develops an expanded capacity to tolerate increasing amounts of affect. The child learns to self-regulate. The attuned resonant relationship between child and therapist and child and caregiver enables the child to make sense (a left-hemispheric function) out of memories, autobiographical representations, and affect (right hemispheric functions). Dyadic Developmental Psychotherapy shares many important elements with optimal, sound social casework and clinical practice. For example, attention to the dignity of the client, respect for the client's experiences, and starting where the client is, are all time-honored principles of social work practice and all are also central elements of Dyadic Developmental Psychotherapy. What distinguishes Dyadic Developmental Psychotherapy from traditional clinical work with children is the strong emphasis on maintaining an affectively attuned relationship with the child, a deep acceptance of the child's affect and experience, and greater emphasis on experience and process rather than on verbalization and content. The practice of Dyadic Developmental Psychotherapy requires the clinician to become affectively attuned with the child, and to develop and maintaining a meaningful emotional connection with the child, often at a nontraditional verbal and experiential level. Dyadic Developmental Psychotherapy requires a greater use of self than, for example, Cognitive-Behavioral Psychotherapy, behavioral approaches, or strategic or structural family therapy interventions.

Specifically, There are several important implications of treatment that flow from the above description. Dyadic Developmental Psychotherapy is an approach to treating trauma-attachment disordered children that is based on attachment theory (Bowlby, 1988; Bowlby, 1980) and the previously mentioned processes. This treatment seeks to remediate the negative working model of such children, using experiential methods that have several important and overlapping dimensions: modeling the healthy attachment cycle, reducing shame, safe and nurturing physical contact that is containing, reexperiencing the affect associated with the trauma in order to integrate the experience and not dissociate, and the interpersonal regulation of affect. Maintaining an affectively attuned relationship with the child enacts these dimensions. Accepting the child's affect, and, more importantly, the motivation behind the behavior or affect, the deeper affective meaning for the child, which is based on early experiences of trauma that created the child's current working model expressed in the present, is central to effective treatment and resolution of attachment difficulties. The use of curiosity and acceptance to uncover that deeper meaning is an important element of Dyadic Developmental Psychotherapy and the creation of a new meaning for the child in the present.

These dimensions are also addressed by the through the use of eye contact, touch, tone of voice, cognitive restructuring, psychodramatic reenactments, and repeated implementations of the first year (needs) and second year (shame) attachment cycles. As a result of treatment, children can affectively internalize their adoptive or foster parent's love, structuring, and nurturing, resulting in increased ability to tolerate affect without becoming dysregulated or dissociated, a more coherent sense of autobiographical memory, increased trust, and increased self-esteem. Overall, these children will use their caregivers as a secure base for comfort and from which they can explore their world. Behaviorally, such children exhibit lower levels of aggression, delinquent behaviors, thought disorders, depression, anxiety, and withdrawn behaviors. It is though the healthy internalization of the caregiver that the child comes to trust the caregiver and experience a drive to please the caregiver. This is the beginning of conscience and morality.

METHOD

Subjects

The sample consisted of two groups. There were thirty-four subjects in the treatment-group and thirty subjects in the usual care group. Subjects were selected from among the case files of The Center For Family Development, Williamsville, New York, using the following criteria:

1. The case was closed in within a twelve-month period.
2. The child received a diagnosis of Reactive Attachment Disorder, 313.89, using the criteria in the Diagnostic and Statistical Manual IV (DSM IV, 1994).

3. Children in the treatment group received Dyadic Developmental Psychotherapy. Children in the usual care group received an evaluation only and did not receive Dyadic Developmental Psychotherapy, although 53% did subsequently receive another form of treatment from other providers, which is being termed "usual care" in this chapter.

4. The child had a significant history of physical abuse, physical or psychological neglect, sexual abuse, or institutional care. These children were experiencing complex Post Traumatic Stress Disorder.

All children were between the ages of five years old and sixteen years old at the time treatment began. Most had at least one prior episode of treatment with the average being 3.4 prior treatment episodes for the treatment group and 2.7 prior treatment episodes for the usual care group.

The sample consisted of children in foster care and adopted children. The children in foster care had all been residing with their foster parents for more than one year. On the demographic variables measured (age at placement, gender, race, number of prior treatment episodes, age when treatment or the evaluation occurred, and length of follow-up time period), the foster children and adopted children were similar. The only significant difference was that 31% of the adopted children were adopted internationally while none of the foster children were born outside the U.S.

Detailed description of the subjects, demographic information, and statistical comparisons of the treatment and control groups may be found in Becker-Weidman 2005a.

MEASURES

The Child Behavior Checklist (CBCL) is composed of several questionnaires and is a parent-report measure designed to assess behavior problems of children 1 ½ to 18 years of age. The CBCL has eight syndrome scales. The child's score is compared with age and gender based norms. The syndrome scales used in this study are: Withdrawn/Depressed, Social Problems, Thought Problems, Attention Problems, Rule-Breaking Behavior, and Aggressive Behavior. The instrument has widely accepted reliability and validity that is reported on extensively in the manual[33].

The Randolph Attachment Disorder Questionnaire assesses Attachment Disorder. It consists of thirty items completed by the caregiver who rates each item on a one to five scale. The manual (Randolph, 2000) describes in detail the development of the test, scoring, reliability, and validity.

All families completed the RADQ and CBCL as part of the evaluation process prior to beginning treatment (Becker-Weidman, 2005c). An extensive examination of records is also part of the evaluation. Prior treatment records, school records, adoption summaries, protective service reports, police reports, termination of parental rights court documents, and other evaluations and reports, as available, were reviewed for each child as part of the assessment process. Evaluations usually consisted of three interviews and several psychological tests and questionnaires. In the first interview, the therapist elicits a detailed child history from the parent(s) and assesses the parent's capacity to implement attachment-based parenting

(Hughes, 1997; Gray, 2002; Thomas, 1997). The parents are given several questionnaires to complete and return at the second interview, which is with the child. These questionnaires usually include the RADQ, CBCL, a Behavior Checklist, and several narratives, including an autobiography of each caregiver and a description of a "day-in-the-life" of the child. The child interview consists of an assessment of the child's capacity to engage in an emotionally attuned relationship and the administration of several psychological tests, such as the House-Tree-Person, Kinetic Family Drawing, Child Apperception Test, and Sentence Completion. The Youth version of the CBCL and the Million Adolescent Personality Inventory are sometimes administered to older children or adolescents. The third interview is with the caregivers to discuss the assessment and treatment plan.

INDEPENDENT VARIABLE: DYADIC DEVELOPMENTAL PSYCHOTHERAPY

Dyadic Developmental Psychotherapy is a treatment developed by Daniel Hughes, Ph.D., (Hughes, 2005, Hughes, 2003, Hughes, 2002; Hughes, 1997). Its basic principals are described by Hughes (2003) and summarized as follows:

1. A focus on both the caregivers and therapists own attachment strategies. Previous research (Dozier, 2001, Tyrell 1999) has shown the importance of the caregivers and therapists state of mind for the success of interventions.
2. Therapist and caregiver are attuned to the child's subjective experience and reflect this back to the child. In the process of maintaining an intersubjective attuned connection with the child, the therapist and caregiver help the child regulate affect and construct a coherent autobiographical narrative.
3. Sharing of subjective experiences.
4. Use of PACE and PLACE are essential to healing.
5. Directly address the inevitable misattunements and conflicts that arise in interpersonal relationships.
6. Caregivers use attachment-facilitating interventions.
7. Use of a variety of interventions, including cognitive-behavioral strategies.

Dyadic Developmental Psychotherapy interventions flow from several theoretical and empirical lines (Becker-Weidman and Shell, 2005). Attachment theory (Bowlby, 1980, Bowlby, 1988) provides the theoretical foundation for Dyadic Developmental Psychotherapy. Early trauma disrupts the normally developing attachment system by creating distorted internal working models of self, others, and caregivers. This is one rationale for treatment in addition to the necessity for sensitive care-giving. As O'Connor and Zeanah (2003, p. 235) have stated, "A more puzzling case is that of an adoptive/foster caregiver who is 'adequately' sensitive but the child exhibits attachment disorder behavior; it would seem unlikely that improving parental sensitive responsiveness (in already sensitive parent) would yield positive changes in the parent-child relationship." Treatment is necessary to directly address the rigid and dysfunctional internalized working models that traumatized children with attachment disorders have developed.

Current thinking and research on the neurobiology of interpersonal behavior (Siegel, 1999, Siegel, 2000, Siegel, 2002, Schore, 2001) is another part of the foundation on which Dyadic Developmental Psychotherapy rests.

The primary approach is to create a secure base in treatment (using techniques that fit with maintaining a healing PACE (Playful, Accepting, Curious, and Empathic) and at home using principals that provide safe structure and a healing PLACE (Playful, Loving, Acceptance, Curious, and Empathic). Developing and sustaining an attuned relationship within which contingent collaborative communication occurs helps the child heal. Coercive interventions such as rib-stimulation, holding-restraining a child in anger or to provoke an emotional response, shaming a child, using fear to elicit compliance, and interventions based on power/control and submission, etc., are never used and are inconsistent with a treatment rooted in attachment theory and current knowledge about the neurobiology of interpersonal behavior.

Dyadic Developmental Psychotherapy, as conducted at The Center For Family Development, uses two-hour sessions involving one therapist, parent(s), and child. Two offices are used. Unless the caregivers are in the treatment room, the caregivers are viewing treatment from another room by closed circuit TV. or a one-way mirror. The usual structure of a session involves three components. First, the therapist meets with the caregivers in one office while the child is seated in the treatment room. During this part of treatment, the caregiver is instructed in attachment parenting methods (Hughes, 1997; Gray, 2002; Thomas, 1997). The caregiver's own issues that may create difficulties with developing affective attunement with their child may also be explored and resolved. Effective parenting methods for children with trauma-attachment disorders require a high degree of structure and consistency, along with an affective milieu that demonstrates playfulness, love, acceptance, curiosity, and empathy (PLACE). During this part of the treatment, caregivers receive support and are given the same level of attuned responsiveness that we wish the child to experience. Quite often caregivers feel blamed, devalued, incompetent, depleted, and angry. Parent-support is an important dimension of treatment to help caregivers be more able to maintain an attuned connecting relationship with their child. Second, the therapist, often with the caregivers, meets with the child in the treatment room. This generally takes one to one and a half hours. Third, the therapist meets with the caregivers without the child. Broadly speaking, the treatment with the child uses three categories of interventions: affective attunement, cognitive restructuring, and psychodramatic reenactments. Treatment with the caregivers uses two categories of interventions: first, teaching effective parenting methods and helping the caregivers avoid power struggles and, second, maintaining the proper PLACE or attitude. The caregivers provide a high degree of structure to provide safety for the child. Within this structured world, the caregiver maintains a high degree of affective attunement that is nurturing and that repeatedly enacts the attachment-cycle of engagement, disruption, and interactive-repair (Siegel, 2001; Schore, 2001).

There are several elements of Dyadic Developmental Psychotherapy, that distinguish it from what might be termed traditional clinical work with children; although it certainly shares many elements in common with sound casework practice. First, Dyadic Developmental Psychotherapy is based on Attachment Theory, not Object-Relations Theory, Cognitive-Behavioral Theory, or other theories of human behavior and its relationship to the social environment. Second, there is a greater emphasis on non-verbal processes rather than on verbal content. Cognitive-Behavioral, Behavioral, Task-Centered Casework, and many other methods do not focus as significantly on non- verbal processes as therapeutic intervention methods. Dyadic Developmental Psychotherapy focuses extensively on the non-verbal experiential level of interaction as a way of addressing negative internal working models and as a way of creating a safe and secure base from which the child can explore past trauma. Third, while many effective treatments rely on empathy, attunement, acceptance, developing a coherent autobiographical narrative, psychodramatic reenactments and role-playing, and nonverbal processes, Dyadic Developmental Psychotherapy is unique in its using all these elements together as an integrated strategy to revise negative internal working models, develop a coherent autobiographical narrative, and foster the development of a secure and healthy attachment. The therapy is an affect-modulating therapy that combines elements of several recognized approaches into a unique reconfigured mix to address the severely dysregulating trauma that chronic maltreatment causes.

Treatment of the child has a significant non-verbal dimension since much of the trauma took place at a pre-verbal stage and is often dissociated from explicit memory. As a result, childhood maltreatment and resultant trauma create barriers to successful engagement and treatment of these children. Treatment interventions are designed to create experiences of safety and affective attunement so that the child is affectively engaged and can explore and resolve past trauma. This affective attunement is the same process used for non-verbal communication between a caregiver and child during attachment facilitating interactions (Hughes, 2002, Siegel, 2001). The therapist and caregivers' attunement results in co-regulation of the child's affect so that is it manageable. Cognitive restructuring interventions are designed to help the child develop secondary mental representations of traumatic events, which allow the child to integrate these events and develop a coherent autobiographical narrative. Treatment involves multiple repetitions of the fundamental caregiver-child attachment cycle. The cycle begins with shared affective experiences, is followed by a breach in the relationship (a separation or discontinuity), and ends with a reattunement of affective states. Non-verbal communication, involving eye contact, tone of voice, touch, and movement, are essential elements to creating affective attunement.

The treatment provided often adhered to a structure with several dimensions. It is pictured in Figure 1, below. First, behavior is identified and explored. The behavior may have occurred in the immediate interaction or have occurred at some time in the past. Using curiosity and acceptance the behavior is explored. Second, using curiosity and acceptance the behavior is explore and the meaning to the child begins to emerge. Third, empathy is used to reduce the child's sense of shame and increase the child's sense of being accepted and understood. Forth, the child's behavior is then normalized. In other words, once the meaning of the behavior and its basis in past trauma is identified, it becomes understandable that the symptom is present. An example of such an interaction is the following:

Wow, I see how you got so angry when your Mom asked you to pick up your toys. You thought she was being mean and didn't want you to have fun or love you. You thought she was going to take everything away and leave you like your first Mom did, like when your first Mom took your toys and then left you alone in the apartment that time. Oh, I can really understand now how hard that must be for you when Mom said to clean up. You really felt mad and scared. That must be so hard for you.

Fifth, the child communicates this understanding to the caregiver.

Sixth, finally, a new meaning for the behavior is found and the child's actions are integrated into a coherent autobiographical narrative by communicating the new experience and meaning to the caregiver.

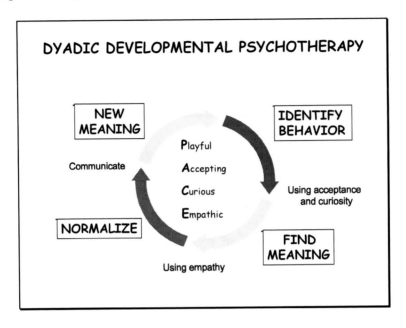

Figure 1

Past traumas are revisited by reading documents and through psychodramatic reenactments. These interventions, which occur within a safe attuned relationship, allow the child to integrate the past traumas and to understand the past and present experiences that create the feelings and thoughts associated with the child's behavioral disturbances. The child develops secondary representations of these events, feelings, and thoughts that result in greater affect regulation and a more integrated autobiographical narrative.

As described by Hughes (1997, 2002), the therapy is an active, affect modulated experience that involves acceptance, curiosity, empathy, and playfulness. By co-regulating the child's emerging affective states and developing secondary representations of thoughts and feelings, the child's capacity to affectively engage in a trusting relationship is enhanced. The caregivers enact these same principals. If the caregivers have difficulty engaging with their child in this manner, then treatment of the caregiver is indicated.

RESULTS

The results for the treatment group show that all the scores remain in the normal range and that after nearly four years the improvements in the behaviors measured remain clinically and statistically significant. Table 2 shows the scores on the Child Behavior Checklist (CBCL) and Randolph Attachment Disorder Questionnaire (RADQ) for the children in the treatment group. The pre-test measure was taken during the evaluation period before treatment began. The first post-test measure was taken an average of 1.1 years after treatment ended. The treatment group received an average of twenty-three sessions of Dyadic Developmental Psychotherapy over eleven months.

The second post-test measure was taken an average of four years after treatment ended. As Table 1 indicates, about fifty percent of the treatment group received additional treatment after Dyadic Developmental Psychotherapy ended, but this was primarily medication management treatment.

Table 2.Statistical Analysis.Treatment Group

measure	mean Pre-test	SD Pre-test	mean Post-test	sd Post-test	t-value	p value	mean 2nd. Post-Test	sd 2nd. Post test	t test prob.
RADQ	65	20.3	20	12.1	12.822	<.0001	15	12	<.0001
CBCL Syndrome Scale Scores									
Withdrawn	65	11.8	54	6.0	4.897	<.0001	56	6	.008
Anxious/D epressed	62	10.5	58	8.1	2.665	.006	58	5	.006
Social Problems	67	9.7	59	5.5	4.376	<.0001	56	5	.001
Thought Problems	68	9.5	56	3.9	6.133	<.0001	60	8	.02
Attention Problems	72	12.5	57	6.1	5.836	<.0001	57	6	<.0002
Rule-Breaking Behavior	69	6.9	53	3.8	12.181	<.0001	52	3	<.0001
Aggressive Behavior	71	9.1	55	4.5	10.576	<.0001	54	4	<.0001

The control group did not fare as well. As we see in Table 3, all of the measured scores increased from pre-test to second post-test and from the first post-test to the second post-test, which was over three years after the pre-test. All the scores remained in the clinical range despite having received on-going treatment averaging fifty sessions. In addition, the deterioration in test scores reached statistically significant levels on Anxious/Depressed, Attention Problems, Rule-Breaking Behavior, and Aggressive Behavior scales of the Child Behavior Checklist.

The control group results are especially disturbing since all the children did receive treatment. The children in the control group received treatment from various agencies and professionals in private practice, none of who are affiliated with The Center For Family Development. As the previous study demonstrated, there was no clinically or statistically significant difference between the control and treatment groups on the variables measures before treatment began. There were statistically and clinically significant changes in the behaviors measured for the treatment group, but not for the control group, after the initial one-year follow-up period. These results strongly suggest that Dyadic Developmental Psychotherapy is an effective treatment and that the results of this treatment are stable for over time. It appears that Dyadic Developmental Psychotherapy effectively helped the children in the treatment group resolve their Reactive Attachment Disorder, while those in the control group worsened.

Table 3.Statistical Analysis.Control Group

measure	mean Pre-test	SD Pre-test	mean Post-test	sd Post-test	t-value	p value	mean 2nd. post test	sd 2nd post test	t-test prob.
RADQ	67	16.6	69	18.5	-1.065	.30	73	9	.3
CBCL Syndrome Scale Scores									
Withdrawn	65	10.5	63	9.4	1.427	.16	71	4	.18
Anxious/ Depressed	62	10.6	60	10.3	1.060	.30	70	10	.03*
Social Problems	64	11.1	65	11.2	-0.854	.40	65	2	.5
Thought Problems	63	8.6	62	8.1	0.984	.33	67	8	.8
Attention Problems	68	11.9	66	10.8	0.927	.36	77	9	.02*
Rule-Breaking Behavior	67	7.4	66	9.6	1.869	.07	81	4	.02*
Aggressive Behavior	70	10.2	68	9.4	0.919	.37	81	4	.02*

* Statistically significant

DISCUSSION

The purpose of the present study was to demonstrate the outcome of Dyadic Developmental Psychotherapy with children who have trauma-attachment disorders in an outpatient setting when provided by a trained clinician. While residential treatment and intensive forms of treatment have been used to treat this population, a method that is usable by trained clinicians in a general office or clinic setting would allow for more efficient and widely available treatment for these children.

Children with the symptoms of attachment disorder and antisocial behaviors are very likely to continue these behaviors in adulthood (Robins and Price, 1991; Loeber, 1991). In addition, children with trauma-attachment disorders are more likely to develop severe personality disorders, such as Borderline Personality Disorder, Sociopathic Personality Disorder, Narcissistic Personality Disorder, and other personality disorders in adulthood (Dozier, et al., 1999). For these reasons, it is vital that effective treatment for children with trauma-attachment problems be developed and validated. Dyadic-Developmental-Psychotherapy, also known as attachment therapy, appears to be one such treatment. Prior to this study, there have been no quantitative studies using an outpatient model, which verified the effectiveness of this type of treatment.

This study found statistically and clinically significant reductions in outcome variables that continued four years after treatment ended. The basis for these changes is that an affectively based treatment will result in integration of trauma, improved affect regulation, and an enhanced, integrated, and coherent autobiographical sense of self. It is suggested that treatment allows the child to develop a healthier attachment to the child's caregiver, increase the child's capacity for self-regulation, empathy, remorse, and toleration of higher levels of stress. The measurable dimensions of these changes are seen in a number of areas: 1) increased capacity to use the caregiver as a secure base for comfort and security as measured by a decrease in the Withdrawn/Depressed scale on the Child Behavior Checklist (CBCL) (Achenback, 1991); 2) reduction in grief and loss issues associated with abuse, neglect, and foster/adoptive placements as measured by a reduction in the Depressed/Anxious Problems scale on the CBCL; 3) improved ability to form social relationships as measured by a reduction on the Social Problems scale on the CBCL; 4) improved cause-effect thinking as measured by a decrease in the Thought Problems scale of the CBCL; 5) reduced aggression as measured by a decrease in the Aggression scale of the CBCL; 6) increased adherence to generally acceptable social behavior as measured by a reduction in the Delinquent Behavior scale of the CBCL.

The conclusion that Dyadic Developmental Psychotherapy may be the cause of the clinically and statistically significant reductions in the measured outcome variables is bolstered by the use of a control group or usual care group. The usual care-group was not statistically different from the treatment-group on such variables as age, gender, race, type of adoption, age at adoption, or number of prior treatment episodes. However, the usual care-group was older than the treatment group.

The treatment group received Dyadic Developmental Psychotherapy while 53% of the original usual care group received "usual-care" but not Dyadic Developmental Psychotherapy. However, 100% of this usual care group received treating during the second follow-up period, while their behavior worsened. This finding strengthens the conclusion that Dyadic Developmental Psychotherapy is an effective method of treating children with attachment-trauma disorders. Individual therapy, play therapy, family therapy, residential treatment, and intensive outpatient treatment are the usual treatment modalities that these children receive. The lack of change and actual worsening in the usual care group's measured outcome variables bolsters the conclusion that usual care methods are not effective in treating such abused and maltreated children while Dyadic Developmental Psychotherapy is an effective treatment method.

The use of the usual care group eliminated the likelihood that time alone cause the positive change in the treatment group on the measured outcome variables. If maturation were a significant factor then one would expect to see a positive reduction in attachment disorder symptoms and other behavioral symptoms among the usual care-group; such a change was not observed in this study.

It is suggested that Dyadic Developmental Psychotherapy is effective because of its reliance on and development of affective attunement between therapist and child, caregiver and child, and therapist and caregiver. The process of maintaining affective attunement allows for dyadic regulation of affect between child and therapist so that the child feels a sense of safety and security and can experience the affect associated with past traumas, allowing for integration of these experiences rather than dissociation of the affect and memory. Furthermore, Dyadic Developmental Psychotherapy's significant involvement of caregivers in treatment facilitates the development of an affectively attuned relationship between the child and caregiver. An affectively attuned relationship may be described as a relationship in which the two persons are experiencing the same affect and that their affect co-varies. Within the safety of the attuned relationship the shame of past trauma and current misbehaviors are explored, experienced, and integrated. The caregiver-child interactions build on a dyadic affect regulation process that normally occurs during infancy and the toddler years. The child's past traumatic history of abuse and neglect strongly suggests that such interaction, which facilitates a health attachment and a trusting and safe relationship, did not occur or occurred in an inadequate manner. Dyadic Developmental Psychotherapy facilitates the development of a healthy attachment between child and caregiver, enables the child to affectively trust the caregiver, and allows the child to secure comfort and safety from the caregiver.

Another limitation of this study is that there is no direct reliable and valid measure of attachment between child and caregiver. There are no existing reliable and valid measures of child-caregiver attachment for the age group in this study. Developing such a measure that can be used in a clinic or office setting should be a priority. Anecdotally, we can report a nearly universal improvement in the treatment group in reported secure base behaviors. For example, before treatment most of the children did not go to their caregiver for care, comfort, or solace. After treatment, there was a marked increase in reports of such use of the caregiver for comfort in times of stress or discomfort. We also found that the treatment group caregivers reported a more authentic and genuine affective relationship with their child. The children were experienced as more spontaneous in their displays of affection (without using affection in a manipulative manner). Children also reported more enjoyment of their caregivers and more interest in seeking out their advice, ideas, approval, and assistance. However, anecdotal evidence of an increase in attachment behaviors lacks the power of a more rigorous and empirically based measure.

Further research is indicted in order to replicate and extend these findings. A larger sample of subjects would allow for an exploration of what factors facilitate or inhibit the effectiveness of psychotherapy. Such factors may include the length of time between the child entering the family and beginning treatment or the number of prior treatments. Our anecdotal experience is that the more previous failed attempts to resolve problems and incorrect diagnoses, the more discouraged, angry, and disheartened are the caregivers. Another set of factors may involve the caregivers' ability to demonstrate playfulness, love, acceptance, curiosity, and empathy (PLACE) with their child, key dimensions to enact affective attunement and maintain a sense of connectedness with the child. These behaviors may be described as representing the caregiver's ability to psychologically maintain a healing PLACE for their child.

CONCLUSION

This study examined the effects of Dyadic Developmental Psychotherapy on children with trauma-attachment disorders who meet the DSM IV criteria for Reactive Attachment Disorder. A treatment group composed of thirty-four subjects and a usual care group composed of thirty subjects was compared. All children were between the ages of five and sixteen when the study began. It was hypothesized that Dyadic Developmental Psychotherapy would reduce the symptoms of attachment disorder, aggressive and delinquent behaviors, social problems and withdrawal, anxiety and depressive problems, thought problems, and attention problems among children who received Dyadic Developmental Psychotherapy. Significant reductions were achieved in all measures studied. The results were achieved in an average of twenty-three sessions over eleven months. These findings continued for an average of 3.9 years after treatment ended for children between the ages of six and fifteen years. There were no changes in the usual care-group subjects, who were re-tested an average of 3.3 years after the evaluation was completed. The results are particularly salient since 82% of the treatment-group subjects and 83% of the usual care-group subjects had previously received treatment with an average of 3.2 prior treatment episodes. This past history of unsuccessful treatment further underscores the importance of these results in demonstrating the effectiveness and efficacy of Dyadic Developmental Psychotherapy as a treatment for children with trauma-attachment problems. In addition, 100% of the usual care-group subjects received "usual care" but without any measurable change in the outcome variables measured. Children with trauma-attachment problems are at significant risk of developing severe disorders in adulthood such as Post Traumatic Stress Disorder, Borderline Personality Disorder, Narcissistic Personality Disorder, and other personality disorders.

This study supports several of O'Connor and Zeanah's conclusions and recommendations concerning treatment. They state (p. 241), "treatments for children with attachment disorders should be promoted only when they are evidence-based." The results of this study are a beginning toward that end. While there are a number of limitations to this study, given the severity of the disorders in question, the paucity of effective treatments, and the desperation of caregivers seeking help, it is a step in the right direction. Dyadic Developmental Psychotherapy is not a coercive therapy, which can be dangerous. Dyadic Developmental Psychotherapy provides caregiver support as an integral part of its treatment methodologies. Finally, Dyadic Developmental Psychotherapy uses a multimodal approach built around affect attunement.

This study indicates that Dyadic Developmental Psychotherapy is an effective intervention for children with trauma-attachment problems. Additional research with a larger sample would be a valuable extension of this study.

REFERENCES

Achenback, T. (1991). *Manual for the Child Behavior Checklist/4-18 and 1991 Profile.* Burlington: University of Vermont Press.

Allan, J. (2001). *Traumatic Relationships and Serious Mental Disorders.* NY: John Wiley.

Andrews, B., Varewin, C.R., Rose, S., and Kirk (2000). Predicting PTSD symptoms in Victims of Violent Crime. *Journal of Abnormal Psychology,* 109, 69-73.

Becker-Weidman, A, *Treatment For Children with Trauma-Attachment Disorders*: Dyadic Developmental Psychotherapy, *Child and Adolescent Social Work Journal,* December 2005a.

Becker-Weidman, A., "Dyadic Developmental Psychotherapy: The Theory." In Becker-Weidman, A., Shell, D., (Eds.), *Creating Capacity for Attachment*, OK: Wood 'N' Barnes, 2005b pp. 7 -- 43.

Becker-Weidman, A., "The Logistics of Providing Dyadic Developmental Psychotherapy." In Becker-Weidman, A., Shell, D., (Eds.), *Creating Capacity for Attachment*, OK: Wood 'N' Barnes, 2005b pp. 43 -- 57.

Becker-Weidman, A., and Shell, D., (Eds.), (2005) *Creating Capacity for Attachment*, OK: Wood 'N' Barnes.

Bowlby, J. (1988). *A Secure Base.* NY: Basic Books.

Bowlby, J. (1980). *Attachment, Separation, and Loss.* NY: Basic Books.

Carlson, E.A. (1988). A prospective longitudinal study of disorganized/disoriented attachment. *Child Development* 69, 1107-1128.

Carlson, V., Cicchetti, D., Barnett, D., and Braunwald, K. (1995). Finding order in disorganization: Lessons from research on maltreated infants' attachments to their caregivers. In D. Cicchetti and V. Carlson (Eds), *Child Maltreatment: Theory and research on the causes and consequences of child abuse and neglect* (pp. 135-157). NY: Cambridge University Press.

Cicchetti, D., Cummings, E.M., Greenberg, M.T., and Marvin, R.S. (1990). An organizational perspective on attachment beyond infancy. In M. Greenberg, D. Cicchetti, and M. Cummings (Eds), *Attachment in the Preschool Years* (pp. 3-50). Chicago: University of Chicago Press.

Dozier, M. Stovall, K.C., Albus, K.E., and Bates, B. (2001) Attachment for Infants in Foster Care: The Role of Caregiver State of Mind. *Child Development,* 70, 1467-1477.

Dozier, M., Stovall, K.C., and Albus, K. (1999) Attachment and Psychopathology in Adulthood. In J. Cassidy and P. Shaver (Eds.). *Handbook of Attachment* (pp. 497-519). NY: Guilford Press.

DSM IV (1994). Washington DC: American Psychiatric Association.

Finzi, R., Cohen, O., Sapir, Y., and Weizman, A. (2000). Attachment Styles in Maltreated Children: A Comparative Study. *Child Development and Human Development,* 31, 113-128.

Gauthier, L., Stollak, G., Messe, L., and Arnoff, J. (1996). Recall of childhood neglect and physical abuse as differential predictors of current psychological functioning. *Child Abuse and Neglect* 20, 549-559.

Gray, D. (2002). *Attaching in Adoption.* Indianapolis: Perspective Press.

Greenberg, M. (1999). Attachment and Psychopathology in Childhood. In J. Cassidy and P. Shaver (Eds.). *Handbook of Attachment* (pp.469-496). NY: Guilford Press.

Hughes, D. (1997). *Facilitating Developmental Attachment.* NJ: Jason Aronson.

Hughes, D. (2002) *The psychological treatment of children with PTSD and attachment disorganization: Dyadic developmental psychotherapy.* Manuscript submitted for publication.

Hughes, D. (2003) Psychological intervention for the spectrum of attachment disorders and intrafamilial trauma. *Attachment and Human Development,* 5, 271-279.

Lachar, P. (1979). *Manual for the Personality Inventory for Children.* National Computer Systems.

Hughes, D., "The Development of Dyadic Developmental Psychotherapy." In Becker-Weidman, A., and Shell, D., (Eds.), *Creating Capacity for Attachment.* OK: Wood 'N' Barnes, 2005, pp vii – xvii.

Loeber, R. (1991). Antisocial behavior: More enduring than changeable? Special section. *Journal of the American Academy of Child and Adolescent Psychiatry,* 30, 393-397.

Lyons-Ruth, K. (1996). Attachment relationships among children with aggressive behavior problems: The role of disorganized early attachment patterns. *Journal of Consulting and Clinical Psychology* 64, 64-73.

Lyons-Ruth, K., Alpern, L., and Repacholi, B. (1993). Disorganized infant attachment classification and maternal psychosocial problems as predictors of hostile-aggressive behavior in the preschool classroom. *Child Development* 64, 572-585.

Lyons-Ruth K. and Jacobvitz, D. (1999) Attachment disorganization: unresolved loss, relational violence and lapses in behavioral and attentional strategies. In J. Cassidy and P. Shaver (Eds.) *Handbook of Attachment.* (pp. 520-554). NY: Guilford Press.

MacMillian, H.L. (2001). Childhood Abuse and Lifetime Psychopathology in a Community Sample. *American Journal of Psychiatry,* 158, 1878-1883.

Main, M., and Cassidy, J. (1988). Categories of response to reunion with the parent at age six: Predictable from infant attachment classifications and stable over a one-month period. *Developmental Psychology,* 24, 415-426.

Main, M. and Hesse, E. (1990) Parents' Unresolved Traumatic Experiences are related to infant disorganized attachment status. In M.T. Greenberg, D. Ciccehetti, and E.M. Cummings (Eds), *Attachment in the Preschool Years: Theory, Research, and Intervention* (pp161-184). Chicago: University of Chicago Press.

Malinosky-Rummell, R. and Hansen, D.J. (1993) Long term consequences of childhood physical abuse. *Psychological Bulletin* 114, 68-69.

McEwen, B. (1999). Development of the cerebral cortex XIII: Stress and brain development – II *Journal of the American Academy of Child and Adolescent Psychiatry,* 38, 101-103.

Millon, T. (1982). *Millon Adolescent Personality Inventory Manual.* National Computer Systems.

O'Connor, T., and Zeanah, C., (2003) Attachment Disorders: Assessment strategies and treatment approaches. *Attachment and Human Development,* 5, 223-245.

Randolph, E. (2000). *Manual for the Randolph Attachment Disorder Questionnaire,* Third Edition. CO: The Attachment Center Press.

Prino, C.T. and Peyrot, M. (1994) The effect of child physical abuse and neglect on aggressive withdrawn, and prosocial behavior. *Child Abuse and Neglect,* 18, 871-884.

Quay, H.C. and Peterson, D.R. (1983). *Interim Manual for the Revised Behavior Problem Checklist.* Coral Gables: University of Miami Press.

Robins, L.N. (1978) Longitudinal studies: Sturdy childhood predictors of adult antisocial behavior. *Psychological Medicine,* 8, 611-622.

Robins, L. and Price, R. (1991). Adult disorders predicted by childhood conduct problems: Results from the NMH Epidemiological Catchment Area Project. *Psychiatry,* 54, 116-132.

Schore, A.N. (2001). The effects of Early Relational Trauma on Right Brain Development, Affect Regulation, and Infant Mental Health. *Infant Mental Health Journal,* 22, 201-269.

Schreiber, R. and Lyddon, W. J. (1998) Parental bonding and Current Psychological Functioning Among Childhood Sexual Abuse Survivors. *Journal of Counseling Psychology,* 45, 358-362.

Siegel, D.J. (1999). *The Developing Mind.* NY: Guilford Press.

Siegel, D.J. (2001). Toward an Interpersonal neurobiology of the Developing Mind. *Infant Mental Health Journal,* 22, 67-94.

Siegel, D.J. (2002). Toward an interpersonal neurobiology of the developing mind: attachment relationships, "mindsight," and neural integration. *Infant Mental Health Journal,* 22, 67-94.

Solomon, J. and George, C. (Eds.) (1999). *Attachment Disorganization.* NY: Guilford Press.

Thomas, N. (1997). *When Love is Not Enough.* CO: NT Press.

Tyrell, C., Dozier, M., Teague, G.B. and Fallot, R. (1999). Effective treatment relationships for persons with serious psychiatric disorders: the importance of attachment states of mind. *Journal of Consulting and Clinical Psychology*, 67, 725-733.

Walker, B., Goodwin, N.J., and Warren, R.C. (1992). Violence: A challenge to the public health community. *Journal National Medical Association,* 84, 490-496.

In: New Developments in Child Abuse Research
Editor: Stanley M. Sturt, pp. 61-72

ISBN 1-59454-980-X
© 2006 Nova Science Publishers, Inc.

Chapter 4

REDUCED AUTOBIOGRAPHICAL MEMORY SPECIFICITY AND TRAUMA IN MAJOR DEPRESSION: ON THE IMPORTANCE OF POST-TRAUMA COPING VERSUS MERE TRAUMA EXPOSURE

Filip Raes[1,*], Dirk Hermans[1], J. Mark G. Williams[2], Els Brunfaut[3], Luc Hamelinck[1,3] and Paul Eelen[1]

[1] Department of Psychology, University of Leuven, Belgium
[2] Department of psychiatry, University of Oxford, UK
[3] University Hospitals Leuven, Belgium

ABSTRACT

Reduced autobiographical memory specificity, or overgeneral memory, is an important feature and vulnerability factor of depression (Williams, 1996) and is closely associated with a trauma or abuse history in childhood (Hermans et al., 2004). The present study examined the relation between autobiographical memory specificity and trauma in 28 patients with major depression. Trauma-related intrusive memories and efforts to avoid such memories were significantly related to reduced autobiographical memory specificity, whereas trauma itself was not. Moreover, this relationship could not be explained by a reduction in working memory capacity. Results further revealed rumination as a moderator of the relation between trauma and overgeneral memory. The results as a whole suggest that how one copes with trauma or abuse afterwards is of more importance for developing overgeneral memory following trauma, than mere trauma experience itself.

* Filip Raes,Department of Psychology,University of Leuven,Tiensestraat 102,3000 Leuven, Belgium, Tel : ++ 32 - (0)16 - 32.58.92,Fax : ++ 32 - (0)16 - 32.60.99,E-mail: filip.raes@psy.kuleuven.be

Keywords: Autobiographical Memory; Trauma; Abuse; Depression; Rumination; Depression.

Past research has shown that people with depression have difficulty retrieving specific autobiographical memories, referring to one-day events (see Williams, 1996, 2004, for a review). When compared to controls, they retrieve relatively more overgeneral memories to given words (Autobiographical Memory Test, AMT; Williams and Broadbent, 1986). In the AMT respondents are asked to retrieve a specific memory to each of a set of cue words (e.g., *happy, sad, interested, alone)*. A specific memory is one that refers to a particular personal event that did not last longer that one day (e.g., "my best friend's wedding last year"). As compared to normal controls, depressed people respond relatively more with overgeneral memories. Memories are overgeneral either because they cover a period that lasts longer than a day (so-called extended memories, e.g., "the last few years", "when I lived in Germany", "when I was still in college"), or because they summarize similar events, without specifying a particular time (so-called categoric memories, e.g., "being around other people", "whenever I get bored", "attending funerals or memorial services").

Reduced autobiographical memory specificity, or *overgeneral memory,* appears to be a stable and clinically important feature. For example, it is predictive of a less favorable outcome in depression and represents a likely vulnerability marker for depression (Brittlebank, Scott, Williams, and Ferrier, 1993; Dalgleish, Spinks, Yiend, and Kuyken, 2001; Mackinger and Svaldi, 2004; Peeters, Wessel, Merckelbach, and Boon-Vermeeren, 2002; but see Brewin, Reynolds, and Tata, 1999). The question then is, what the underlying mechanisms are, connecting reduced memory specificity to depression or depressive relapse. How does lack of memory specificity put people at risk for depression and negatively influence the further course of depression? There are a range of hypotheses about how this association could be conceptualized (see Hermans, Raes, and Eelen, 2005). One possible way through which reduced specificity negatively affects depression is that it hinders effective problem solving (e.g., Raes, Hermans, Williams, Demyttenaere et al., 2005; Watkins and Baracaia, 2002). Second, lack of memory specificity might contribute to depression through its negative impact on imageability of specific images of the future (e.g., Williams et al., 1996). A third way in which reduced memory specificity might lead to (more) depression, pertains to the relative lack of exposure to the full brunt of negative memories (e.g., Hermans and de Decker, 2001). A fourth route via which reduced specificity may render people vulnerable for depression or impede recovery from it, is through a spiraling, reciprocal relationship with depressive rumination (Williams, 1996, 2004).

But how does this overgeneral memory develop? Williams (1996) hypothesized that some people, especially those who have experienced adversities such as abuse or neglect in childhood, may have adopted such a less specific retrieval style as a means of regulating negative affect. This so-called affect regulation model for autobiographical memory specificity proposes that it essentially concerns a form of cognitive avoidance behaviour (Hermans and de Decker, 2001). This retrieval strategy of overgeneral memory is reinforced by the absence of painful emotions attached to the retrieval of specific painful memories. Recent studies have provided preliminary evidence for this avoidance character of reduced memory specificity (Hermans, Defranc, Raes, Williams, and Eelen, in press; also see Raes, Hermans, Williams, and Eelen, in press): reduced memory specificity was found to be significantly related to multiple forms of avoidance, that is, the more avoidance the less specific memories are retrieved. Although possibly advantageous in the short-run, this overgeneral memory is thus thought to put people at risk for depression in the long-run.

In further accordance with this affect-regulation model, a number of studies has shown that people with a *trauma history* indeed display reduced autobiographical memory specificity or overgeneral memory (e.g., Dalgleish et al., 2003; de Decker, Hermans, Raes, and Eelen, 2003; Henderson, Hargreaves, Gregory, and Williams, 2003; Kuyken and Brewin, 1995; see Hermans et al., 2004 for a review). Some studies, however, failed to replicate this finding (e.g., Wessel, Meeren, Peeters, Arntz, and Merckelbach 2001). Elsewhere, we (Hermans et al., 2004; Raes, Hermans, Williams, and Eelen, 2005) suggested that the relation between reduced autobiographical memory specificity and trauma most likely is not a one-to-one relation, and that various variables might be moderating or mediating this relation.

Rather than trauma per se, we believe that how an individual copes with trauma, for example, might be of greater importance in the development of overgeneral memory. For example, McNally, Lasko, Macklin, and Pitman (1995) found that within a group of Vietnam veterans with PTSD, those who still wore war-regalia (e.g., combat medals, military clothing) retrieved significantly fewer specific memories on the AMT, relative to those who wore no such Vietnam regalia. Moreover, the latter group did not differ with respect to memory specificity from control participants (i.e. Vietnam veterans without PTSD). The authors suggest that regalia-wearing may be emblematic of psychological fixation (p. 619) to the Vietnam War. These findings indeed seem to suggest that the way in which trauma is dealt or coped with is important to take into account in the study of the impact of trauma on autobiographical memory specificity (see also Hermans et al., 2004).

In a recent study (Raes, Hermans, Williams, and Eelen, 2005), we found further empirical support for the idea that the way in which trauma is being processed might play an important role in the development of overgeneral memory. In that study, which was conducted in a group of first-year psychology students, we explored the importance of the level of support received after the trauma as a possible moderating variable in the development of reduced autobiographical memory specificity. Lack of (social) support is a well-known risk factor for developing emotional disorders following (childhood) trauma or stressful events (e.g., Brewin, Andrews, and Valentine, 2000; Llabre and Hadi, 1997; Testa, Miller, Downs, and Panek, 1992; Wasserstein and La Greca, 1996). We reasoned that in case of abuse, non-supported individuals would be less specific with respect to autobiographical memory retrieval than individuals who did receive some support. Adopting a less specific retrieval style as a functional (avoidance) strategy to deal with the negative feelings, thoughts and memories might be an alternative for less supported individuals [cf. Williams' (1996) affect-regulation hypothesis].[1] Results showed that students who had not received any support for the (emotional) abuse showed a trend towards retrieval of fewer specific memories as compared with those who had received support. As such, these results suggest that receiving support following the abuse might protect individuals from developing reduced autobiographical memory specificity. So again, these findings suggest that the way trauma is processed is important to take into account when studying the role of trauma in the development of overgeneral autobiographical memory.

---

[1] In line with this reasoning, Bal, Crombez, Van Oost, and Debourdeaudhuij (2003) found that in adolescents who reported a non-sexually abusive stressful event, a high level of support from the family was related to lower levels of avoidant coping.

A number of studies that have reported a relation between reduced autobiographical memory specificity and *intrusions and/*or *efforts to avoid* memories for past traumatic events are also relevant here (Brewin et al., 1999; Kuyken and Brewin, 1995; Stokes, Dritschel, and Bekerian, 2004; Wessel, Merckelbach, and Dekkers, 2001; for a non-replication, see de Decker et al., 2003; Henderson et al., 2002; Hermans et al., 2004). Such intrusive recollections and the tendency to consciously avoid or suppress such intrusions might be informative as to the way in which trauma is dealt with (see Hermans et al., 2004).

Another possible moderator in the relation between trauma and reduced autobiographical memory specificity is *rumination.* Past studies have found a relation between depressive rumination and reduced autobiographical memory specificity (e.g., Park, Goodyer, and Teasdale, 2004; Raes, Hermans, Williams, Demyttenaere et al., 2005; Ramponi, Barnard, and Nimmo-Smith, 2004; Watkins and Teasdale, 2001, 2004; Watkins, Teadale, and Williams, 2000). But the role of rumination in the relation between trauma and overgeneral memory has not yet been investigated. We hypothesize that whether trauma is related to overgeneral memory depends on peoples' tendency to ruminate, such that trauma only or especially leads to overgeneral memory when one has a ruminative style of thinking.

In summary, the present study investigates whether (1) trauma and (2) intrusive trauma-related memories and the avoidance of such memories are related to reduced autobiographical memory specificity. A third objective was to explore the moderating role of rumination in the relation between trauma and reduced autobiographical memory specificity.

METHOD

Participants

Participants were 28 patients (19 women) from three hospitals: Sint-Pieter Hospital from the University Hospitals (Leuven; $n = 15$), Psychiatric Hospital Sint-Norbertus (Duffel; $n = 9$), and University Centre Sint-Jozef (Kortenberg; $n = 4$). All met criteria for current major depressive disorder (American Psychiatric Association, 1994) on the Structured Clinical Interview for DSM-IV Axis-I Disorders (SCID-I; First, Spitzer, Gibbon, and Williams, 1996; Dutch version by van Groenestijn, Akkerhuis, Kupka, Schneider, and Nolen, 1999). The interviewer (Filip Raes) received a SCID training at the Stanley Foundation Bipolar Network in Utrecht (The Netherlands) with R. W. Kupka en G. W. Akkerhuis, both authors of the Dutch translation of the SCID-I/P. Exclusion criteria were (a) electroconvulsive therapy (ECT) in the previous six months, and (b) a diagnosis of bipolar disorder, substance abuse, or organic brain disease. No exclusion was made on any other Axis-I or Axis-II pathology.

Mean age of the total sample was 40.2 years ($SD = 11.6$; range = 21–65). Twenty-one participants were inpatients and 7 outpatients. Nine participants presented MDE for the first time (single episode); the other 19 were recurrent depressives who had a history of 1 or 2 previous episodes ($n = 12$) or 3 or more past episodes ($n = 7$). The sample had a mean duration of current episode of 5.6 months ($SD = 4.7$; range = 2–23). For 16 participants, it was their first admission to a hospital for MDD; the other 12 had a history of previous admissions (1 to 2 for $n = 7$, and 3 or more for $n = 5$). The most common comorbid diagnoses in the sample were personality disoders ($n = 14$) and anxiety disorders ($n= 2$).[2] In terms of education, a majority of the participants (79%; $n= 22$) completed high school (50% from the vocational track; 50% from the academic track).[3] All but four participants were receiving antidepressant medication, and a majority (82%; $n = 23$) had just started receiving individual supportive psychotherapy with either a cognitive-behavioural therapist ($n = 14$) or a client-centered therapist ($n = 9$) depending on the particular setting.

MATERIALS

Autobiographical Memory Test (Amt)

An extended version of the Dutch AMT of de Decker et al. (2003; also see de Decker, 2001) was used (original version by Williams and Broadbent, 1986). Participants are asked to recall a *specific memory* to 18 cue words (60s for each cue): nine positive and nine negative, matched for familiarity, imageability, and emotionality. Words are presented orally by the experimenter in a fixed order, with positive and negative words alternating: *happy, sad, safe, angry, interested, clumsy, successful, emotionally hurt, surprised, lonely, relaxed, guilty, proud, scared, pleasurable, cowardly, carefree, and lazy.*[4] A specific memory refers to an event that happened on a particular day at least one week before. To familiarize participants with the procedure, and to ensure they understand the instructions, three practice words are given (*to enjoy, friendly, and naughty*).[5] Responses are coded as specific or as non specific. Non specific memories are further qualified as an overgeneral categoric memory (e.g., "Talking to my therapist whenever I see her"), an overgeneral extended memory (e.g., "When I was in therapy for about a year"), no memory (e.g., verbal associations such as "My cat" or "My dad"), no response (i.e., omission), same event (i.e., event already mentioned), or incorrect-specific (i.e., event from the past week). Using this scoring procedure, previous studies obtained good reliability (Pousset, Raes, and Hermans, 2004; Raes, Hermans, de Decker, Eelen, and Williams, 2003) with interrater agreement ranging from 92% to 99% ($K = .83-.96$).

Traumatic Experiences Checklist (TEC; Nijenhuis, Van der Hart, and Vanderlinden, 1999) is a self-report questionnaire including 29 types of traumatic experiences. Trauma area severity scores are calculated for emotional neglect, sexual approach, and emotional, physical, and sexual abuse. A total composite trauma score is computed by summing trauma area scores ($\alpha = .86-.90$; Nijenhuis, Van der Hart, and Kruger, 2002).

Impact of Event Scale (IES). The IES (Horowitz, Wilner, and Alvarez, 1979; Brom and Kleber 1985) is a self-report scale assessing current subjective stress as a result of a specific event from the past. It includes two subscales: Intrusion ($\alpha = .72$) and Avoidance ($\alpha = .66$,

---

[2] Personality Disorders were: Borderline and Not Otherwise Specified (both $n = 5$), Dependent ($n = 2$), Antisocial and Histrionic (both $n = 1$). Anxiety disorders were Panic Disorder With ($n = 1$) and Without Agoraphobia ($n = 1$).

[3] Level of education was scored on an 9-point scale (*primary   school level to university degree*).

[4] In Dutch these words are, respectively: gelukkig, verdrietig veilig, kwaad, belangstellend, onhandig, succesvol, emotioneel gekwetst, verrast, eenzaam, ontspannen, schuldig, trots, bang, prettig, laf, zorgeloos, and lui.

[5] In Dutch these practice words are, respectively: *genieten, vriendelijk, and stout.*

measuring the intrusiveness of the memories for the event and the extent to which such memories are avoided. A total score ($\alpha = .71$) is obtained by summing subscale scores.

Rumination measures. The Ruminative Response Scale (RRS; Nolen-Hoeksema and Morrow, 1991) is composed of 22 items measuring ruminative responses to depressed mood. Each item is rated on a 4-point scale (almost never to almost always) for the extent to which it reflects a participant's thoughts or actions when feeling depressed. Adequate reliability is reported for this instrument (Luminet, 2004). The Rumination on Sadness Scale (RSS; Conway, Csank, Holm, and Blake, 2000) is a 13-item questionnaire measuring rumination on sadness. Items are rated on a 5-point scale (not at all to very much) for the extent to which they reflect the participant's responses to sadness. All items are preceded by the frame sentence "When I feel sad, down, or blue …". The RSS has good psychometric qualities (Conway et al., 2000). For both rumination questionnaires, the Dutch versions by Raes, Hermans and Eelen (2003) were used ($\alpha = .88$ and $.84$ for the Dutch RRS and RSS, respectively). Because the scores on both scales were highly correlated ($r = .81$, $p < .001$), one composite rumination score was calculated by averaging the scales' standardized scores.

Hamilton Rating Scale for Depression (HRSD). The HRSD (Hamilton, 1960) is a widely used observer-rated instrument measuring severity of depressive symptoms. For the present study, the Dutch version by Schotte (1996) was used, for which adequate reliability is reported ($\alpha = .70$).

Letter-Number Sequencing (LNS). The LNS measures working memory (WAIS-III; Wechsler, 1997; Dutch version by Swets and Zeitlinger, 2000).

PROCEDURE

Participants were tested individually. Following the Structured Clinical Interview for DSM-IV Axis-I Disorders (SCID) and informed consent, the Hamilton Rating Scale for Depression (HRSD) was administered. Next, they completed the Ruminative Response Scale (RRS), the Rumination on Sadness Scale (RSS), and the Autobiographical Memory Test (AMT). One or two days later they were administered the Letter-Number Sequencing (LNS), the Traumatic Experiences Checklist, and the Impact of Event Scale (IES). Participants filled out the IES only if they had mentioned an 'IES-relevant' traumatic experience in the TEC, which was defined as a past traumatic event that still caused intrusive thoughts as well as attempts to avoid such thoughts.

RESULTS

Pearson correlations were calculated between all *TEC*-scores and AMT performance indices. None of these correlations was significant: all *ps* > .10.

Nineteen participants filled out the *IES*. The total number of specific memories (in response to negative cue words) was negatively correlated with total IES scores, Intrusion scores, and Avoidance scores (Table 1). These associations remained significant after controlling for level of depressive symptomatology (HRSD scores) and severity of trauma history (TEC trauma scores). The correlation with total IES scores remained significant when controlled for working memory capacity (LNS), $r(17) = -.56, p < .05.$[6]

Table 1.Correlations Between Scores on the Autobiographical Memory Test and the Impact of Event Scale (n = 19)

Variable	S	S+	S−	OG	OG+	OG−
IES-Total	-.60**	-.38	-.70***	.44†	.19	.57*
IES-Intrusion	-.46*	-.25	-.59**	.44†	.20	.55*
IES-Avoidance	-.58**	-.42†	-.62**	.32	.12	.42†

Note. S = Number of specific first memories to all cue words; S+ = Number of specific first memories in response to positive cue words; S− = Number of specific first memories in response to negative cue words; OG = Number of overgeneral first memories to all cue words; OG+ = Number of overgeneral first memories in repsonse to positive cue words; OG− = Number of overgeneral first memories in response to negative cue words; IES = Impact of Event Scale.
†$p < .10$. *$p < .05$. **$p < .01$. ***$p < .001$.

To investigate the moderating role of *rumination* in the relation between trauma and overgeneral memory, a 2 (Trauma: High vs. Low) × 2 (Rumination: High vs. Low) ANOVA was performed. For this, two median splits were performed on composite rumination scores and TEC composite trauma scores, resulting in four groups: low-trauma, low-rumination ($n = 7$), low-trauma, high-rumination ($n = 7$), high-trauma, low-rumination ($n = 6$), high-trauma, high-rumination ($n = 8$). For the number of overgeneral memories in repsonse to negative cue words, this ANOVA yielded a marginally significant main effect of rumination, $F(1, 24) = 3.20, p < .09$: High-ruminators tended to produce more overgeneral memories (to negative cue words) than low-ruminators, respective means being 3.07 ($SD = 1.49$) and 2.15 ($SD = 1.46$). The effect of traumatization was not significant, $F < 1$. Of most importance, the ANOVA revealed the expected interaction, $F(1, 24) = 5.45, p < .05$. One-degree-of-freedom contrasts showed that with low level of traumatization, high- and low-ruminators produced about the same amount of overgeneral memories, $F < 1$ (high-rumination $M = 2.57, SD = 0.98$; low-rumination $M = 2.86, SD = 0.98$). In respondents with higher levels of traumatization, high-ruminators produced significantly more overgeneral memories than low-ruminators, $F(1, 24) = 8.41, p < .01$; (high-rumination $M = 3.50, SD = 1.77$; low-rumination $M = 1.33, SD = 1.21$).

DISCUSSION

The present results failed to replicate earlier findings on *trauma* being associated with reduced autobiographical memory specificity (see Hermans et al., 2004, fro a review). Convergent with others (e.g., Wessel et al., 2001), we did not find empirical support for such a relationship. A possible explanation for the absence of such association in our study is the relative absence of traumatization within its sample. For example, scores on the TEC, when compared to data reported by Hermans et al. (2004), suggest rather low levels of trauma in our sample.

---

[6] $n = 17$ for LNS analyses, because 2 participants were not able to fluently cite the alphabet.

We did found, however, convincing evidence supporting the claim that how one deals with the trauma afterwards is of more importance relative to the mere experiencing of trauma per se. First, IES results replicated those of Kuyken and Brewin (1995) and Wessel, Merckelbach and Dekkers (2002) indicating a mood-independent association between reduced autobiographical memory specificity and trauma-related *intrusions* and attempts to *avoid* such intrusive memories. Kuyken and Brewin (1995) suggested that high IES scores might be related to reduced memory specificity because of a reduction in working memory capacity caused by trauma-related memories intruding and the effort devoted to avoiding or suppressing such memories. However, when controlled for working memory capacity, as an extension to previous studies, higher IES scores were still inversely related to autobiographical memory specificity, suggesting that working memory resource depletion cannot fully account for the link between intrusion/avoidance and lack of autobiographical memory specificity.

Second, *rumination* moderated the relation between trauma and overgeneral memory. Results suggest that for those who have experienced high levels of traumatization, low rumination, relative to high rumination, might be protective against the development of overgeneral memory. Only further, in particular longitudinal research can address this issue more directly and further clarify the relation between rumination in the face of trauma and lack of memory specificity.

As a whole, the results of the present study further add to a growing body of evidence suggesting that the known relationship between a traumatic past and reduced autobiographical memory specificity is not a direct linear one. Most likely, moderating variables such as coping-style determine the extent to which trauma indeed leads to reduced memory specificity (also see Hermans et al., 2004; Raes, Hermans, Williams, and Eelen, 2005). In the PTSD literature, the importance of trauma characteristics and moderating variables such as social support — besides the mere exposure to trauma — is increasingly being acknowledged in explaining the development of PTSD (see Brewin et al., 2000).

Given that reduced memory specificity appears to put people at risk for developing depression, it is important to obtain a better understanding of the factors involved here, that is, getting a clearer view on which factors are protective or maladaptive in developing overgeneral memory. By doing so, we might be able to protect people from adopting or developing an overgeneral retrieval style following trauma, and thus prevent them from going down at least one path to depression, that is, overgeneral autobiographical memory.

ACKNOWLEDGMENTS

We thank Koen Demyttenaere, Sieglinde Meganck, Bart Janssen, Bernard Sabbe, Carmen De Grave, Stefaan Vertommen, and Guido Pieters who assisted us in the conduct of this study.

REFERENCES

American Psychiatric Association (1994). *Diagnostic and statistical manual of mental disorders* (4th ed). Washington, DC: Author.

Bal, S., Crombez, G., Van Oost, P., and Debourdeaudhuij, I. (2003). The role of social support in well-being and coping with self-reported stressful events in adolescents. *Child Abuse and Neglect, 27,* 1377-1395.

Brewin, C. R., Andrews, B., and Valentine, J. D. (2000). Meta-analysis of risk factors for posttraumatic stress disorder in trauma-exposed adults. *Journal of Consulting and Clinical Psychology, 68,* 748-766.

Brewin, C. R., Reynolds, M., and Tata, P. (1999). Autobiographical memory processes and the course of depression. *Journal of Abnormal Psychology, 108,* 511-517.

Brittlebank, A. D., Scott, J., Williams, J. M. G., and Ferrier, I. N. (1993). Autobiographical memory in depression: State or trait marker? *British Journal of Psychiatry, 162,* 118-121.

Brom, D., and Kleber, R. J. (1985). De Schok Verwerkings Lijst [The Impact of Event Scale]. *Nederlands Tijdschrift voor de Psychologie, 40,* 164-168.

Conway, M., Csank, P. A. R., Holm, S. L., and Blake, C. K. (2000). On assessing individual differences in rumination on sadness. *Journal of Personality Assessment, 75,* 404-425.

Dalgleish, T., Spinks, H., Yiend, J., and Kuyken, W. (2001). Autobiographical memory style in seasonal affective disorder and its relationship to future symptom remission. *Journal of Abnormal Psychology, 110,* 335-340.

Dalgleish, T., Tchanturia, K., Serpell, L., Hems, S., Yiend, J., de Silva, P., and Treasure J. (2003). Self-reported parental abuse relates to autobiographical memory style in patients with eating disorders. *Emotion, 3,* 211-222.

de Decker, A. (2001). *The specificity of the autobiographical memory retrieval style in adolescents with a history of trauma.* Unpublished doctoral dissertation, University of Leuven, Leuven, Belgium.

de Decker, A., Hermans, D., Raes, F., and Eelen P. (2003). Autobiographical memory specificity and trauma in inpatient adolescents. *Journal of Clinical Child and Adolescent Psychology, 32,* 23-32.

First, M. B., Spitzer, R. L., Gibbon, M., and Williams, J. B. W. (1996). *Structured Clinical Interview for DSM-IV Axis I Disorders: Patient Edition (SCID-I/P, Version 2.0).* Washington, DC: American Psychiatric Press.

Hamilton, M. (1960). A rating scale for depression. *Journal of Neurology, Neurosurgery and Psychiatry, 23,* 56-62.

Henderson, D., Hargreaves, I., Gregory, S., and Williams, J. M. G. (2002). Autobiographical memory and emotion in a non-clinical sample of women with and without a reported history of childhood sexual abuse. *British Journal of Clinical Psychology, 41,* 129-141.

Hermans, D., and de Decker, A. (2001, December). *Adaptive aspects of overgeneral memory: Part 2.* Paper presented at at the Second Autobiographical Memory Workshop, Cambridge, UK.

Hermans, D., Defranc, A., Raes, F., Williams, J. M. G., and Eelen, P. (in press). Reduced autobiographical memory specificity as an avoidant coping style. *British Journal of Clinical Psychology.*

Hermans, D., Raes, F., and Eelen, P. (2005). Mood and memory. A cognitive psychology perspective on maintenance of depressed mood and vulnerability for relapse. In J. Corveleyn, P. Luyten and S. J. Blatt (Eds), *The theory and treatment of depression: Towards a dynamic interactionism model* (pp. 43-66). Leuven, Belgium/Mahwah, NJ: Leuven University Press/Lawrence Erlbaum Associates.

Hermans, D., Van den Broeck, K., Belis, G., Raes, F., Pieters, G., and Eelen, P. (2004). Trauma and autobiographical memory specificity in depressed inpatients. *Behaviour Research and Therapy, 42*, 775-789.

Horowitz, M., Wilner, N., and Alvarez, W. (1979*). Impact of Event Scale: A measure of subjective stress*. Psychosomatic Medicine, 41, 209-218.

Kuyken, W., and Brewin, C. R. (1995). Autobiographical memory functioning in depression and reports of early abuse. *Journal of Abnormal Psychology, 104*, 585-591.

Llabre, M. M., and Hadi, F. (1997). Social support and psychological distress in Kuwati boys and girls exposed to the gulf crisis. *Journal of Clinical Child Psychology, 26,* 247-255.

Luminet, O. (2004). Measurement of depressive rumination and associated constructs. In C. Papageorgiou and A. Wells (Eds.), *Depressive Rumination: Nature, theory and treatment* (pp. 187-215). Chichester, UK: John Wiley and Sons.

Mackinger, H. F., and Svaldi, J. J. (2004). Autobiographical memory predicts cognitive but not somatic change in sleep apnea patients vulnerable for affective disorder. *Journal of Affective Disorders, 81,* 17-22.

McNally, R. J., Lasko, N. B., Macklin, M. J., and Pitman, R. K. (1995). Autobiographical memory disturbance in combat-related posttraumatic stress disorder. *Behaviour Research and Therapy, 33,* 619-630.

Nijenhuis, E. R. S., Van der Hart, O., and Kruger, K. (2002). The psychometric characteristics of the Traumatic Experiences Checklist (TEC): First findings among psychiatric outpatients. *Clinical Psychology and Psychotherapy, 9,* 200-210.

Nijenhuis, E. R. S., Van der Hart, O., and Vanderlinden, J. (1999). The Traumatic Experiences Checklist (TEC). In E. R. S. Nijenhuis (Ed.), *Somatoform dissociation: Phenomena, measurement, and theoretical issues* (pp. 188-193). Assen, the Netherlands: Van Gorcum.

Nolen-Hoeksema, S., and Morrow, J. (1991). A prospective study of depression and posttraumatic stress symptoms after a natural disaster: The 1989 Loma Prieta earthquake. *Journal of Personality and Social Psychology, 61,* 115-121.

Park, R. J., Goodyer, I. M., and Teasdale, J. D. (2004). Effects of induced rumination and distraction on mood and overgeneral autobiographical memory in adolescent major depressive disorder and controls. *Journal of Child Psychology and Psychiatry, 45,* 996-1006.

Peeters, F., Wessel, I., Merckelbach, H., and Boon-Vermeeren, M. (2002). Autobiographical memory specificity and the course of major depressive disorder. *Comprehensive Psychiatry, 43,* 344-350.

Pousset, G., Raes, F., and Hermans, D. (2004). *Correlates of autobiographical memory specificity in a non-clinical student population*. Unpublished manuscript.

Raes, F., Hermans, D., de Decker, A., Eelen, P., and Williams, J. M. G. (2003). Autobiographical memory specificity and affect regulation: An experimental approach. *Emotion, 3,* 201-206.

Raes, F., Hermans, D., and Eelen P. (2003). De Nederlandstalige versie van de RRS-NL en de RSS-NL [The Dutch version of the RRS-NL RSS-NL]. *Gedragstherapie, 36,* 97-104.

Raes, F., Hermans, D., Williams, J. M. G., Demyttenaere, K., Sabbe, B., Pieters, G., and Eelen, P. (2005). Reduced specificity of autobiographical memories: A mediator between rumination and ineffective social problem-solving in major depression? *Journal of Affective Disorders, 87,* 331-335.

Raes, F., Hermans, D., Williams, J. M. G., and Eelen, P. (2005). Autobiographical memory specificity and emotional abuse. *British Journal of Clinical Psychology, 44*, 133-138.

Raes, F., Hermans, D., Williams, J. M. G., and Eelen, P. (in press). Reduced autobiographical memory specificity and affect regulation. *Cognition and Emotion.*

Ramponi, C., Barnard, P. J., and Nimmo-Smith, I. (2004). Recollection deficits in dysphoric mood: An effect of schematic models and executive mode? *Memory, 12*, 655-670.

Schotte, C. (2001). *Descriptieve psychodiagnostiek van unipolair depressieve stoornissen* [Descriptive assessment of unipolar depressive disorders]. Unpublished doctoral dissertation, Vrije Universiteit Brussel, Belgium.

Stokes, D. J., Dritschel, B. H., and Bekerian, D. A. (2004). The effect of burn injury on adolescents autobiographical memory. *Behaviour Research and Therapy, 42*, 1357-1365.

Swets and Zeitlinger (2000). *Handleiding bij de Nederlandse bewerking van de WAIS-III* [Manual of the Dutch version of the WAIS-III]. Lisse, the Netherlands: Author.

Testa, M., Miller, B., Downs, W., and Panek, D. (1992). The moderating impact of social support following childhood sexual abuse. *Violence and Victims, 7*, 173-186.

Van Groenestijn, M. A. C., Akkerhuis, G. W., Kupka, R. W., Schneider, N., and Nolen, W. A. (1999). *Gestructureerd Klinisch Interview voor de vaststelling van DSM-IV As I Stoornissen* [Structured Clinical Interview for DSM-IV Axis I Disorders]. Lisse, the Netherlands: Swets and Zeitlinger.

Wasserstein, S. B., and La Greca, A. M. (1996). Can peer support buffer against behavioral consequences of parental discord? *Journal of Clinical Child Psychology, 25*, 177-182.

Watkins, E., and Baracaia, S. (2002). Rumination and social problem-solving in depression. *Behaviour Research and Therapy, 40*, 1179-1189.

Watkins, E., and Teasdale, J. D. (2001). Rumination and overgeneral memory in depression: Effects of self-focus and analytic thinking. *Journal of Abnormal Psychology, 110*, 353-357.

Watkins, E., and Teasdale, J. D. (2004). Adaptive and maladaptive self-focus in depression. *Journal of Affective Disorders, 82*, 1-8.

Watkins, E., Teasdale, J. D., and Williams, R. M. (2000). Decentering and distraction reduce overgeneral autobiographical memory in depression. *Psychological Medicine, 30*, 911-920.

Wechsler, D. (1997). *Wechsler Adult Intelligence Scale – third edition*. San Antonio, TX: The Psychological Corporation.

Wessel, I., Meeren, M., Peeters, F., Arntz, A., and Merkelbach, H. (2001). Correlates of autobiographical memory specificity: The role of depression, anxiety and childhood trauma. *Behaviour Research and Therapy, 39*, 409-421.

Wessel, I., Merckelbach, H., and Dekkers, T. (2002). Autobiographical memory specificity, intrusive memory, and general memory skill in Dutch-Indonesian survivors of the World War II era. *Journal of Traumatic Stress, 15*, 227-234.

Williams, J. M. G. (1996). Depression and the specificity of autobiographical memory. In D. C. Rubin (Ed.), *Remebering our past: Studies in autobiographical memory* (pp. 244-267). Cambridge, UK: Cambridge University Press.

Williams, J. M. G. (2004). Experimental cognitive psychology and clinical practice: Autobiographical memory as a paradigm case. In J. Yiend (Ed.), *Cognition, Emotion and Psychopathology* (pp. 251-269). Cambridge, UK: Cambridge University Press.

Williams, J. M. G., and Broadbent, K. (1986). Autobiographical memory in suicide attempters. *Journal of Abnormal Psychology, 95*, 144-149.

Williams, J. M. G., Ellis, N. C., Tyers, C., Healy, H., Rose, G., and MacLeod, A. K. (1996). The specificity of autobiographical memory and imageability of the future. *Memory and Cognition, 24,* 116-125.

In: New Developments in Child Abuse Research
Editor: Stanley M. Sturt, pp. 73-93

ISBN 1-59454-980-X
© 2006 Nova Science Publishers, Inc.

Chapter 5

HEARSAY TESTIMONY IN CHILD SEXUAL ABUSE CASES

Julie A. Buck

The University of Tennessee at Chattanooga

ABSTRACT

As children have become more involved in the legal system as victims or witnesses, special accommodations for child witnesses have been developed and utilized. One often used accommodation is hearsay testimony in place of, or in conjunction with, the child's in-court testimony. Although hearsay has traditionally been inadmissible, there are numerous exceptions to the hearsay rule that are relevant to child sexual abuse trials. In this chapter the legal standards for admitting hearsay testimony and relevant US Supreme Court cases addressing accommodations for child witnesses are discussed in the context of hearsay evidence. Research has only just begun to empirically explore the impact of hearsay testimony on trial results. The following areas of research relating to hearsay testimony are discussed: 1) the accuracy of hearsay witnesses' reports of children's statements and 2) jurors' reactions to hearsay testimony. Finally, the legal implications of this research are analyzed.

INTRODUCTION

The legal system has attempted to make a special effort to provide accommodations for child witnesses whose testimony may be of key importance in court cases. This situation is particularly likely in cases involving child sexual abuse, as the perpetrator and child are likely to be the only eyewitnesses to the event in question. Therefore, when legally pursuing such cases the child's statements are of critical importance. To allow the child to successfully communicate to the jury, courts have allowed the child to testify using closed circuit television or a screen shielding the defendant from the child. Also, children's out of court statements have been admitted through hearsay testimony, which is "a statement, other than one made by the declarant while testifying at the trial or hearing, offered in evidence to prove the truth of the matter asserted" (Federal Rules of Evidence 801[c]). The declarant is the witness to the original event.

Due to questions about the reliability of hearsay testimony, it has not traditionally been allowed in the courts (Myers, 1992). Also, hearsay is often viewed as unconstitutional because it may violate the defendant's Sixth Amendment right to confront and cross-examine the person making the accusation (Mason, 1992) and the defendant's Fourteenth Amendment right to due process (Tobey, Goodman, Batterman-Faunce, Orcutt, and Sachsenmaier, 1995).

LEGAL STANDARDS FOR HEARSAY TESTIMONY

The Federal Rules of Evidence present twenty-nine exceptions to the inadmissibility of hearsay testimony. Therefore, there are a number of instances in which hearsay may be admitted. As the state codes and rules of evidence are modeled after the Federal Rules of Evidence (McGough, 1994), this discussion will focus on the Federal Rules of Evidence rather than specific state codes.

Hearsay Exceptions When the Declarant is Available to Testify

Twenty-three of the exceptions to the hearsay rule are made "even though the declarant is available" (Federal Rules of Evidence, 803). For such exceptions, the reliability of these statements due to the circumstances under which they were made is believed to be so strong that the declarant does not have to testify (McGough, 1994). Many of these exceptions relate only to official records or written documentations. However, four of these exceptions are particularly applicable to cases involving children. Although they apply to adults as well, these exceptions include *present sense impression; excited utterance; then existing mental, emotional or physical condition*; and *statements for purposes of medical diagnosis or treatment* (Federal Rules of Evidence, 803 [1-4]).

To meet the *present sense impression* exception, the statement must be "describing or explaining an event or condition made while the declarant was perceiving the event or condition, or immediately thereafter" (Rule 803 [1]). Requiring the statement to be made during or immediately following the event reduces several risks involved in the use of hearsay. Since the statement is made during or immediately after the event, there is minimal risk of the declarant's memory fading and the declarant is not likely to have the time to fabricate a story (Myers, 1992). However, this exception "arises infrequently" in child sexual abuse cases, because it is unlikely that a person other than the child and the perpetrator would be present during or immediately following the abuse (Myers, 1992, p. 156).

For the *excited utterance* exception to apply, the declarant must be in an excited state due to stress caused by the event in question. Similar to the *present sense impression* exception, the logic behind the *excited utterance* exception is that the declarant's statements made under such circumstances are likely to be truthful because the declarant made them spontaneously and the declarant did not have the opportunity or mental capacity to fabricate the statement

(Ross, Lindsay, and Marsil, 1999). Also, the statements were made shortly after the event occurred, preventing memory decay (Ross, Lindsay, and Marsil, 1999; Schoenfeld, 1985).

The *then existing mental, emotional, or physical condition* exception applies to statements regarding "the declarant's then existing state of mind, emotion, sensation, or physical condition" (Rule 803 [3]). The rationale for this exception is that the declarant's own description of his or her emotional or physical state, made while experiencing this condition, should be accurate (McGough, 1994). Again, since the declarant must be describing existing physiological or emotional conditions, the risk of memory loss is minimal (Myers, 1992).

Statements are "made for purposes of medical diagnosis or treatment" (Rule 803 [4]) are admissible under the *medical diagnosis or treatment* exception. The argument is that a person would not be dishonest to a mental health or medical professional treating him or her, because it could potentially harm the individual or hinder their successful treatment. While the use of this exception is fairly clear for physicians, it is more ambiguous when the child is treated by a mental health professional. The general trend in child sexual abuse cases has been to allow mental health professionals to testify in cases involving child sexual abuse when the professional is testifying that abuse occurred (Guyer, 1991). However, in most cases, experts are not allowed to testify regarding statements made by the child if the expert was consulted only to testify as a hearsay witness, but not to treat the child (see Guyer, 1991 for more information).

Hearsay Exceptions When the Declarant is Unavailable

Under Rule 804 of the Federal Rules of Evidence there are exceptions to the hearsay rule that may be made only if the declarant is unavailable to testify. These statements are thought to be less reliable than statements meeting Rule 803. The declarant is considered unavailable if he/she is exempt from testifying, refuses to testify, "testifies to a lack of memory of the subject matter", is unavailable due to death or a "then existing physical or mental illness or infirmity", or "the proponent of a statement has been unable to procure the declarant's attendance" (Federal Rules of Evidence, 804). When the declarant is a child, it is most likely that the child will be unavailable because the child refuses to testify, the child testifies that he or she can not remember the event in questions, or the child is unavailable due to physical or mental illness.

Of the hearsay exceptions that require the declarant to be unavailable to testify, only two are likely to be used in cases involving children. The first is *former testimony* (Rule 804 [1]). Under this exception, testimony made in court by the declarant is admissible if the party who is currently being prosecuted had the opportunity to direct or cross-examine the declarant. For example, if a child's testimony was videotaped during a deposition and the child was cross-examined by the defendant's attorney, then that recording may later be shown during a trial to prosecute the accused. The other exception is a *statement against interest* (Federal Rules of Evidence, 804 [3]). For example, if the declarant makes a statement that is self-incriminating, it may be admissible under this rule. It is thought that the declarant would not make such a statement, unless the statement is actually true. Therefore, if the declarant is unavailable such hearsay evidence would be admissible because it is necessary to pursue the case at hand.

Residual Exception

Finally, there is also a "residual exception" to the hearsay rule (Federal Rules of Evidence, 807), which allows hearsay testimony to be admitted if it has "circumstantial guarantees of trustworthiness". Although many of these exceptions lack clear standards, the residual exception is particularly vague and allows the courts to make a decision about the admissibility of hearsay "on a case-specific basis" (McGough, 1994, p. 145).

Most states also have special exceptions to the hearsay rule when the declarant is a child who has allegedly been sexually abused (Myers, 1996). Under these exceptions there are generally more specific guideless for the admissibility of hearsay. However, unlike most of the other hearsay rules, both the child declarant and a hearsay witness may testify (McGough, 1999). For example, after an abusive incident, the child declarant may make a statement to a childcare provider explaining what took place during this incident. Assuming the case is legally pursued, then the child declarant and/or the childcare provider may be asked to testify. If, due to the circumstances under which the child's statement was made to the adult (i.e., the potential hearsay witness), the statement meets an existing hearsay exception, then the prosecuting attorney may decide that hearsay testimony should be used during the trial. When the case is brought to trial, then the trial judge must determine whether the hearsay testimony meets an exception to the hearsay rule and is admissible.

RELEVANT US SUPREME COURT CASES

To clarify what accommodations are acceptable for use in cases involving children, US Supreme Court decisions in similar trials are often consulted. In *Coy v. Iowa* (1988), the Supreme Court reversed a guilty verdict in a case involving two 13-year-old children who reported that the defendant sexually assaulted them. In this case a screen was used to shield the children from viewing the defendant during their in-court testimony. Although the child witnesses were not able to see the defendant, the defendant was able to hear and see them through the screen. The Supreme Court ruled that by using the screen, the defendant's Sixth Amendment right to confront his accusers was violated. The Supreme Court reported that there was no evidence that these child witnesses needed special accommodations and the defendant's conviction was reversed. This ruling suggests that it is unacceptable to shield a child from the person being accused when there is not evidence that doing so is necessary.

Another case involving the use of accommodations for child witnesses is *Maryland v. Craig* (1990). In this case, one-way closed circuit television was used in place of the child testifying in court, because it was determined that "the child's courtroom testimony would result in the child suffering serious emotional distress such that he or she could not reasonably communicate" (*Maryland v. Craig,* 1990). In this case, the defendant was charged with sexually abusing a six-year-old girl. The child was subject to cross-examination and the jury was able to observe, on a television screen, the child's demeanor during the child's testimony, but the child could not see the jury or the defendant. In this case, the Supreme Court ruled that the use of one-way closed circuit television did not violate the defendant's Sixth Amendment right to confront the accuser. This ruling set the precedent that in cases where the child is not likely to be able to "reasonably communicate" in court due to the stress of confronting the defendant, closed circuit television is an acceptable alternative because the child is still cross examined, the jury is able to observe the child's demeanor, and the child is under oath. However, this decision suggests that such an accommodation should only be used when it is necessary to shield the child witness from the trauma of confronting the defendant.

In a third case (*Idaho v. Wright,* 1990), the US Supreme Court directly addressed the issue of hearsay testimony is child sexual abuse cases. Wright was charged with lewd conduct with her two daughters, ages 5 and 2 years old. Hearsay testimony by the younger daughter's pediatrician was admitted under the residual hearsay exception. The Supreme Court found that "the admission of the child's hearsay statements violated Wright's Confrontation Clause rights" (*Idaho v. Wright,* 1990, pp. 813-827). The Court ruled that hearsay testimony must meet one of the "firmly rooted" hearsay exceptions or show "particularized guarantees of trustworthiness" to possess "adequate indicia of reliability" (*Idaho v. Wright,* 1990). In this case, the court ruled that these hearsay statements did not meet these standards, and was therefore inadmissible. The Court argued that if the hearsay exception is not firmly rooted, then the indicia of reliability should relate to the circumstances under which the statement was made, and corroborating evidence supporting the accusation should not be used as such indicia of reliability. In cases involving child abuse, such indicia of reliability include "the declarant's mental state and the use of terminology unexpected of a child of similar age", the spontaneity of the statement, the child repeating an accusation consistently, and the child's motivation to lie (*Idaho v. Wright,* 1990).

In a more recent case, *White v. Illinois* (1992), the defendant was convicted of sexually assaulting a 4-year-old girl. In this case five hearsay witnesses testified, including the babysitter, mother, investigating officer, a doctor, and an emergency nurse. These witnesses were allowed to testify under the medical examination and excited utterances exceptions to the hearsay rule. The US Supreme Court denied White's appeal. Even though the child declarant was available and still did not testify, the Supreme Court said that the use of hearsay testimony in this case did not violate White's right to confront the accuser, because the hearsay exceptions used were "firmly rooted" (*White v. Illinois,* 1992). The Supreme Court suggested that in cases in which hearsay is admitted through firmly rooted exceptions, it is not necessary to have the child testify or for the child to be unavailable to testify to admit hearsay testimony because, due to the circumstances under which the statement was originally made, it is seen as sufficiently reliable.

In these cases, the Supreme Court supported the use of accommodations such as closed circuit TV and screens, but only when the child appeared to be unable to "reasonably communicate" through typical means (*Coy v. Iowa,* 1988; *Maryland v. Craig,* 1990). Based on *Idaho v. Wright* (1990) and *White v. Illinois* (1992), the Supreme Court ruled that it does not violate the Confrontation Clause of the Sixth Amendment to admit hearsay, even if the child declarant is available to testify and does not testify, as long as the hearsay statement meets either a firmly rooted exception or has "adequate indicia of reliability" (*Idaho v. Wright,* 1990). However, in the most recent Supreme Court case addressing hearsay evidence (*Crawford v. Washington,* 2004), the Supreme Court took a more conservative stance on the admissibility of hearsay testimony.

In *Crawford v. Washington* (2004) the US Supreme Court ruled against the admissibility of hearsay testimony in a case involving allegations of assault and attempted murder. Unlike the previously discussed cases, *Crawford v. Washington* involved the use of hearsay evidence when the declarant was an adult. The defendant's wife made a statement to the police which was audio-recorded. This recording was originally admitted as hearsay testimony under the *statement against interest* exception (Federal Rules of Evidence, 804 [3]). The Supreme Court overturned this ruling, stating that the only indicia of reliability that would have been sufficient to admit the out of court statement would have been the confrontation or cross-examination of the witness. The Court stated that in cases were "testimonial" evidence is used the witness must be unavailable and the defendant must have had the opportunity to confront the witness prior to the admission of such hearsay testimony. As the Supreme Court did not specifically address hearsay testimony in cases involving child witnesses in *Crawford v. Washington,* it is not clear whether the same standards for admitting hearsay evidence are to apply to cases where the declarant is a child. However, this ruling suggests that in child sexual abuse cases the child must be both unavailable to testify and the child must have been previously cross-examined if "testimonial" hearsay statements are to be admitted. Therefore, under such a ruling it is likely that statements made by children to social work professionals or police officers who are in the process of investigating allegations of abuse would not be admissible as hearsay testimony.

THE ADMISSIBILITY OF HEARSAY TESTIMONY

Why Allow Hearsay Testimony?

While exceptions to the Federal Rules of Evidence were originally designed for cases involving adult declarants, there are several reasons why the courts have also allowed these exceptions to apply to cases involving children. One of the primary reasons why hearsay is allowed in cases involving child declarants is to protect the child from trauma due to testifying. The American Psychological Association argued in an amicus curaie brief for the *Maryland v. Craig* case that, "the right of face-to-face confrontation should give way in a case where a child victim-witness would likely suffer serious emotional distress from such a confrontation" (Goodman, Levine, Melton, and Ogden, 1991, p. 17).

Children may also be inaccurate or not disclose in court, perhaps due to the stress of confronting the defendant or because the child wishes to protect the defendant (Ross, Warren, and McGough, 1999). Therefore, hearsay testimony may be introduced under some circumstances to pursue a case that might not otherwise be pursued because there is little evidence beyond the child's claims, and the child is unable or unwilling to accurately testify in court. As Myers (1996) argues, hearsay testimony may be the most compelling evidence supporting the abuse, the child may not be capable of testifying, or there may be no other corroborating evidence besides the hearsay testimony supporting the allegations of abuse. In such a case, hearsay testimony may be the only means of prosecuting the defendant.

Arguments Against the Admissibility of Hearsay Testimony

While there are several reasons why hearsay testimony should be admissible in cases involving child sexual abuse, there are also many reasons why it may be problematic to admit hearsay testimony. For example, the use of hearsay testimony may violate the accused's right to confront the witness against him or her based on the Sixth Amendment (Ross, Lindsay, and Marsil, 1999). By allowing hearsay testimony of the child's statement, the defendant's right to confront the child in court is removed. A similar argument for not allowing hearsay testimony is that the declarant is not under oath when making statements to the hearsay witness (Schoenfeld, 1985). Therefore, the declarant may be more likely to lie and cannot be prosecuted for perjury. Further, the declarant is not cross-examined (Ross, Lindsay, and Marsil, 1999) and cross-examination may reveal inaccuracies or problems with the testimony (Schoenfeld, 1985). However, we do not know if children are less likely to lie when testifying in-court as opposed to giving an out of court statement.

By having a hearsay witness testify in place of the child, the jury may find it difficult or impossible to assess the child's accuracy (see Kovera, Park, and Penrod, 1992, Ross, Lindsay, and Marsil, 1999). It has been argued that "the appearance, demeanor, and courtroom conduct of the witness" (Schoenfeld, 1985, p. 120) may be vital to the jury in judging the accuracy of the statement. The jury may be more successful in determining whether the witness is accurate if given the opportunity to observe the witness' demeanor while testifying. However, if a hearsay witness testifies in place of a child declarant, then the jury is not given this opportunity and may be less capable of evaluating the witness' truthfulness.

Another argument against the admissibility of hearsay testimony in child sexual abuse cases is that by having a hearsay witness testify instead of the child eyewitness, jurors may assume that the defendant is guilty (Ross, Lindsay, and Marsil, 1999), thereby violating the defendant's Fourteenth Amendment right to due process. Jurors may believe that the child was too traumatized by the abuse to testify in front of the defendant.

Admitting hearsay testimony may affect jurors' perceptions of the testimony or the defendant, but it might also affect the accuracy of the actual testimony. The use of hearsay testimony may increase the possibility that inaccurate or false testimony will be given. First, the hearsay witness has the opportunity to fabricate or modify his or her statement (Kovera et al., 1992; Marks, 1995). Second, the hearsay witness may have simply misunderstood or misinterpreted the child's behavior or statements, perhaps because they were ambiguous (Marks, 1995; McGough, 1994). Third, the child declarant may have lied or misinterpreted the original event or the child may have simply forgotten information relating to the event in question. As McGough (1994) suggested, "distortions of the account" take place in three places. These distortions take place when the child gives an account of the event to a hearsay witnesses, when the hearsay witness "hears and stores" (p. 148) the account, and when the hearsay witness reports the account to the court. Therefore, hearsay testimony has the potential to protect the child eyewitness, but possibly at the cost of increasing the opportunity for inaccurate testimony to be presented to the jury.

SCIENTIFIC RESEARCH ON HEARSAY TESTIMONY

Although hearsay testimony is currently used in child sexual abuse cases, there are relatively few scientific studies evaluating its accuracy or impact. While a few studies have explored the accuracy of hearsay testimony, the majority of the research has evaluated jurors' reactions to hearsay testimony. This research has looked at jurors' competence to assess hearsay testimony, the affect of the age of the declarant on jurors' perceptions of hearsay testimony, and whether the hearsay witness' relationship to the child affects jurors' views of the testimony.

The Accuracy and Quantity of Information Reported by Hearsay Witnesses

If we are to determine whether hearsay should be admissible in child sexual abuse trials, it is vital that we determine how accurate and complete hearsay testimony is in such cases. Several studies have attempted to explore this issue when the declarant is a child. These studies have evaluated how accurate or trustworthy hearsay testimony is, and how much information pertaining to the interview is actually reported by hearsay witnesses (i.e., memory quantity).

In one such study conducted by Warren and Woodall (1999), 27 experienced interviewers conducted 15-minute interviews with children (ages 3 through 5 years old). The children had participated in either a magic show or a doctor exam one month prior to the interview. The interviewers averaged almost 11 years of experience (R = 4-21 years) in "forensic/child protective services" (Warren and Woodall, 1999, p. 359). Immediately after the interview was completed each interviewer was questioned about the child's statements. The interviewers were asked to report the child's verbatim answers to their questions and the types of questions they used to elicit the child's response. Finally, the interviewers were asked to write in transcript form everything that was said during the interview.

Interviewers made fairly accurate and complete reports of the primary activities correctly recalled by the children, reporting approximately 80% of these activities. However, interviewers reported fewer details (65%) recalled by the children and less information that the children inaccurately reported (60%). Less than 20% of the exact questions or content of the questions that they asked the children were reported, but the questions that were recalled were very accurate. While most of the interviewers' questions (80%) were either specific or closed ended questions, the interviewers reported asking mostly open-ended questions. Therefore, while the interviewers' reports of the gist of the children's statements were quite accurate, they had trouble accurately recalling the types of questions that they asked the children and the details of the children's statements.

Similar results were found by Bruck, Ceci, and Francoeur (1999) in a study that evaluated mothers' abilities to accurately and completely recall information reported by their children (age ranging from 3 to 4 years old). In this study children interacted with a research assistant for a short period of time. Immediately following this interaction, mothers interviewed their children about the event. Prior to the interview, approximately half of these mothers were told that several days later they would be asked to recall what the child reported in the interview. The other mothers were not told that they would be questioned about the interview. Three or four days later, the mothers were asked to recall the interview in dialogue format and to report the activities that the child mentioned. Finally, each mother evaluated twenty passages taken from their interview of the child, some of which had been altered. The mothers were asked to determine what was inaccurate or accurate about each passage.

Warning the mothers that they would be asked to recall the interview did not affect the results (e.g., amount of information accurately reported). Although the gist and verbatim information that the mothers reported was fairly accurate and the mothers reported most of the gist information (88%), only 66% of the primary activities that the children reported during the interview were recalled by the mothers and even fewer of the details relating to these events were recalled (35%). Similar to Warren and Woodall's (1999) findings, only 17% of the questions that the mothers asked while interviewing their children were later recalled by the mothers. When mothers were asked to recognize passages from their interview of the child the findings were comparable. Mothers were better able to identify passages in which the meaning (gist) of the passage had been changed than if the changes did not affect the meaning (e.g., making the child's statements appear more spontaneous). While the information reported by mothers was very accurate, these mothers were particularly unlikely to report details relating to the events in question or the manner in which they elicited information from the child.

To determine if equivalent results would be found if interviewers were questioning children about child sexual abuse, Lamb, Orbach, Sternberg, Hershkowitz, and Horowitz (2000) examined twenty transcripts of actual forensic interviews of alleged victims of child sexual abuse and compared them to the notes made by the interviewers during the interview. The interviewers' notes were "designed to record the substantive conversations in their entirety" (p. 700) and therefore these notes are likely to be more accurate and complete than typical interview notes. All of the interviewers had years of experience conducting interviews (R = 6-23 years, M = 12 years) and taking verbatim notes of the interviews. The notes and the transcripts of the interviews were separately coded for the details reported by the child relating to the alleged event and the manner in which the interviewer elicited the information.

Twenty-five percent of the details specifically relevant to the abuse were not recorded in the notes. Of these substantive details, 18% of the central details (i.e., "allegation-specific details", p. 702) reported by the children were also not recorded by the interviewer. However, it was extremely rare that the interviewer would inaccurately report information. Therefore, although the interviewers left out relevant information that the child reported, the information recorded by the interviewer was an extremely accurate reflection of what the child reported and rarely included information that the child did not report. However, the interviewers reported less than 50% of their own utterances made during the interview, and, much like the prior studies, interviewers were more likely to report their free-recall prompts than their more suggestive and directive prompts, thereby misrepresenting how the information was elicited from the children.

Based on these studies it seems that interviewers are able to accurately report most of the gist information recalled by the child declarant, but they report fewer of the details reported by the child. Interviewers tend to be much less accurate and complete when reporting how the information was elicited from the child. Interviewers report that the questions they asked were more open-ended and less suggestive and specific than they were in reality. However, this creates a substantial problem, as research has consistently demonstrated that the accuracy of children's reports is greatly influenced by the manner in which the child is interviewed. For example, repeating questions and asking leading or specific questions has been shown to increase the probability that children will report inaccurate information (Ceci, Huffman, Smith, and Loftus, 1994; Poole and Lamb, 1998). Therefore, it is extremely important that jurors understand how the child was interviewed. Since research on hearsay reports shows that interviewers do not accurately recall the manner in which they interviewed the child (i.e., recalling few of the actual questions asked and being more likely to recall open-ended questions than more specific or leading question), jurors exposed to a hearsay report of an interview of a child are likely to believe that the child's report was more spontaneous than it was in reality.

Jurors' Evaluations of Hearsay Testimony

To date, only one study has evaluated jurors' reactions to actual trials involving hearsay testimony. In this study, Myers, Redlich, Goodman, Prizmich, and Imwinkelried (1999) had 248 actual jurors who served in child sexual abuse criminal trials (42 trials), complete a questionnaire shortly after deliberating (i.e., within a few days of the trial). The questionnaire contained a series of questions regarding basic trial information (e.g., demographic information about the child witness, juror, and defendant), perceptions of the main child witness and the main hearsay witness, and perceptions of the child's pre-trial statements made to the hearsay witness. In all of these trials both a child eyewitness testified in court and at least one hearsay witness testified.

Interestingly, police officers (38% of the cases) and mothers (20%) accounted for over half of the main hearsay witnesses testifying in these trials. Other hearsay witnesses were fathers, other relatives, social workers, doctors, friends, and teachers. In this study, children's in-court statements were seen as significantly more important in determining a verdict than the hearsay testimony. But the adult hearsay witnesses were seen as more accurate, consistent, confident, and less suggestible than the children. As the age of the child testifying increased, the child was also seen as less suggestible and the hearsay witness was seen as more credible. Since jurors were questioned about actual child sexual abuse trials, aspects of these trials could not be manipulated. Therefore, causal inferences can not be made based on these results. However, this study raises important issues that should be further studied, such as the affect of the child victim's age and the influence of the relationship between the hearsay witness and the child.

While the study conducted by Myers et al. (1999) gives us an idea of how jurors react to actual trials involving hearsay testimony, several other experiments have attempted to further evaluate jurors' reactions to hearsay testimony by determining jurors' abilities to assess hearsay testimony in mock child sexual abuse trials. Two such studies were conducted by Golding, Sanchez, and Sego (1997). In their first experiment, mock jurors read a trial summary of a criminal case involving charges of child sexual abuse against the child's uncle. The age of the child (6 or 14 years old) and the presence and type of testimony (no testimony, hearsay testimony, child victim's testimony, or child and hearsay testimony) were varied. In this mock trial, hearsay was admitted under the excited utterances exception.

Not surprisingly, in the no witness condition, the defendant was seen as more believable, was less likely to receive a guilty verdict, and jurors found it less likely that the abuse occurred than in any of the other conditions. However, there were no other affects of type of testimony. While the age of the child did not affect verdicts, guilt ratings, or belief that the incident occurred, the defendant was given a longer sentence when the child was younger. Also there was an interaction between gender of the participant and the age of the victim. Female participants tended to believe the child and the hearsay witness more than males did only when the child was younger (6-years-old). Also, females were more likely to believe that the event really occurred, gave the defendant higher ratings of guilt, found the defendant less believable, and gave more guilty verdicts than did males.

A follow-up study was conducted by Golding and his colleagues (1997) that further investigated the affects of hearsay testimony. In this study, a condition involving a 4-year-old victim was added and the gender of the hearsay witness, who was the child's teacher, was varied to see if this affected the trial outcomes. The condition involving both hearsay testimony and child testimony was not included in this study since this variation did not significantly affect trial results in the previous study. Therefore, either no witness testified, the child testified, a female hearsay witness testified, or a male hearsay witness testified. All other aspects of this trial were the same as the summary used in the prior study.

Similarly to study 1, the child victim was seen as less believable, jurors found it less likely that the child was abused, and guilt ratings were lower in the no witness condition than in the conditions with hearsay or child testimony. There was not a significant difference between the believability ratings or verdicts in the conditions involving either the child or hearsay witness's testimony. As a whole, the gender of the hearsay witness had little effect on trial outcomes (e.g., verdict, belief in the event, and guilt ratings).

In study 2, hearsay testimony was more affective in cases involving younger children, than for older children because in the hearsay condition the percentage of guilty verdicts and believability ratings of the witness was highest when the child was only 4 and lowest when the child was 14. However, guilty verdicts remained relatively stable regardless of age when the child testified. A post-hoc control group was added to this study to determine if participants in the no witness condition might have had artificially low ratings of guilty verdicts because the case was weak. The control condition included the testimony of a psychologist saying that the child exhibited signs of abuse. However, similar results were found and the post-hoc control did not significantly vary from the original control group. These findings support the authors' assertion that hearsay testimony is "believed to a considerable degree" (p. 309) because having hearsay testimony leads to more guilty verdicts than not having a witness testify. Also since the hearsay condition and the child condition did not significantly vary in ratings such as believability and guilt of the defendant, it appears that hearsay testimony and child eyewitness testimony are affecting the trial outcomes in similar manners. However, it appears that hearsay testimony may be particularly affective for younger children.

Another study by Golding and his colleagues further investigated the affects of hearsay testimony (Golding, Alexander, and Stewart, 1999) by varying the age of the hearsay witness. In this study, either the child victim's sister (7-, 16-, or 25-years-old) testified as a hearsay witness, the child testified (6- or 15-years-old), or only the child's psychologist testified in the control condition. A psychologist testified in all conditions saying that the child described the abuse to her and in her opinion the abuse occurred. Participants were told that this expert witness was hired primarily for the purpose of determining whether the child was abused.

Participants in the condition involving the hearsay witness were more likely to find the defendant guilty than participants in the control condition, while the control group and child witness condition did not significantly vary by verdict. Again, females were more supportive of the child victim (e.g., giving higher pro-victim ratings) than were males.

A post hoc control condition was added to examine the affect of having no witness testify. In this condition, a friend of the victims testified that the victim told her that she was a home alone with the defendant, but no witness was called to testify about the event in question. The no witness condition lead to fewer guilty verdicts than the other three conditions.

In these studies (Golding et al., 1999; Golding et al., 1997), the presence of hearsay testimony led to more guilty verdicts than having no witness testify. Golding et al. (1997) argued that jurors find child sexual abuse to be such a terrible crime that they are likely to convict with limited evidence. Therefore, jurors may be eager to believe any testimony, including hearsay testimony. In these studies (Golding et al., 1999; Golding et al., 1997), females were more supportive of the child victims than males. There were also various interactions between the gender of participants and other variables, including the age of the victim, the age of the hearsay witness, and the gender of the hearsay witness. While it is clear that these are important variables to consider when investigating hearsay testimony, these interactions are difficult to interpret because the findings did not yield consistent patterns.

The above studies did not use videotaped mock trials, but instead had mock jurors read a trial summary, which may limit the applicability of such findings to actual court cases. Ross, Lindsay, and Marsil (1999) attempted to determine if the results of prior studies generalize to a more realistic mock trial. In this study, mock jurors viewed part of a videotaped mock trial involving hearsay testimony. The mock trial was created based on court transcripts of child sexual abuse cases and was videotaped in a courtroom. In the videotape, either the alleged child victim (10 years old) testified or the child's mother testified as a hearsay witness. The defendant (the child's father) denied the charges, saying that the child's mother encouraged the child to fabricate allegations of abuse so that the mother could gain custody of the child. Mock jurors saw only the opening statements and the testimony of either the child or the mother. They were given judge's instructions prior to reaching individual verdicts. Mock jurors were more likely to convict the defendant if they saw the child testify rather than the mother (53% vs. 24% guilty verdicts). Also, the child was rated as more credible when she testified than when her mother testified. Women generally found the hearsay witness to be more credible than did men.

A follow up study (Ross, Lindsay, and Marsil, 1999) was conducted to determine if the relationship of the hearsay witness to the child affects juror's views of the hearsay testimony and to see if the results of the previous study generalize to a written trial summary. In this second study, jurors read a trial summary involving charges of sexually abusing a 9-year-old girl. The defendant, a male neighbor, either denied the allegation stating that the parents of the girl planned to sue because the defendant was wealthy, or the defendant simply denied the allegations and presented no explanation for why the child may have lied. In each trial one witness testified, either the child or a hearsay witness (i.e., the child's mother, doctor, teacher, or neighbor). Hearsay testimony led to more convictions than having the child testify (39% vs. 23% guilty verdicts), except for the neighbor hearsay witness. The conditions with either the neighbor or the child did not significantly vary. However, when the defense's case was strong (i.e., the defendant gave a reason why the child would lie), the rates of conviction did not differ by who testified. The child's mother was seen as less credible than the other hearsay witnesses (doctor, teacher, or neighbor). The defendant was seen as less credible when the doctor or teacher testified than when the child testified, suggesting that the doctor and teacher were seen as the most credible witnesses.

This second study suggests that the relationship between the hearsay witness and the child declarant is an important consideration when trying to predict how jurors will react to hearsay testimony. Since this is the only study to date that has investigated the influence of the relationship between the declarant and the hearsay witness, this is an area of research that should be further investigated. Past research has shown that police officers are commonly used as hearsay witnesses in child sexual abuse trials (Myers et al., 1999), but the affect of having a police officer as a hearsay witness was not investigated in this study. Therefore, future research should specifically evaluate the affect of having a police officer testify as a hearsay witness in comparison to other hearsay witnesses. In some ways the results of these two studies by Ross et al. (1999) are contradictory. While having the child testify led to more guilty verdicts than having the hearsay witness testify in their first study, the opposite was found in their second study.

In the first of two studies, Warren, Nunez, Keeney, Buck, and Smith (2001) directly investigated the impact of method of presenting testimony (i.e., either videotape or written transcript). The child (4 years old) was questioned about three activities, two of which really took place and one that the child did not participate in. Later, the interviewer of this child was videotaped giving two scripted statements regarding what the child reported. One of the statements was a verbatim hearsay statement, in which the interviewer reported all of the information reported by the child and the manner in which the child was questioned. In the second statement, the interviewer gave a gist summary of what the child reported, which is more typical of what a hearsay witness is likely to report. In the gist hearsay condition, the interviewer gave a less specific description regarding how the information was elicited from the child, but accurately reported a summary of what the child reported. To determine whether mock jurors react differently to transcripts of interviews or videotapes of interviews, participants either read a transcript of the videotaped testimony or saw a videotape of the actual testimony. Therefore, a factorial design with the mode of presentation (videotape vs. transcript) by type of testimony (child, verbatim hearsay, vs. gist hearsay) was used.

For the most part, the manner in which the testimony was presented (i.e., videotape or transcript) did not interact with mock jurors' reactions to hearsay testimony. The adult interviewer was seen as all together more credible than the child (i.e., more truthful, having a better and more accurate memory, and more confident than the child). Also, the type of testimony participants observed did affect their reactions. Participants were more likely to believe that the child actually experienced a falsely reported event when participants observed the gist hearsay testimony than if they observed the verbatim hearsay testimony or the child's direct testimony. The child's statement was also seen as more believable in the gist condition than in the other two conditions, and the interview was seen as more spontaneous, less suggestive, and more open-ended in the gist condition than in the child condition. These findings suggest that in the more realistic hearsay condition (gist), jurors tended to believe the child more than in the conditions where the actual questions that the interviewer asked could be observed. In the gist condition, jurors were not able to observe the entire interview and therefore may not have realized that the interview was highly suggestive. This lack of information about the interview format may have lead jurors to rate the child's statement as more believable.

Too determine if these results generalize to actual child sexual abuse interviews, a second study using two actual interviews of children who were allegedly sexually abused was conducted (Warren et al., 2001). The children interviewed were 4 and 8 years old. These two interviews were selected from a number of other interviews because they were similar in many aspects (e.g., relationship between the child and the alleged perpetrator, and similar degree and type of abuse). However, the quality of the interviews could not be controlled, and it was determined that the interview of the 4-year-old was of a higher quality than the interview of the 8-year-old. The 4-year-old gave longer statements in response to questions and the interviewer asked fewer leading questions than in the 8-year-old's interview. Therefore, the age of the child was reversed in some conditions so that the quality of the report was not confounded with the age of the child. Similar to the previous study, gist and verbatim hearsay transcripts were created.

In this study, verdict was not affected by condition. Also the age of the child and the quality of the interview did not consistently interact with the type of testimony presented. Participants in the conditions with the higher quality original interview rated the child's case as stronger, found the statement more believable and more spontaneous, and rated the witness as having a better memory than participants who were in the conditions with the lower quality interview. Therefore, it appears that participants were able to evaluate the quality of the interview at least to a certain extent. Consistent with the prior study, in the gist condition the child's statement was rated as less suggestive and more open-ended than in the child and the verbatim hearsay conditions. Also, in the gist interview condition, the child's disclosure was seen as more spontaneous than in the child interview condition. Again, the adult interviewer in the gist and verbatim condition was seen as more truthful and having a better memory than the child.

These two studies (Warren et al., 2001) suggest that jurors may find adult interviewers more credible than children. Therefore, jurors may be skeptical of children's direct testimony and may be more likely to believe an adult's hearsay statements than a child's actual account. Also, in Warren et al.'s (2001) study jurors exposed to the gist hearsay testimony thought that the children's reports were more spontaneous than jurors who were exposed to the actual interview. As we know from other studies (Bruck et al., 1999; Lamb et al., 2000; Warren and Woodall, 1999), hearsay witnesses are likely to leave out information regarding how the child was questioned and report that the child was questioned in a less suggestive manner than was actually used. Therefore, it is not surprising that jurors observing typical gist hearsay testimony are also likely to assume that the interview was more spontaneous and of a higher quality than jurors observing the actual interview.

While Warren and colleagues (2001) began to explore the impact of interview quality on hearsay testimony, Pathak and Thompson (1999) also explored this issue by manipulating the accuracy of the child declarant's testimony by varying how the interview of the child was conducted. To manipulate the accuracy of the child's testimony, children were questioned about a staged event (i.e., a janitor cleaning or playing in the child's presence) in either a neutral manner or a leading manner. All of the children who were questioned in a leading manner changed their responses in the suggested direction, while the children interviewed in the neutral condition were relatively accurate. Adult participants (i.e., hearsay witnesses) were then randomly assigned to watch one of the videotapes of a child being interviewed. Later each adult was asked to recount what the child reported and rate on a 5-point scale whether the janitor cleaned or played. Prior to viewing the videotape, half of the adults were told that the janitor was suppose to clean and half were told that the janitor was suppose to play. This last manipulation was added to see if adults' pre-conceptions affect their opinions about what the declarant said, but this manipulation did not influence the results.

As expected, adult participants in the suggestive condition said that the children were influenced more by the interviewer than participants in the neutral condition. However, while participants in the neutral condition were fairly accurate at determining what the children witnessed, participants in the suggestive condition were unable to determine what the children actually witnessed. Next the adults (hearsay witnesses) were videotaped recounting what the children said. These videotapes were then viewed by a second group of participants acting as mock jurors. The mock jurors were asked what the child witnessed (either cleaning or playing) and whether the interviewer influenced the child. Although the hearsay witnesses realized that suggestive questioning in the leading condition influenced the children, they were not able to relay this information to mock jurors, as mock jurors did not think that the children in the leading condition were influenced by the suggestive interviewing any more than the children in the neutral condition. As the authors note (Pathak and Thompson, 1999), in the neutral condition, the hearsay witnesses and the jurors' responses to the question of whether the janitor cleaned or played were towards the direction of the actually experienced event, but jurors seemed to be unsure of their responses. Jurors' responses to the question regarding what the child witnessed tended to be closer to the middle of the 5-point scale than to the end points representing playing or cleaning. Jurors who were exposed to the hearsay testimony in the leading condition were simply unable to determine what the child witnessed. However, these jurors did not make incorrect judgments based on the hearsay testimony, but instead realized that they could not determine what had actually taken place. Clearly there was a loss of information when jurors observed the hearsay testimony in place of the child's statements, making it difficult for them to determine what really took place.

To further evaluate the impact of interview quality on perceptions of hearsay testimony, Buck, Warren, and Brigham (2004) used actual interviews of children making allegations of sexual abuse. In their study, a 2 (type of testimony: child interview or hearsay) by 2 (child's age: 4 or 10 years old) by 3 (interview quality: poor, typical, or good) factorial design was employed. In this study, the information reported by the child was identical for all conditions, while the language and age of the child was systematically varied to be consistent with the language of a 4 year old or a 10 year old. The quality of the interview was also varied, and, then based on these interviews of varying qualities, the hearsay statements were created to be consistent with what is typically reported by hearsay witnesses. Therefore, while the primary activities recalled by the child were all reported by the interviewer, few (22%) of the interviewers exact questions were reported in the hearsay testimony. Also, in this study, unlike prior research, participants deliberated and reached jury verdicts in this child sexual abuse case.

Jurors in the child interview conditions (i.e., mock jurors reading the actual interview with the child) were quite sensitive to the quality of the interview. If they read the actual interview, jurors rated the interview as less suggestive in the higher quality interview condition, and jurors were more likely to convict in the condition with the higher quality child interview than in the typical or poor interview conditions. However, when jurors were only exposed to the hearsay testimony, interview quality ratings and verdicts did not significantly vary as a product of the quality of the interview that the hearsay statements were based on. Therefore, when exposed only to hearsay testimony it appears that jurors do not have enough information about the interview quality to take this into account when reaching a verdict.

CONCLUSION

So what do these two bodies of research suggest? It is clear that there is significant information loss with the use of hearsay testimony in place of the actual interview with the child. For example, even when interviewers are reporting the information immediately after interviewing a child, interviewers are unable to accurately recall how they questioned the child, making the child's disclosure appear more spontaneous than it was in reality. Interviewers fail to report more than 50% of their own utterances and more than 80% of the questions they asked the child declarant. Also, interviewers appear to have a systematic bias to be more likely to recall less suggestive, more open-ended prompts than the more leading questions they asked. However, the hearsay witnesses reports of the primary events recalled by the children tended to be quite accurate and complete. As reports by the hearsay witnesses in these studies were made within a few days of the actual interview or even immediately after interviewing the child, it is reasonable to predict that far less information would be reported by hearsay witnesses after a longer delay, which would typical for a child sexual abuse case.

Research has shown that memory is colored by our expectations, stereotypes, and schemas (e.g., Dunning, 1999). However, research on hearsay testimony has not evaluated how interviewers' expectations impact what they later report. People who regularly interview victims of child abuse are likely to develop a schema or script about how child sexual abuse generally occurs and how a typical interview is conducted. This information may then be incorporated into the interviewer's hearsay report of the child's testimony making the hearsay report more coherent than the child's disclosure.

Many aspects of hearsay testimony, including the relationship between the declarant and the hearsay witness, the age of the declarant, and the age of the hearsay witness have been explored empirically. But many of these studies yielded contradicting results. The majority of the studies assessing how hearsay testimony affects verdicts found that verdicts were not influenced by the use of hearsay testimony in place of the declarant's testimony (e.g., Golding et al., 1999; Golding et al., 1997; Warren et al., 2001). However, two studies conducted by Ross, Lindsay, and Marsil (1999) found that this was not the case. In the first study, participants were more likely to convict the defendant of child abuse if the child testified rather than the hearsay witness, but in their second study, mock jurors were more likely to convict if the hearsay witness testified instead of the child. In the first study by Ross, Lindsay, and Marsil (1999) the mother was the hearsay witness and was attempting to gain custody of the child declarant. Therefore, jurors may have found the hearsay witness (the mother) to be biased and perhaps a less credible source. Since all possible results have been found in these studies, it is difficult to determine exactly how hearsay testimony compares to the child's testimony, and it appears that other variables may mediate this relationship (e.g., the child's age, the quality of the interview, and the relationship between the child and the hearsay witness).

A few experiments (Buck et al., 2004; Golding et al., 1999; Golding et al., 1997; Warren et al., 2001) have manipulated the age of the child declarant. In Golding et al.'s (1997) study, hearsay testimony was more affective for younger children than for older children. That is, when the hearsay witness testified there was a higher percentage of guilty verdicts if the child was younger. However, when the child testified the verdicts were similar for the different age groups. Myers et al. (1999) found that when jurors participating in actual trials involving child sexual abuse were questioned, younger children were seen as more suggestible than older children. Since children are viewed as more suggestible than adults, jurors may be more skeptical of a younger child's testimony than hearsay testimony. Other research (Buck et al., 2004; Warren et al., 2001) found that age did not interact with the conditions involving either hearsay testimony or the child's testimony. Therefore, it is difficult to determine how age influences trial outcomes as the results were not consistent across these studies. As Goodman and Schwartz-Kenney suggested, "many factors influence a child's ability and willingness to report an event accurately" other than just the child's age (1992, p. 30). In the studies discussed in their chapter, factors such as reinforcement, nature of the reported event, and whether the children were asked to keep the event a secret all reduced or eliminated age differences in the amount and accuracy of the information reported. Therefore, consistent affects of the declarant's age may not have been found in studies exploring the impact of hearsay testimony because jurors may realize that factors other than the child's age influence the accuracy of the report.

Researchers are beginning to explore jurors' reactions to hearsay testimony when the quality of the original interview with the child varies. When typical hearsay testimony (which is fairly accurate, but incomplete) is used in mock trials, jurors tend to believe that the child declarant made a more spontaneous report than jurors exposed to the child's statement, especially when the interview is of a lower quality (Buck et al., 2004; Warren et al., 2001). Jurors exposed to hearsay testimony appear to be unable to determine the suggestive nature of the original interview or evaluate the context of the disclosure (Buck et al., 2004; Pathak and Thompson, 1999). Generally, mock jurors in these studies tended to think that the child was interviewed in a less suggestive manner when hearsay was used than when the child interview was observed. This is not surprising based on the research evaluating the accuracy of hearsay testimony, which suggests that hearsay witnesses are likely to report that the interview as more open-ended and less leading than it was in reality.

There are limitations to these studies that should be taken into account when applying these results to actual court cases. For example, most of these studies only used trial summaries. In actual trials, the testimony of the child may be more compelling than the summaries and transcripts of their testimony used in many of these studies. Actual jurors who served on child sexual abuse trials found that the child's in court testimony was more influential when reaching a verdict (most of which were guilty) than was the hearsay testimony (Myers et al., 1999).

While the research on hearsay testimony has greatly contributed to our understanding of the impact of hearsay testimony, there are still many topics that the research has yet to address. Currently all of the studies relating to hearsay testimony in child sexual abuse cases have used hearsay witnesses for the prosecution. However, the defense could also call a hearsay witness. For example, the child declarant could make a statement to an adult that contradicted his/her previous statements and would benefit the defendant. Also, the majority of studies relating to hearsay testimony when the declarant is a child have used mock criminal trials. However, the use of hearsay testimony may be even more common in civil proceedings, in which the judge has more flexibility to accommodate child witnesses (Myers, 1996). Hearsay testimony may impact trial results more in civil trials than in criminal cases, due to the more lenient burden of proof (i.e., preponderance of the evidence).

Specific characteristics of an individual trial are also likely to influence trial results. For example, the exception under which hearsay is admitted, the child's or the hearsay witness' appearance of credibility, the nature of the abuse, the use of multiple hearsay witnesses, and the child's demeanor when testifying are all likely to affect trial outcomes. However, to date, these case characteristics have not been studied.

While the possible problems with the use of hearsay testimony are numerous, the legal system appears to be particularly concerned with the possible violation of the Confrontation Clause of the Sixth Amendment, and the fact that the child is not under oath when making the statement and is not cross-examined. The reason why it is important that the declarant confront the defendant, be under oath, and be cross-examined is to insure that the declarant is making an accurate and truthful report. However, we do not know whether any of these safeguards actually increase children's accuracy or jurors' ability to determine the child's accuracy. Therefore, it is difficult to conclude that hearsay testimony should be inadmissible based on these arguments.

As previously discussed, research has shown that hearsay witnesses do not recall all of the information reported by children in interviews and, importantly, there is a systematic bias for interviewers to report that the child's statements were more spontaneous than they were in reality. This is very problematic as research has demonstrated the significant impact that the manner in which a child is questioned has on the accuracy of children's reports. Given this important limitation of hearsay testimony, the use of videotaped testimony in place of having a hearsay witness testify seems promising. If the videotaped interview of the child was shown to the jury, the child's interest would be protected and the child would not have to undergo the stress of testifying in court. Also, the testimony of the child would be preserved in its original form and, therefore, further memory decay would be a less of an issue. Showing the jury the videotaped testimony of the child would also allow jurors to evaluate the child's demeanor and language when describing the abuse, which may increase jurors' ability to determine the child's accuracy. For these reasons, the best alternative to having a hearsay witness testify would be to use a videotaped interview of the child in place of the child's in-court testimony. This option seems to present the best compromise between protecting the defendant's rights and the rights of the child declarant.

REFERENCES

Brigham, J. C. (1998). Adults' evaluations of characteristics of children's memory. *Journal of Applied Developmental Psychology, 19,* 15-39.

Bruck, M., Ceci, S. J., and Francoeur, E. (1999). The accuracy of mothers' memories of conversations with their preschool children. *Journal of Experimental Psychology: Applied, 5,* 89-106.

Buck, J. A., Warren, A. R., and Brigham, J. C. (2004). When does quality count?: Perceptions of hearsay testimony about child sexual abuse interviews. *Law and Human Behavior, 28 (6),* 599-621.

Ceci, S. J., Huffman, M. L. C., Smith, E., and Loftus, E. F. (1994). Repeatedly thinking about a non-event: Source misattributions among preschoolers. *Consciousness and Cognition,*

3, 388-407. *Coy v. Iowa,* 487 U.S. 1012 (1988).*Crawford v. Washington,* 541 U.S. 36 (2004).

Dunning, D. (1999). On the social psychology of hearsay evidence. *Psychology, Public Policy, and Law, 5,* 456-472.

Federal Rule of Evidence 801 (c).

Federal Rule of Evidence 803.

Federal Rule of Evidence 803 (1).

Federal Rule of Evidence 803 (2).

Federal Rule of Evidence 803 (3).

Federal Rule of Evidence 803 (4).

Federal Rule of Evidence 804.

Federal Rule of Evidence 804 (1).

Federal Rule of Evidence 804 (3).

Federal Rule of Evidence 807.

Golding, J. M., Alexander, M. C., and Stewart, T. L. (1999). The affect of hearsay witness age in a child sexual assault trial. *Psychology, Public Policy, and Law, 5,* 420-438.

Golding, J. M., Sanchez, R. P., and Sego, S. A. (1997). The believability of hearsay testimony in a child sexual assault trial. *Law and Human Behavior, 21,* 299-325.

Goodman, G. S., Levine, M., Melton, G. B., and Ogden, D. (1991). Child witnesses and the confrontation clause: The American Psychological Association brief in *Maryland v. Craig. Law and Human Behavior, 15,* 13-29.

Goodman, G. S. and Schwartz-Kenney, B. M. (1992). Why knowing a child's age is not enough: Influences of cognitive, social, and emotional factors on children's testimony. In H. Dent and R. Flin (Eds.), *Children as Witnesses,* (pp. 15-32). West Sussex, England: John Wiley and Sons Ltd.

Guyer, M. J. (1991). Psychiatry, law and child sexual abuse. In A. Tasman and S. M. Goldfinger (Eds.), *American Psychiatric Press Review of Psychiatry,* (pp.367-390). Washington, DC: American Psychiatric Press, Inc.

Herbest, R. M., Steward, M. S., Myers, J. E. B., and Hansen, R. L. (1999). Young children's understanding of the physician's role and the medical hearsay exception. In M. Siegal and C. C. Peterson (Eds.), *Children's Understanding of Biology and Health* (pp. 235-256). United Kingdom: Cambridge University Press.

Hovland, C. I., and Weiss, W. (1951). The influence of source credibility on communication effectiveness. *Public Opinion Quarterly, 15,* 635-650.*Idaho v. Wright,* 497 U.S 805 (1990).

Kelman, H. C. and Hovland, C. I. (1953). "Reinstatement" of the communicator in delayed measurement of opinion change. *Journal of Abnormal and Social Psychology, 48,* 327-335.

Kovera, M. B., Park, R. C., and Penrod, S. D. (1992). Jurors' perceptions of eyewitness and hearsay evidence. *Minnesota Law Review, 76,* 703-722.

Lamb, M. E., Orbach, Y., Sternberg, K. J., Hershkowitz, I., and Horowitz, D. (2000). Accuracy of investigators' verbatim notes of their forensic interviews with alleged child abuse victims. *Law and Human Behavior, 24,* 2000.

Landsman, S., and Rakos, R. F. (1991). Research essay: A preliminary empirical inquiry concerning the prohibition of hearsay evidence in American courts. *Law and Psychology Reviews, 15,* 65-85.

Manson, M. A. (1992). Social workers as expert witnesses in child sexual abuse cases. *Social Work, 37,* 30-34.

Marks, R. G. (1995). Should we believe the people who believe the children? The need for a new sexual abuse tender years hearsay exception statue. *Harvard Journal on Legislation, 32,* 207-253.*Maryland v. Craig,* 497, U.S. 836 (1990).

McGough, L. S. (1994). *Child witness: Fragile voices in the American legal system.* New Haven, CT: Yale University Press.

McGough, L. S. (1999). Hearing and believing hearsay. *Psychology, Public Policy, and Law, 5,* 485-498.

Myers. J. E. B. (1992). *Evidence in child abuse and neglect* (2nd ed.). New York: Wiley Law Publications.

Myers, J. E. B. (1996). A decade of international reform to accommodate child witnesses. *Criminal Justice and Behavior, 23,* 402-422.

Myers, J. E. B., Redlich, A. D., Goodman, G. S., Prizmich, L. P., and Imwinkelried, E. (1999). Jurors' perception of hearsay in child sexual abuse cases. *Psychology, Public Policy, and Law, 5,* 388-419.

Pathak, M. K. and Thompson, W. C. (1999). From child to witness to jury: Affects of suggestion on the transmission and evaluation of hearsay. *Psychology, Public Policy, and Law, 5,* 372-387.

Poole, D. A. and Lamb, M. E. (1998). *Investigative interviews of children.* Washington, DC: American Psychology Association.

Rakos, R. F. and Landsman, S. (1992). Researching the Hearsay Rule: Emerging findings, general issues, and future directions. *Minnesota Law Review, 76,* 655-682.

Ross, D. F., Lindsay, R. C. L., and Marsil, D. F. (1999). The impact of hearsay testimony on conviction rates in trials of child sexual abuse: Toward balancing the rights of defendants and child witnesses. *Psychology, Public Policy, and Law, 5,* 439-455.

Ross, D. F., Warren, A. R., and McGough, L. S. (1999). Foreword: Hearsay testimony in trials involving child witnesses. *Psychology, Public Policy, and Law, 5,* 251-254.

Ross, L. (1977). The intuitive psychologist and his shortcomings: Distortions in the attribution process. In L. Berkowitz (Ed.), *Advances in Experimental Social Psychology* (pp. 174-221). New York: Academic Press.

Schoenfeld, C. G. (1985). A psychoanalytic approach to the law of evidence. *The Journal of Psychiatry and Law,* 109-135.

Tobey, A. E., Goodman, G. S., Batterman-Faunce, J. M., Orcutt, H. K., and Sachsenmaier, T. (1995). Balancing the rights of children and defendants: Affects of closed-circuit television on children's accuracy and jurors' perceptions. In M. S. Zaragoza, J. R. Graham, G. C. N. Hall, R. Hirschman, and Y. S. Ben-Porath (Eds.), *Memory and Testimony in the Child Witness* (pp. 214-239). Thousand Oaks, CA: Sage.

Warren, A. R., Nunez, N., Keeney, J. M., Buck, J. A., and Smith, B. (2002). The believability of children and their interviewers' hearsay testimony: When less is more. *Journal of Applied Psychology, 87,* 846-857.

Warren, A. R. and Woodall, C. E. (1999). The reliability of hearsay testimony: How well do interviewers recall their interviews with children? *Psychology, Public Policy, and Law, 5,* 355-371.

Wells, G. L., Turtle, J. W., and Luus, C. A. E. (1989). The perceived credibility of child eyewitnesses: What happens when they use their own words. In S. J. Ceci, D. F. Ross, and M. P. Toglia (Eds.), *Perspectives on Children's Testimony* (pp.23-36). New York, NY: Springer-Verlag New York Inc. *White v. Illinois,* 502 U.S. 346 (1992).

In: New Developments in Child Abuse Research
Editor: Stanley M. Sturt, pp. 95-111

ISBN 1-59454-980-X
© 2006 Nova Science Publishers, Inc.

Chapter 6

EXPERT WITNESSES AND THE SEARCH FOR JUSTICE – A UK PERSPECTIVE

John Hartshorne and José Miola
Faculty of Law, University of Leicester, England, UK

ABSTRACT

In the past year, expert testimony and its role in child abuse trials has received much unwelcome publicity in the United Kingdom. The case of Angela Cannnings, wrongfully convicted on the basis of testimony by Professor Sir Roy Meadow, has not been unique. Rather, it is only one of several instances where the testimony of experts has, directly or indirectly, caused courts to decide cases wrongly. This chapter will first describe the instances where this phenomenon has been seen to occur, then continue by analysing what lessons may be learnt in order to minimise the chances of a recurrence. The chapter will thus consider how the courts should treat medical experts and their evidence in future. In particular, it focuses on a paradox that exists in the UK between the civil and criminal courts. In the former, recent developments have ensured that medical evidence is critically evaluated by the judge - a response to perceived medical dominance and a reassertion of the role of the judiciary as the ultimate arbiters of behaviour. In the criminal courts, in the wake of the successful appeal by Angela Cannings, the opposite has occurred. The courts now hold that, in the criminal sphere, expert evidence for the defence should be taken as demonstrating 'reasonable doubt', and thus requiring acquittal. The chapter argues that the approach taken by the criminal courts is counterproductive, and does not prevent miscarriages of justice. It concludes by suggesting proposals for how courts should treat medical experts and their evidence.

INTRODUCTION

Events in the United Kingdom in the recent past have made life somewhat uncomfortable for medical expert witnesses. In particular, a series of scandals concerning experts and their evidence have had the consequence of begging the question of how the courts should treat the evidence of medical experts in courtrooms. In this chapter, we begin by examining the perceived 'problem' with this evidence and its use. This enables us to highlight the issues that we shall discuss. We then continue by considering the way in which the civil and criminal courts have treated the evidence of experts. We identify not only a marked difference in the way in which such evidence is treated by the courts, but also the fact that the criminal courts, in response to the 'scandals', are in danger of falling into a trap that the civil courts took forty years to extricate themselves from. We end by providing our own proposals for how the courts should treat expert evidence in all courts.

First, then, we must identify the 'problem' that the law has had to deal with. Essentially, it is that a lack of trust in the medical profession (and thus medical practitioners) has developed, and that this has been exacerbated by the fact that some of the 'scandals' have concerned the provision of expert evidence in the criminal courts. That the first part of the last sentence is the case can be seen in several ways. First, it is perhaps no coincidence that, of the eight non-fiction contributions to *The Lancet* special edition in 2004 emanating from the United Kingdom, half concerned an analysis of medical 'scandals'.[1] All of the articles express concern regarding the current profile of the medical profession. Ian Ellis notes that "[t]he reputation of Britain's medical profession has taken a battering after a series of very public … scandals".[2] Rosemary Field and Alastair Scotland, meanwhile, argue that "doctors have been seen to be fallible in ways unimaginable a generation ago" due to "high-profile medical scandals in the UK [that] have followed one another relentlessly".[3] Brian Hurwitz expresses concern that "Shipman must not be allowed to kill off the notion of the virtuous and humane GP", but admits that he has "brought forward the day when unbridled medical power and paternalism over patients and their bodies" will have ended in the UK.[4] José Miola simply argues that "[i]f this is not yet a crisis, then it cannot be too far from one".[5] Secondly, as demonstrated later in this chapter, in 2001 even the then Lord Chief Justice identified the erosion of trust in the medical profession as a reason why the courts were determined to be 'less deferential' to the medical profession.[6]

As for the second part, at least two recent 'scandals' involving expert evidence have meant that the courts have had to assess exactly how they deal with expert evidence. First, there is the case of Professor Sir Roy Meadow. Professor Meadow was struck off the medical register as a result of the evidence that he gave at the trial of another parent accused of killing her child – Sally Clark. While his general theory of Munchausen Syndrome by Proxy remains generally uncontested, his statistical analysis of cot death was found to be misleading. Rather than the actual 1 in 77 chance of two cot deaths in the same family, Professor Meadow had stated at the trial of Ms Clark that the figure was 1 in 73 *million*.[7] This informed the infamous "Meadow's Law", which stated that whilst one death was unfortunate, two effectively constituted murder. It is the legal reaction to the subsequent appeal against conviction by Angela Cannings that is the catalyst for the issues dicussed in this article. However, there is also the case of Dr Colin Paterson, highlighted by Clare Dyer in the *Guardian* newspaper in the UK.[8] According to Dyer, Paterson,

"a retired chemical pathologist from Dundee, peddled a theory around courts in England, Scotland and eventually America which few specialists believe has any basis in reality. Dozens of children with fractures apparently caused by their parents were actually suffering from "temporary brittle bone disease" (TBBD), he argued, a condition whereby babies are prone to fractures in their first few months but grow out of it by a year or so. He also readily attributed fractures to osteogenesis imperfecta, a genuine but rare disorder in which brittle bones are permanent, or to copper deficiency".[9]

He was eventually reported to the General Medical Council (GMC) by a senior judge, and it was found that he was acting as an advocate of his theory rather than a dispassionate and objective witness in cases in which he appeared. The consequence of the 'scandals', and the crux of the issue of what to do with expert evidence, is that the courts were asked to find a way to minimise the perceived infiltration of 'junk scientists' and 'junk science' into British courtrooms.[10] This was, indeed, a crucial issue in the appeal by Angela Cannings against her conviction based partly on the evidence of Professor Meadow. Essentially, the options available to the courts are either to scrutinise the evidence more or less. As we shall see, both solutions have been tried by both the civil and criminal courts, paradoxically in an attempt to achieve the same solution to the same problem.

THE POSITION IN ENGLISH CRIMINAL PROCEEDINGS PRIOR TO THE DECISION IN *R V. CANNINGS*

Prior to the trilogy of cases that rocked the confidence of the English senior judiciary over the use of expert opinion evidence in criminal proceedings for child abuse – Clark,[11] Patel[12] and Cannings[13] – English judges adopted a robust approach towards the admissibility and use of expert evidence in such proceedings. Admissibility, being a question of law, was determined in the absence of the jury whose primary role was to resolve whether the facts of the prosecution's case were proved to the requisite standard. In contrast to the position in the United States,[14] English judges have adopted a "lighter touch" approach towards the admissibility of expert opinion evidence. Provided that the case was one in which expert evidence appeared to be necessary because it would "furnish the court with scientific information which is likely to be outside the experience and knowledge of a judge or jury",[15] then the "better, and now more widely accepted, view is that so long as the field is sufficiently well-established to pass the ordinary tests of relevance and reliability, then no enhanced test of admissibility should be applied, but the weight of the evidence should be established by the same adversarial forensic techniques applicable elsewhere."[16] On the question of reliability the issue for the court was "whether the subject matter of the opinion forms part of a body of knowledge or experience which is sufficiently organised or recognised to be accepted as a reliable body of knowledge or experience, a special acquaintance with which by the witness would render his opinion of assistance to the court."[17] Whilst judges have not been entirely consistent in their willingness to acknowledge the reliability of emerging areas of expertise,[18] in general it has been the policy of the English courts to be flexible in admitting expert evidence and to enjoy the advantages to be gained from new techniques and new advances in science.[19] For example in R v Clarke the Court of Appeal asserted that there "are no closed categories where such evidence may be placed before a jury. It would be entirely wrong to deny to the law of evidence the advantages to be gained from new techniques and new advances in science."[20]

Provided that the tests of relevance and reliability were passed, it was the task of the jury to determine what, if any, weight it was appropriate to place upon the opinion of the expert, subject where appropriate to guidance from the trial judge. In the adversarial tradition jurors were entitled to approach expert testimony in the same fashion as they might approach other forms of testimony, without necessarily being expected to accord any particular weight to the expert's opinion through deference to the expert's standing or qualifications.[21] So in Davie v Magistrates of Edinburgh, for example, Lord President Cooper ordained that "[e]xpert witnesses, however skilled or eminent, can give no more than evidence. They cannot usurp the functions of the jury."[22] Furthermore in R v Stockwell the Lord Chief Justice emphasised that it was "important that the judge should make clear to the jury that they are not bound by the expert's opinion, and that the issue is for them to decide."[23] In several reported cases juries appear to have done exactly this, apparently preferring to believe extraneous facts rather than the testimony of an expert whose opinions have gone unchallenged by experts acting for the opposite party.[24] However where no extraneous evidence existed which a jury could prefer over the uncontradicted opinion of an expert, then a rejection of the expert's opinion would result in a finding not based on evidence and would accordingly be deemed unreasonable.[25] So in R v Bailey the Lord Chief Justice remarked that the Court of Appeal "has said on many occasions that of course juries are not bound by what the medical witnesses say, but at the same time they must act on evidence, and if there is nothing before them, no facts and no circumstances shown before them which throw doubt on the medical evidence, then that is all that they are left with, and the jury, in those circumstances, must accept it."[26] Similarly in R v Sanders, decided in the context of the defence of diminished responsibility, Watkins LJ, having reviewed the relevant authorities in the area, stated that "if there are no other circumstances to consider, unequivocal, uncontradicted medical evidence favourable to a defendant should be accepted by a jury and they should be so directed."[27] Where expert opinion evidence was admitted for both the prosecution and the defence upon a particular issue therefore, the jury was entitled to determine for itself which body of opinion it preferred.

THE DECISION IN *R. V. CANNINGS*

The decision in R v Cannings undoubtedly alters the position described above in so far as prosecutions of parents for murder following multiple infant deaths are concerned, and has contributed to a sea change in the public's perception of the role of experts in criminal proceedings.[28] The wider implications of Cannings and associated decisions are still being worked out by the courts, the prosecuting agencies and the expert witness industry itself, however. Angela Cannings had given birth to four children in total, Gemma, Jason, Jade and Matthew. All except Jade had died in infancy. Mrs Cannings was initially accused of murdering each of her deceased children, although at trial she was tried on two counts of murder only, count one relating to Jason and count two Matthew. The prosecution's case was that Mrs Cannings had smothered Jason and Matthew. In support of this it was contended that Gemma's death, and two "Acute" or "Apparent Life Threatening Events" (ALTEs) which Jason and Jade had both experienced, were also the result of smothering by Mrs Cannings, and that the deaths of Jason and Matthew therefore formed part of an overall "pattern" consistent with an intention on Mrs Cannings' part to kill or cause really serious bodily harm to her children. Beyond the views of the experts called by the prosecution there was no extraneous direct evidence and very little indirect evidence to substantiate this argument. The prosecution's case was advanced against an evidential backdrop in which Mrs Cannings was described as a loving mother who was apparently free of any personality disorder or psychiatric condition. The defence case was that all three deaths were natural if unexplained incidents, falling to be classified as "cot death" or Sudden Infant Death Syndrome (SIDS), and that the ALTEs were similarly natural if unexplained incidents. Defence experts challenged the opinions offered by the prosecution experts. Confronted with a choice of finding that the deaths were either natural or unnatural, the jury chose the latter and Mrs Cannings was convicted on both counts of murder.

Mrs Cannings appealed against her convictions to the Court of Appeal. The Court of Appeal was willing to receive fresh evidence from additional experts on the question of whether Jason and Matthews' deaths were natural if unexplained, or unnatural. Having examined all the evidence the Court of Appeal was struck by the fact that this was a field where there was a great deal about death in infancy, and its causes, which remained as yet unknown and undiscovered. The judgment is lengthy and detailed and it is unnecessary for the purposes of this essay to analyse in depth the nature and implications of the fresh evidence which the court was willing to receive, but in summary this additional evidence consisted of: evidence that there might have been a genetic cause, as yet unidentified, for the deaths; evidence of a substantial body of research suggesting that three unexplained infant deaths can occur naturally within the same family; evidence that babies who died during the daytime could appear apparently well fewer than ten minutes before they were found dead; and evidence undermining the significance of an ALTE preceding an infant's death. The Court of Appeal found that the expert evidence adduced by the prosecution had played a critical role in the conviction of Mrs Cannings, and ruled that the fundamental basis of the prosecution's case, resting as it did upon the extreme rarity of three separate infant deaths within the same family, and the pattern of events within the Cannings family in particular, had been demonstrably undermined by the fresh evidence. Moreover the Court of Appeal was satisfied that there was a realistic, if as yet undefined, possibility of a genetic problem within the Cannings family, which might serve to explain the tragic events.

The decision to allow the appeal in Cannings was therefore based predominantly upon arguments derived from the evidence. Despite this essentially factual basis for the decision, the Court of Appeal used the appeal as an opportunity to reshape the law in the sphere of prosecutions following multiple infant deaths, prompted by the fact that this was third case of its type considered before the courts in controversial fashion in 2003. The passage which is crucial to this development merits full rehearsal:

> "Experts in many fields will acknowledge the possibility that later research may undermine the accepted wisdom of today. "Never say never" is a phrase which we have heard in many different contexts from expert witnesses. That does not normally provide a basis for rejecting the expert evidence, or indeed for conjuring up fanciful doubts about the possible impact of later research. With unexplained infant deaths, however, as this judgment has demonstrated, in many important respects we are still at the frontiers of knowledge. Necessarily, further research is needed, and fortunately, thanks to the dedication of the medical profession, it is continuing. All this suggests that, for the time being, where a full investigation into two or more sudden unexplained infant deaths in the

same family is followed by a serious disagreement between reputable experts about the cause of death, and a body of such expert opinion concludes that natural causes, whether explained or unexplained, cannot be excluded as a reasonable (and not a fanciful) possibility, the prosecution of a parent or parents for murder should not be started, or continued, unless there is additional cogent evidence, extraneous to the expert evidence... which tends to support the conclusion that the infant, or where there is more than one death, one of the infants, was deliberately harmed. In cases like the present, if the outcome of the trial depends exclusively or almost exclusively on a serious disagreement between distinguished and reputable experts, it will often be unwise, and therefore unsafe, to proceed.[29]

In expressing ourselves in this way we recognise that justice may not be done in a small number of cases where in truth a mother has deliberately killed her baby without leaving any identifiable evidence of the crime. That is an undesirable result, which however avoids a worse one. If murder cannot be proved, the conviction cannot be safe. In a criminal case, it is simply not enough to be able to establish even a high probability of guilt. Unless we are sure of guilt the dreadful possibility always remains that a mother, already brutally scarred by the unexplained death or deaths of her babies, may find herself in prison for life for killing them when she should not be there at all. In our community, and in any civilised community, that is abhorrent."[30]

The Court of Appeal also singled out for criticism what they described as an "over-dogmatic" approach by experts who were willing to assume that an unnatural cause of death in infants had been established unless it was possible to demonstrate a natural explanation for death. The infamous "Meadow's Law" (One sudden infant death is a tragedy, two is suspicious and three is murder until proved otherwise)[31] was not something that the law of criminal evidence countenanced. The decision therefore serves to remind experts that their foremost duty is to the court and not to the party calling them, and that their role, as was stated in 1953, "is to furnish the Judge or jury with the necessary scientific criteria for testing the accuracy of their conclusions, so as to enable the Judge or jury to form their own independent judgment by the application of these criteria to the facts proved in evidence."[32]

THE IMPLICATIONS OF *R V. CANNINGS*

The decision in Cannings is a highly significant one in that it removes from the province of the jury the responsibility for resolving a category of dispute. Interpretation of the Court of Appeal's guidance is a troublesome affair. A literal interpretation would confine the implications of the decision narrowly to cases where two or more sudden unexplained infant deaths have occurred in the same family. Even here, however, it is far from clear as to precisely when it will be inappropriate to commence or continue with a criminal prosecution for murder. For example Walker and McCartney have questioned "what constitutes "serious disagreement"? Who are "reputable" experts, and who makes that judgment?"[33] On this latter point, presumably the answer is someone within the Crown Prosecution Service, but without further guidance, how are they to assess whether the experts are "reputable" or whether the "disagreement" is indeed "serious"?

On a wider level, however, the Court of Appeal cannot possibly make utterances about the need for caution where the frontiers of knowledge are developing without inviting debate about whether it would be inappropriate for any prosecution to proceed where there is a serious disagreement between experts and paucity of extraneous evidence bearing on the issue. Indeed appeals have already been mounted on this very basis and the Court of Appeal has been obliged to fight a rearguard action to circumscribe the limits of its decision in Cannings, albeit with varying degrees of success. In R v Kai-Whitewind,[34] for example, one of the defendant's three children died leading to the defendant's subsequent conviction for his murder following a trial at which the experts for the prosecution and the defence had disagreed over the cause of death and the conclusions to be drawn from the findings at the post-mortem. On appeal it was argued that the conviction was unsustainable in the light of the decision in Cannings. The Court of Appeal disagreed emphasising that Cannings had no direct application to the present appeal. The court explained that in Cannings the "judgment as a whole, and para.178 itself demonstrates that the Court had in mind "cases like the present", that is, Cannings itself, which depended on the inferences based on coincidence, or the unlikelihood of two or more infant deaths in the same family, or one death where another child or other children in the family had suffered unexplained ALTEs."[35] The court continued: "In reality, the problem with the argument based on reading para.178 of Cannings outside its context is that, carried to its logical conclusion, the submission would mean that whenever there is a conflict between expert witnesses the case for the prosecution must fail unless the conviction is justified by evidence independent of the expert witnesses. Put another way, the logical conclusion of what we shall describe as the overblown Cannings argument is that, where there is a conflict of opinion between reputable experts, the expert evidence called by the Crown is automatically neutralised. That is a startling proposition, and it is not sustained by Cannings."[36]

Despite the attempts by the Court of Appeal in Kai-Whitewind to contain what it described as the "overblown Cannings argument", and to limit the guidance in Cannings to the literal circumstances of the case itself, a hare has nevertheless been set running by Cannings which looks awkward to corner. For example in the conjoined appeals of R v Harris, Rock, Cherry and Faulder[37] the defendants appealed against convictions arising out of alleged non-accidental head injuries to children (NAHI), more commonly referred to as "shaken baby syndrome". At its heart the appeal consisted of a challenge to the accepted hypothesis concerning findings of a triad of intracranial injuries in such cases. The court received fresh evidence from a body of medical opinion which did not accept that the triad was an infallible tool for diagnosis, and who cautioned against its use as a certain diagnosis in the absence of other evidence. Counsel for the prosecution invited the court to find that the triad was proved as a fact and not just a hypothesis. On the evidence before it the court did not think it was possible for them to do so. Whilst being a strong pointer to NAHI on its own, the court did not think that it was possible to find that it must automatically and necessarily lead to a diagnosis of NAHI. All the circumstances, including the clinical picture, had to be taken into account. In light of the fresh evidence the court felt that the safety of several of the convictions had therefore properly been called into question. Counsel for the prosecution submitted to the court that the appeals demonstrated that there had been a significant failure within the criminal justice system to control and manage expert evidence. He argued that there must be a change in approach and invited the court to consider giving guidance. The Court of Appeal was reluctant to provide any new guidance on expert evidence arising from the facts of the cases, but felt that it might, however, be helpful to re-iterate current guidance concerning the duties of expert witnesses. The court quoted from two previous decisions, The

Ikerian Reefer,[38] and Re AB (Child Abuse: Expert Witnesses).[39] In the former case Creswell J stated inter alia that:

> "An expert witness should state the facts or assumptions on which his opinion is based. He should not omit to consider material facts which detract from his concluded opinions... An expert should make it clear when a particular question or issue falls outside his expertise... If an expert's opinion is not properly researched because he considers that insufficient data is available then this must be stated with an indication that the opinion is no more than a provisional one."[40]

In the latter case Wall J stressed that in cases in which there is a genuine disagreement on a scientific or medical issue, or where it is necessary for a party to advance a particular hypothesis to explain a given set of facts then:

> "the expert who advances such a hypothesis owes a very heavy duty to explain to the court that what he is advancing is a hypothesis, that it is controversial (if it is) and placed before the court all material which contradicts the hypothesis. Secondly, he must make all his material available to the other experts in the case. It is the common experience of the courts that the better the experts the more limited their areas of disagreement, and in the forensic context of a contested case relating to children, the objective of the lawyers and the experts should always be to limit the ambit of disagreement on medical issues to the minimum."[41]

The Court of Appeal in *R v Harris, Rock, Cherry and Faulder* also exhorted trial judges to make use of new rules of criminal procedure. These make provision for judges to direct experts to consult with each other, and if possible identify points of agreement or disagreement with a summary of reasons before trial, with a view to narrowing the areas of dispute and limiting the volume of expert evidence which the jury will have to consider.

With respect to the Court of Appeal in *R v Harris, Rock, Cherry and Faulder*, however, reminding experts of their duty to the court is a rather limp response to a perceived "failure" within the criminal justice system to control and manage expert opinion evidence. The decision in *Cannings* is therefore likely to generate further controversy in the sphere of expert evidence. This must be inevitable because, as Walker and McCartney have observed, does "the basic scientific methodology of ongoing falsification not mean that all science is "at the frontiers of knowledge"? Indeed, if a science ceases to have frontiers where received wisdom is questioned, then it should be debunked as dogma or as unscientific."[42]

THE *BOLAM* EXPLOSION – EXPERT EVIDENCE IN THE CIVIL COURTS

Medical evidence in the civil courts has always been treated differently from that in the criminal sphere. Partly, this may be because 'medical law' as a subject is a relatively recent phenomenon. As Ian Kennedy and Andrew Grubb argue, what is now 'medical law' was, before, simply a tort, criminal law or contract law case involving medical practitioners.[43] In this sense, then, there was no need for one, single way to treat medical experts who gave testimony. Quite simply, in the criminal courts they were treated under the rules of criminal evidence, while in the civil courts they were treated under the rules of that court.

If nothing else, the different standards of proof required by the two spheres would in themselves make it inevitable that the approaches would differ. Nevertheless, readers may find what follows somewhat surprising. First, as we shall see, despite the lesser burden of proof required by the civil law, the approach taken by the criminal court in the *Cannings* appeal was, until recently, effectively the same as that formerly used by the civil courts. Secondly, the case which established this in English jurisprudence was a first instance instruction to the jury in a negligence and informed consent case – a most unlikely source of precedent. Indeed, the development of the law in the civil sphere may be seen as something of a lesson for the criminal courts, in the sense that the approach now advocated by the latter has been tried, and rejected, by the former.

The case of *Bolam* v. *Friern Hospital Management Committee* is an unusual contender for the status of, arguably, the most important case in English medical law.[44] The facts are that the plaintiff, John Bolam, was a voluntary psychiatric patient who suffered from a depressive illness. The consultant at the hospital, Dr de Bastarrechea, advised him that he ought to undergo electro-convulsive therapy (ECT). Mr Bolam agreed to the treatment, and signed a consent form. However, he had not been warned of the risk of fracture that can occur during ECT treatment. He received the treatment at the hands of another doctor, Dr Allfrey, but was also not given any relaxant drugs, which made the risk of fracture that much higher. As a result of this, he received several injuries, including dislocation of hip joints, and fractures to his pelvis on both sides caused by the femur on both sides being driven through the cup of the pelvis. He claimed damages from the hospital, arguing that the ECT without relaxant drugs, or at least manual restraint, amounted to negligence. The judge, McNair J., began his summing up to the jury by noting that ECT was a technique that was, at that time, 'progressive', and that there was no standard or set method of its use which all doctors agreed on. Thus the question to be answered by the jury was whether the doctor, following the techniques that he had learned in the hospital, negligent in his failure to use relaxant drugs? The question was not one of bad faith, but simply one of a lack of skill. McNair J. began by defining negligence itself. The quote is lengthy, but perhaps worthy of full reproduction here :

"in an ordinary case which does not involve any special skill, negligence in law means this: some failure to do some act which a reasonable man in the circumstances would do, or doing some act which in the circumstances a reasonable man would not do ... How do you test whether this act or failure is negligent? In an ordinary case it is generally said, that you judge that by the action of the man on the street. He is the ordinary man. In one case it has been said that you judge it by the conduct of the man at the top of the Clapham omnibus ... But where you get a situation which involves the use of some special skill or competence, then the test whether there has been negligence or not ... is the standard of the ordinary skilled man exercising and professing to have that special skill ... A man need not possess the highest skill at the risk of being found negligent ... [I]t is sufficient if he exercises the ordinary skill of an ordinary competent man exercising that particular art."[45]

Thus, we can see that the standard that the doctor must attain to satisfy the law is that of the 'ordinary' doctor. She must be competent – nothing more, nothing less. However, the judge continued by defining how the jury should ascertain whether the doctor has reached the required standard, and it was the interpretation of this quote that was to define English medical law:

"A doctor is not guilty of negligence if he has acted in accordance with a practice accepted as proper by a responsible body of medical men skilled in that particular art ... Putting it the other way round, a doctor is not negligent, if he acting in accordance with such a practice, merely because there is a body of opinion that takes the contrary view."[46]

Whether the doctor has attained the required level of the 'ordinary' doctor will thus depend on whether she can find a 'responsible body' of medical opinion that will say that it would have done as she did in the circumstances. However, this definition presents a problem, particularly with respect to the second sentence of the above quote. Put simply it is not clear whether, providing that the defendant doctor can find others who say that they might have done as she did, it is open for a judge to nevertheless find her to have acted below the standard expected of her as a doctor. This lack of clarity is exacerbated when the language used by the judge is examined a little more closely. At several points in the judgment, McNair J. uses the words 'ordinary', 'reasonable', 'responsible' and 'respectable' to describe the nature of the doctor's duty and the standard required. However, these words would indicate different approaches, for, as Kenneth Norrie has highlighted, they actually mean different things.[47] Thus, the word 'ordinary' suggests that the test of a doctor's competence should be descriptive – to attain the relevant standard the defendant must simply do what *others do*. There is no critical analysis of the profession's practices. Alternatively, the words 'reasonable, 'responsible' and 'respectable' are normative. In other words, they allow for critical analysis of the practice, as they ask not what *was* done by the profession in the relevant situation but, rather, what *ought to have been done*.

Thus *Bolam* begged, but did not answer, the question of whether, presuming that there was medical evidence on both sides, a judge had the right to find for the plaintiffs at all. There was, needless to say, evidence to support both sides of the argument. On one hand, it is possible to argue that the case relied upon by McNair J., the Scottish case of *Hunter* v. *Hanley*, used descriptive rather than normative language to establish its own test:

"In the realm of diagnosis and treatment there is ample scope for genuine difference of opinion, and one man clearly is not negligent merely because his conclusion differs from that of other professional men, or because he has displayed less skill or knowledge than others would have shown. The true test for establishing negligence in diagnosis or treatment on the part of the doctor is whether he has been proved to be guilty of such failure as no doctor of *ordinary* skill would be guilty of if acting with *ordinary* care."[48]

On the other hand, there are also strong reasons to hold that McNair J. did not intend to remove the court's right to be the ultimate arbiter of the issue. Indeed, simply by referring the question of the defendant's negligence to the jury, the judge must be acknowledging that the jury has an actual decision to make. If they were not allowed to find for the plaintiff, then there would be no case to answer, and the jury would not need to become involved at all. This argument is strengthened by way in which the judge framed his question to the jury – clearly leaving them with a choice:

"[I]t is not essential for you to decide which of two practices is the better practice, as long as you accept that what Dr Allfrey did was in accordance with a practice accepted by responsible persons; but if the result of the evidence is that you are satisfied that this practice is better than the practice spoken of on the other side, then it is a stronger case."[49]

The way in which *Bolam* was to be interpreted was of major significance to English medical law, for two reasons. First, *Bolam* grew out of control. As one author noted, the policy of the courts became "when in doubt, *Bolamise*".[50] Thus what was originally supposed to be a test for negligence was to become, to give one example, the arbiter of patients' 'best interests', making the medical profession responsible for determining whether and how to treat incompetent patients.[51] Secondly, alongside this abrogation by the courts to the medical profession of issues that were, at best, only tangentially medical, the difference between a normative and descriptive interpretation of *Bolam* meant the difference between the court being able to retain control or not. This is because the descriptive interpretation of the test meant that, in effect, the only role for the court was to identify whether the defendant had expert witnesses. If so, the defendant won the case. There was no provision for any critical engagement with the evidence – the court was there merely to verify its existence.

That this was the case can be seen in the case of *Maynard*.[52] The facts are that two consultants were treating Mrs Maynard for a chest infection. They believed that she was suffering from tuberculosis, but thought that there was a possibility that she was suffering from Hodgkin's disease. As Hodgkin's is fatal unless treated early the consultants decided not to wait for the tests to see whether she had tuberculosis, and conduct an exploratory operation to see whether she had Hodgkin's. The operation was carried out properly, and showed that she had tuberculosis rather than Hodgkin's. However, an inherent risk in the surgery was that there could be nerve damage to the vocal cords causing speech impairment. Unfortunately, this risk materialised. Mrs Maynard sued on the basis that the consultants should have waited for the tuberculosis test results before proceeding with the test for Hodgkin's. At first instance, the trial judge was most impressed by the expert for the plaintiff, and thus found for Mrs Maynard. The Appeal Court reversed this finding, and Mrs Maynard then appealed to the highest court in England, the House of Lords. The question of law to be considered was whether the trial judge had the right to 'prefer' the evidence of the plaintiff's expert to that of the defendant's. The House found, strongly, that he should not have done so:

"I have to say that a judge's 'preference' for one body of distinguished professional opinion to another also professionally distinguished is not sufficient to establish negligence in a practitioner whose actions have received the seal of approval of those whose opinions, truthfully expressed, honestly held, were not preferred. If this was the real reason for the judge's finding, he erred in law even though elsewhere in his judgment he stated the law correctly. For in the realm of diagnosis and treatment negligence is not established by preferring one respectable body of professional opinion to another. Failure to exercise the ordinary skill of a doctor (in the appropriate speciality, if he be a specialist) is necessary."[53]

This judgment represents what is possibly the hiatus of the English courts' deference to the medical profession. All that Lord Scarman appears to require from medical experts is that their evidence is 'honestly expressed and honestly held'. The role of the court was merely, as argued above, to verify the existence of the defendant's evidence. As José Miola and Margot Brazier have argued, all that was necessary was to "[l]ine up your expert in sober garb and with letters after his name and the defendant could not fail".[54] This was not to be the only case where this approach was adopted. Rather, it was the dominant ethos of the courts for fully forty years after *Bolam* was decided – "[it] ... was interpreted, whatever judges might say, to allow judgment by colleagues to substitute judgment by a court".[55] Moreover, the defendant always had the advantage afforded to the champion boxer of retaining his title in the event of a draw.

Needless to say, this approach did not escape severe criticism. For Sally Sheldon, for example, the interpretation of *Bolam* could be understood in the context of class, race and gender, in the sense that judges and doctors are likely to come from the same social strata.[56] Harvey Teff argues that the courts have failed to grasp the distinction between involving themselves in decisions and interfering in clinical freedom.[57] Meanwhile, Sheila MacLean simply notes that the law had proved itself "unable, unwilling or inefficient" in the regulation of the medical profession's conduct.[58] For the purposes of this chapter, however, it is sufficient to note that these criticisms all emanate from the fact that *Bolam* virtually nullified the chances of a plaintiff seeking redress for injury suffered iatrogenically. In essence, then, the way that experts are treated, and their evidence considered, is a hindrance rather than a help in the quest for a fair result. Moreover, it is difficult to argue with this proposition – as whenever such an advantage is given to one side, the result cannot be considered 'fair'. Yet it is exactly this approach that the criminal courts appeared to be moving towards in *Cannings*.

However, if there is a lesson to be learned from the civil law, then it is that, as we shall see, the approach could not survive indefinitely. Essentially, this was because it took all decision-making power from the court and gave it to the expert witnesses. The reasonableness, and thus the question of whether the defendant doctor had achieved the requisite standard of care to escape liability, came to be defined by the medical profession rather than the judge. Doctors became judges in their own cause - a recipe for paternalism. The effect of this was not lost on Lord Donaldson in the Court of Appeal in the middle of the 1980s:

> "[The Courts] cannot stand idly by if the [medical] profession, by an excess of paternalism, denies its patients a real choice. In a word, the law will not permit the medical profession to play God ... I think that, in an appropriate case, a judge would be entitled to reject a unanimous medical view if he were satisfied that it was manifestly wrong and that the doctors must have been misdirecting themselves as to their duty in law."[59]

The House of Lords in that case was to decide to use Bolam in its simple form, despite this warning from the lower court. What was particularly perplexing about the courts' treatment of medical practitioners was that they were treated differently to other professions. Indeed, at around the same time as the House of Lords in cases such as *Maynard*, the courts had been finding even the universal practice of, for example, solicitors and ships' captains to be negligent, despite expert evidence being adduced by the defence.[60] In those cases the courts found that, despite the fact that the defendants had not deviated from the common practice of their professions, their actions were nevertheless negligent because they were held not to stand up to scrutiny by the judge. Eventually, the courts were to treat the medical profession as they do any other, and this occurred in 1997 – the 40th anniversary of the *Bolam* judgment – in a case called *Bolitho*.[61]

BOLITHO – A CHANGE OF APPROACH

In *Bolitho*, the House of Lords finally realised that it could no longer justify treating the medical profession differently from others. One of the specific issues in the appeal to the House of Lords was the question of whether *Bolam* required judges to accept automatically truthful evidence from experts. Lord Browne-Wilkinson held that the adjectives used by McNair J. in *Bolam* – 'reasonable', 'responsible' and 'respectable' – all pointed towards an approach that suggest that a judge must be satisfied that the evidence has a logical basis. Thus, his Lordship continued by stating that "if, in a rare case, it can be demonstrated that the professional opinion is not capable of withstanding logical analysis, the judge is entitled to hold that the body of opinion is not reasonable or responsible".[62]

Why, though, did the courts suddenly change their approach to these cases? In a most illuminating article Lord Woolf, then Lord Chief Justice of England and Wales, explained the change in attitude.[63] First, he admitted that the courts had indeed "treated the medical profession with excessive deference".[64] Among the reasons for this, he argued, was the fact that the courts were "understandably reluctant to second-guess the conduct and opinions of respected professionals practising in their field of expertise".[65] Moreover, the "horror stories emanating from the litigation culture of the USA" encouraged courts to find ways to prevent the "importing of the same disease" into England's courts.[66] It is not difficult to see, if we accept this analysis, exactly why *Bolam* developed and was interpreted in the way that it was.

The causes of change identified by Lord Woolf were equally profound. He began by arguing that, quite simply, "the courts have [developed] a less deferential approach to those in authority".[67] This would lead to an increased willingness to engage in judicial activism in order to right perceived wrongs. Lord Woolf's identification of another factor, the extremely low proportion of successful medical negligence claims (17 per cent), provided the 'wrong' to 'right'. His Lordship felt that the courts became "conscious of the difficulties which bona fide claimants had in successfully establishing claims".[68] This factor was perhaps exacerbated by the fact that *Bolam* was being rejected in other jurisdictions such as Canada, Australia and Germany without a descent into a dreaded 'litigation culture'.[69] Yet another of his factors, however, is the most important for the purposes of this chapter. For Lord Woolf, an intrinsic lack of confidence in the medical profession contributed to the change:

> "[T]he 'automatic presumption of beneficence' has been dented by a series of well-publicised scandals. The judges were not oblivious to these scandals … Almost daily there are reports in the media suggesting that there is something amiss with our health treatment".[70]

It is indeed perhaps the ultimate irony that one of the main reasons for the reassessment of *Bolam* (and the subsequent introduction of judicial scrutiny of medical evidence) was a lack of trust in the medical profession. In effect, it was seen as a 'closed shop', protective of its own members to the detriment of the 'rights' of patients. At that time, oversight by the courts was seen as the panacea that would rein in a profession that had become out of control. Thus oversight by the courts was seen as the only way in which some measure of control could be applied, and the fist principle was that from then on medical evidence would be subject to scrutiny and logical analysis.

Of course, that is completely different to the approach taken by the Court of Appeal in the *Cannings* case. In *Cannings* it was decided that the panacea was to return to the 'old' method of allowing the medical profession to set its own standards in response to a lack of trust in medical professionals – exactly the opposite of the conclusion that the civil courts had come to less than a decade earlier. The differing conclusions may be explained by simple expediency. *Cannings* appears to be something of a 'knee-jerk' reaction to one man's evidence. It can be seen as a specific reaction to a specific situation in a specific case. As previous sections of this chapter have argued, the criminal courts are now seeking to find ways to limit the effect of what was said in *Cannings*. Certainly, it would appear to be incongruous to argue that the best way to achieve oversight is to examine evidence less rather than more. The confusion displayed by the courts does, however, beg the question: what is the correct way to treat expert testimony?

Conclusion

It is somewhat perplexing, and not a little paradoxical, that the criminal Court of Appeal in *Cannings* sought to adopt precisely the approach to medical expert evidence recently rejected by the civil courts to what is effectively the same problem. It is not difficult to understand, however, why they felt that they should do this. They would argue that their proposals would stop another Roy Meadow. But would it have stopped Colin Paterson? The answer, of course, must be that it would not have. Indeed, the inevitable consequence of the *Cannings* ruling is that it gives almost all of the decision-making power to the defence expert – his evidence alone may completely exonerate the defendant.

Yet the protection that *Cannings* attempts to import into the courtroom only works as long as the mistake emanates from the prosecution witness. While a Roy Meadow would have had less influence, so a Colin Paterson would have had more. Here, then, is the inherent flaw in the approach of the Court of Appeal in *Cannings*: it makes no logical sense to attempt to lessen the power of the expert witness by giving even more power to *another* expert witness. The civil courts found that they could no longer justify, in a climate mistrustful of the medical profession, allowing medical practitioners to be judges in their own cause. The incongruity of what the criminal court in *Cannings* sought to do is striking, and it is not in the least surprising that subsequent cases have attempted to dampen the ardour of that decision.

What, though, is the answer? How may courts ensure that errant experts on both sides of cases are identified and their evidence (or, more precisely, the inaccurate portions of their evidence) disregarded? Despite the adversarial climate that this would create amongst experts, we would favour a system where the courts are not only able to scrutinise evidence, but are also encouraged to do so. We hold this view for several reasons. First and foremost, it is simply the case that it is now impossible to justify allowing medical experts to be the effective judges in cases. Not only is this considered to be unacceptable by society but, given that medical experts have been shown to be less than accurate in the past (not least by the recent 'scandals'), once again such an approach cannot be justified. It is, in part at least, for exactly these reasons that the civil courts have rejected the old, descriptive interpretation of *Bolam* in favour of the greater scrutiny available through *Bolitho*.

On the other hand, there are advantages to the more adversarial system. First, in the criminal sphere, peoples' liberty may be at stake. Justice is served neither by the innocent being convicted, nor by the guilty being acquitted on the basis of inaccurate testimony from medical experts. Given the stakes, it should not be thought of as too much to ask that such experts are required to justify the opinions they propound. Indeed, it might be argued that an expert's opinion that cannot by justified has no place in the courtroom in the first place.

The other option of course, is to attempt to scrutinise the expert before he even gets to court, in order to weed out the 'junk scientist'. This, however, is a blunt instrument. The worst scientist may be right on occasion, and the best may similarly be wrong (let us not forget that the vast majority of the evidence provided by Professor Meadow was accurate). While it is true that the likelihood of accurate evidence from the best scientists is higher, and *vice versa*, the root of the problem is not the expert but the evidence itself. For this reason, the best method of finding the truth is to subject the actual evidence to scrutiny. Even if the judicial process becomes more awkward for experts, they will surely agree that the benefits – in the form of more correct decisions – would render their sacrifice worthwhile.

REFERENCES

[1]   The articles concerning 'scandals' are: B. Hurwitz, "Murder Most Medical, Disposal Most Discrete" (2004) 364(S) *The Lancet* 38 and R. Field and A. Scotland, "Medicine in the UK After Shipman: Has 'All Changed, Changed Utterly'?" (2004) 364(S) *The Lancet* 40 (both concern Dr Harold Shipman, a general practitioner who murdered his patients); I. Ellis, "Beyond Organ Retention: The New Human Tissue Bill" (2004) 364(S) *The Lancet* 42 ((the 'organ retention scandal' where thousands of organs of dead children were kept, without consent, by a hospital in Liverpool. A national investigation subsequently found the practice to be widespread); and J. Miola, "Medicine and the Law" (2004) 364(S) *The Lancet* 48 ('scandals' involving expert evidence, particularly that of Professor Sir Roy Meadow).

[2]   *Op cit* at page 42.

[3]   *Op cit* at page 40.

[4]   *Op cit* at page 39.

[5]   *Op cit* at page 48.

[6]   Lord Woolf, "Are the Courts Excessively Deferential to the Medical Profession?" (2001) 9 *Med. L. Rev.* 1

[7]   See R. Escobales and D. Batty, "Paediatrician Struck Off" *The Guardian,* July 15 2005.

[8]   C. Dyer, "Inexpert Witness" *Guardian*, 6 April 2004.

[9]   *Ibid.*

[10]   For an explanation of these terms see J. Miola, "Medicine and the Law", *op cit*, at page 48.

[11]   *R v. Clark (Sally) ((Appeal against Conviction) (No.2))* [2003] 2 F.C.R. 447.

[12]   *The Guardian*, 11 June 2003.

[13]   [2004] 2 Cr. App. R. 7.

[14]   *Daubert* v. *Merrell Dow Pharmaceuticals* 509 U.S. 579 (1993).

[15]   *R v .Turner* (1974) 60 Cr.App.R. 80 at page 83, per Lawton L.J.

[16]   C. Tapper, *Cross and Tapper on Evidence*, 9th edn. (Butterworths: London, 1999) at
       523, quoted with approval by Kennedy L.J. in *R* v. *Dallagher* [2003] 1 Cr. App. R. 12
       at para. 29.

[17]   *R.* v *Bonython* (1984) 38 S.A.S.R. 45, King C.J. at p.46, quoted with approval by Rose
       L.J. in *R* v. *Luttrell and others* [2004] 2 Cr. App. R. 31 at para 32.

[18]   See for example the dismissal by the Court of Appeal in *R* v. *Gilfoyle* [2001] 2 Cr. App.
       R. 5 of the defence application to adduce evidence of a "psychological autopsy" upon
       the deceased victim in a case where the issue was whether the deceased had committed
       suicide or been murdered by the defendant. This decision may be contrasted with that in
       R v. *Dallagher* above concerning the admissibility of expert evidence pertaining to ear-
       print identification.

[19]   Per Rose L.J. *R* v. *Luttrell* at para 37.

[20]   Per Steyn L.J. [1995] 2 Cr. App. R. 425 at 429.

[21]   *R* v. *Lanfear* [1968] 2 Q.B. 77.

[22]   1953 S.C. 34 at 41.

[23]   *R.* v. *Christopher James Stockwell* [1993] 97 Cr. App. R. 260 at 266.

[24]   See for example *R* v. *Stefan Ivan Kiszko* (1979) 68 Cr. App. R. 62, and *Walton* v. *R*
       [1978] A.C. 788 P.C.

[25]   *R* v. *Matheson* [1958] 1 W.L.R. 474.

[26]   (1978) 66 Cr. App. R. 31 at 32.

[27]   [1991] 93 Cr. App. R. 245 at 249 (emphasis supplied by author). See also *Anderson* v.
       R [1972] A.C. 100 P.C.

[28]   See *The Guardian*, 18 June 2004.

[29]   n. 13 above para 178.

[30]   Ibid.

[31]   R. Meadow (ed.), *The ABC of Child Abuse*, 3rd edn. (BMJ Publishing: London, 1997).

[32]   *Davie* v. *Magistrates of Edinburgh* 1953 S.C. 34 at 41.

[33]   C.P. Walker and C. McCartney, "Evidence: expert witnesses seriously disagreeing as to
       whether cause of death of infants natural or unnatural" [2005] Crim L.R. 126, at 128.

[34]   [2005] 2 Cr. App. R. 31.

[35]   Per Judge L.J., ibid at para. 82.

[36]   Per Judge L.J., above n. 34 at para. 84.

[37]   Unreported 21 July 2005.

[38]   [1993] 2 Lloyds Rep. 68

[39]   [1995] 1 F.L.R. 181

[40]   Above, n 38 at 81.

[41]   Above n 39 at 192.

[42]   Above n33 at 128.

[43]   I. Kennedy and A. Grubb, *Medical Law* (3rd Edition, Butterworths, 2000).

[44]   *Bolam* v. *Friern Hospital Management Committee* [1957] 2 All E.R. 118

[45]   *Ibid* at page 121.

[46]   *Ibid* at page 122.

[47]   K. Norrie, "Common Practice and the Standard of Care in Medical Negligence" [1985]
       Juridical Review 145.

[48]   *Hunter* v. *Hanley* [1955] S.L.T. 213. Emphasis added.

[49]   *Bolam* at page 122.

[50] M. Davies, "The 'New *Bolam*': Another False Dawn for Medical Negligence?" (1996) 12 *Professional Negligence* 10.

[51] See M. Brazier and J. Miola, "Bye Bye Bolam: A Medical Litigation Revolution?" (2000) *8 Medical Law Review* 85.

[52] *Maynard* v. *West Midlands Regional Health Authority* [1985] 1 All E.R. 635.

[53] *Ibid* at page 639, *per* Lord Scarman.

[54] M. Brazier and J. Miola, *op. cit.* at page 89.

[55] *Ibid.*

[56] S. Sheldon, "Rethinking the *Bolam* Test" in S. Sheldon and M. Thomson (Eds), *Feminist Perspectives on Health Care Law* (Cavendish Press, 1998).

[57] H. Teff, *Reasonable Care* (Clarendon Press, 1994).

[58] S. MacLean, *"Old Law, New Medicine: Medical Ethics and Human Rights"* (Pandora Press, 1999) at page 2.

[59] *Sidaway* v. *Board of Governors of Bethlem Royal Hospital* [1984] 1 All ER 1018 at page 1028.

[60] See *Edward Wong Finance Co.* v. *Johnson, Stokes and Master* [1984] AC 296 and *Re Herald of Free Enterprise, The Independent*, 18 December 1987 respectively.

[61] *Bolitho* v. *City and Hackney Health Authority* [1998] AC 232. Although the citation is from 1998, the case was actually decided by the House of Lords in 1997.

[62] *Ibid* at page 243.

[63] Lord Woolf, "Are the Courts Excessively Deferential to the Medical Profession?" *op cit.*

[64] *Ibid.*

[65] *Ibid.*

[66] *Ibid*, at page 2.

[67] *Ibid.*

[68] *Ibid* at page 3.

[69] *Ibid.*

[70] *Ibid.*

In: New Developments in Child Abuse Research
Editor: Stanley M. Sturt, pp. 113-128

ISBN 1-59454-980-X
© 2006 Nova Science Publishers, Inc.

Chapter 7

CHILD SEXUAL ABUSE: THE HIDDEN EPIDEMICS. CHILD SEXUAL ABUSE PREVALENCE RATE AND CHARACTERISTICS OF SEXUAL VICTIMIZATION AS REPORTED BY A SAMPLE OF 3000 STUDENTS LIVING IN MILAN

Alberto Pellai, Luca Bassoli, Beatrice Castelli,
Rossella Curci, Dario Signorelli, Marisa Lanzi°,
Antonietta Provinzano and Anna Sacchetti°
Department of Public Health, Microbioligy, Virology – Milano State University
° Department for Children and Family at Milano Health Service Agency

ABSTRACT

How many are the victims of child sexual abuse? Of course, there is no univocal and certain answer to the question. For a trustworthy assessment of the problem, all victims should in fact disclose what happened to them to the police or, otherwise, describe and register in a special "anonymous notepad" every episode of violence, so that not a single incident would be lost. Anyhow, even if this was the case, the actual number of sexually abused victims would still be obscure. It stands to reason that the obscured rate of child sexual abuse, along with that "hidden number" to it related, are so far quite elevated. In spite of that, many other countries tried to define by means of reliable surveys the true extent of the problem.

INTRODUCTION

How many are the victims of child sexual abuse?

Of course, there is no univocal and certain answer to the question. For a trustworthy assessment of the problem, all victims should in fact disclose what happened to them to the police or, otherwise, describe and register in a special "anonymous notepad" every episode of violence, so that not a single incident would be lost. Anyhow, even if this was the case, the actual number of sexually abused victims would still be obscure, because so far:

a) Researchers have not yet come to an agreement on the terminology unilaterally employed to define both sexual abuse and the period contemplated as "early childhood". For many, those episodes of "passive" abuse, with the child-victim not directly involved in, but a mere witness of incidents or exhibitions of sexual nature, are to be left out from incidence and prevalence surveys. (Finkelhor, 1990; Finkelhor, 1994; Zerilli, 2002);

b) Children victimization is not officially reported on a national scale, whereas it is in other countries (among them the USA, Canada and UK);

c) A wide number of health care providers are still officially completing their professional training without being properly educated or informed about child sexual victimization, a matter remaining therefore underestimated. Most training experiences in this field are in fact included in post-diploma courses, willingly selected by operators already having a deeper comprehension of the problem.

On the basis of the above considerations, it stands to reason that the obscured rate of child sexual abuse, along with that "hidden number" to it related, are so far quite elevated. In spite of that, many other countries tried to define by means of reliable surveys the true extent of the problem.

INTERNATIONAL EPIDEMIOLOGICAL SURVEYS

In 1994, D. Finkelhor, among the most important researchers in the field, analysed all the epidemiological surveys defining the prevalence rate of sexual abuse on the female population. He examined data taken from 21 different nations, 19 of them economically developed, with a resulting min. prevalence rate of 7% (1 woman out of 15), and a max. of about 36% (nearly 1 woman out of 3). The survey by Finkelhor is a milestone in the field, since it asserts that sexual victimization in childhood is quite common, independently of the cultural level of a nation, of its economic development or the religion mainly observed, and that it is experienced by at least one woman out of 15. Furthermore, the survey by Finkelhor puts in evidence that most episodes of child sexual abuse cannot be counted as incest cases (in the above literature the reported frequency varying between 14% and 56%).

In conclusion, further to a global analysis of the epidemiological surveys available in literature, even of those supported by research methods less "sound and trustworthy", no investigation on adult population shows a prevalence rate of child sexual abuse lower than 5%. Essentially in retrospective studies, as to say, with adults interviewed on their past childhood and adolescence, the percentage of one or more reported episodes of sexual victimization in infancy appears quite high, with a relative frequency from 3 to 10 times more elevated (according to the examined survey) in women. Some examples:

- Russel (1983) pointed out that in California, nearly 4 women out of 10 had experienced sexual abuse before their 18th birthday, and they were able to report on it.
- In one of his earliest studies, through self-report questionnaires investigating a sample of parents, Finkelhor (1984) evidenced that 15% of mothers and 6% of fathers had experienced a form of sexual abuse in their infancy.

The same authors, however, point out that some limitations of their epidemiological surveys lie in the basic methodology, since, in case of adults interviewing, detecting the prevalence rate is essentially based on recollections of events occurred in childhood. This method is not fully contemplated as scientifically reliable, as facts can sometimes be misrepresented by "false memories", a phenomenon quite relevant in the last few years for researchers on the topic (Epstein, 2000; Sandler 1997; Terr, 1996). Moreover, the time lag between the abuse suffered and its recollection as reported by the researcher may contribute to alter the description of the actual events. In spite of all the above difficulties, all surveys on adult population are however based on the method of mnemonic "recalls". Furthermore, thanks essentially to these surveys, it has been possible to define variety and extent of sexual abuses on children, thus bridging the wide gap existing between official statistics and assessments and actual (or at least likely) rates, providing a truthful perspective on the problem and its spreading worldwide.

The fact that sexual abuse is spread in all societies, independently both of their geographical position and of their economical development is evidenced in a number of other surveys of scientific literature.

Studies carried out in countries quite distant from the USA, such as Costa Rica, Pakistan, El Salvador and Malaysia, have detected a prevalence rate rather close to the American one, with rates in female population comprised between 8.3% and 32% (Barthauer LM, Leventhal JM, 1999).

Considering moreover the most recurring features of the single episodes of sexual victimization, many are the common aspects overlapping transversally in the various surveys. Independently of the country of the survey, it can be noticed that (Finkelhor, 1992):

a) Most children experience sexual victimization from well-known perpetrators.
b) Incest episodes committed by the father are 7-8% only of all sexual incidents, exceeded in frequency by cases of abuse coerced by other members of the family, direct or enlarged (quite often uncles or elder brothers) and mostly by family friends, who are well-known to their victims and perpetrate abuse with a frequency varying between 32% and 60% of all cases.
c) Most sexual abuses on children are libidinous actions that do not involve penetration, the latter coerced or at least attempted in one case out of three.
d) The highest frequency of sexual victimization occurs on children ranging between 9 and 12 years of age; at least 25% of all accidents on younger children, although.

Nations where a large number of surveys were carried into effect with the purpose to know the true extent of sexual victimization on children are often those with the best and most efficacious preventive programs and care-taking actions. These nations are therefore capable, today, of demonstrating the efficacy of their politics aimed at protecting children from the risk of sexual victimization. In the last three years, the attention of researchers, health care providers, directors and politicians has been drawn on a number of surveys documenting how in the '90s the incidence rate of sexual abuses on children in the USA was lowered by 39%, decrease detected through the analysis of the "substantiated" cases number (in other words, checked as actual assaults coerced on children) reported to the State Social Services (from 150.000 episodes verified as truly happened in 1992 down to 92.000 in 1999 - Jones L.M., Finkelhor D, Kopiec K 2001). The number of suspected cases reported to the local agencies (abuse suspect cases) was reduced by 22%, from 429.000 reported assaults in 1991 down to 336.000 in the year 1999.

The above decrease might be indicative of an effective reduction in the actual incidence of the problem, due to the efficacy of public sensitisation campaigns as well as of preventive and care programs developed and spread on the whole American country in '80s and '90s. The same programs have been carried into effect in many other nations of the western world, with a corresponding recent diminution of the incidence rate, equal to, if not even higher than the American one. In Ontario, Canada, for example, in the five-year-period 1993-98, the rate of new cases of children sexual abuse was abated by 49%, while, on the other hand, episodes of general violence and maltreatment on children have considerably increased in the same period (Trocmè N, Fallon B, MacLaurin B, Copp B, 2002). A similar decrease can be noticed in Australia and Ireland (Jones LM, Finkelhor D, 2003), where the topic of sexual abuses on children has been dealt with within the last two decades by means of systematic methodology and programs on national scale.

If this is the situation on an international level, how is Italy facing the problem of child sexual abuse?

THE SITUATION IN ITALY

The Italian situation is far less known and defined, the whole epidemiological analysis being there often based on official data which refer to crimes of abuse and violence on children denounced to and registered by the Department of Justice. Considering the reported cases of child sexual abuse in the decade 1990-2000, it is evident that the lower number (132 cases) occurred in 1990 and the highest in 2000 (705 reported cases). As a matter of fact, in the years 1996-2000, there has been a progressive increase in cases officially acknowledged, which means an augmentation not in episodes of child sexual abuse themselves, but rather in their identification and recognition at social and educational sites where children spend their time (and can therefore be closely observed). It is certainly confirmed by the above data that teachers, social assistants, paediatricians and educators in general have gained deeper competences and a stronger capability of noticing the abuse, if occurring. Besides, it cannot be denied that the Italian situation, as represented in official statistics, appears, if compared to other countries (USA first of all), at any rate unreal. In comparison with the 92,000 cases of child sexual abuse substantiated in 1999 in USA, the episodes numbered in Italy in the same year were only 511, the ratio between Italian and American official figures being up to 5/1000 (while overall population in Italy is only 1/5 of the U.S. one).

It is worth mentioning that official figures include "substantiated cases" only, namely those officially verified as actual cases of sexual abuse on children, leaving all the undisclosed episodes out (a rather relevant percentage in the USA, too) which leads to partially underestimate the actual extent of the problem. On the basis of the above short notes, it can be easily imagined how the problem is widespread within the Italian society.

Child sexual abuse was defined in 1995 by the same American Medical Association (AMA) as a true "silent epidemic" (BP Fontanarosa, 1995).

A "Tailored" Survey, to Know the Actual Numbers

To gain an assessment of the prevalence rate of child sexual abuse in Italy as much as possible realistic, a survey based on the method of the "mnemonic recollection" has been carried out, the method consisting in asking grown-up people to report on memories retained of events occurred in their childhood. One survey only of the kind (M.Zerilli, S.Rigoni, L.Caldana, C.Magrin, L.Schon, R.Valentini, 2002) is available in Italy so far; it defined, by the same method, the prevalence rate of sexual abuse suffered in infancy by the population of a small but rather meaningful territory. The conclusion by the authors of the survey is quite interesting, as it points out that, in the territory taken into consideration ..... "it has been detected a higher percentage of victimized children than in foreign literature, with a prevalence of girls among victims. Interfamilial abuses are common, while those by unknown perpetrators rare (…). The reality of sexual abuses has come to such a level of evidence to make preventive programs necessary both for victims and perpetrators".

The study evidenced that 24.4% of victims were girls (10.8% of them severely and 13.6% slightly abused), while 14.2% were boys (2.8% of them severely and 11.4% slightly abused).

The above-mentioned survey was carried into effect in Venetia and it opened up a window of undoubted importance. It can be by full right considered the "milestone" of the national epidemiological surveys on child sexual abuse.

Further to the light shed on the subject by the Venetian survey, it has been determined to gain a deeper comprehension of the topic by means of a study carried out in the town of Milan in the year 2002.

Milan was chosen as a proper site for the current research owing to the following reasons:

a) For years the town of Milan has been in the van in providing services specialised in the care of sexual abuse victims;

b) The ASL (Local Health Agency) City of Milan is at the moment controlling the most advanced systematic project which connects all area utilities and facilities with the town schools with the purpose of primary and secondary prevention;

c) The ASL City of the city of Milan is at present the only in Italy capable of providing to all primary schools within its jurisdiction a project of child sexual abuse primary prevention, with dedicated sections applying to students, parents and teachers (Pellai A., 2002);

d) A future distribution and organization enhancement of the utilities provided by the ASL will be possible only on the basis of a real knowledge and not of a mere supposition of the problem true figure, as it is happening today;

e) An actual evaluation of all utilities provided to the citizens of Milan in these years will be possible only through the survey of any variation in the incidence/prevalence rates of episodes of child sexual abuse. The knowledge of the true prevalence rate of sexual abuses among 18-year-old boys and girls is the aim of the present survey; the same rate will provide a valuable element for a future analysis of the problem and its evolution.

On account of the above considerations, a research was carried out with the following purposes:

a) Defining the prevalence rate of exposure to sexual victimization among a cohort of students attending the V-year-courses of a group of high schools in Milan.
b) Defining the features of the sexual victimization episodes suffered in childhood according to the following parameters: nature of the abuse, identity of the perpetrator, age of the victim when abused, disclosure to confidants, frequency of abuse occurrence, and eventual intervention of health professionals to provide the victim with support.

MATERIALS AND METHODS

The survey was carried out on the model of epidemiological retrospective studies through distribution of anonymous self-adminstered questionnaires to a representative sample of students attending the V year of Milan high schools. Participants were recruited by the method of cluster sampling among the students of those state high schools voluntarily offered. Specifically, the research protocol was firstly submitted to the directions of the various state high schools in town, the study procedure was fully explained on the occasion of a meeting among directors and the research staff. Each school afterwards voluntarily decided whether to participate or not in the survey. All pupils from the V year-courses of the schools giving their assent were recruited as respondents.

a) Survey Tool

The questionnaire of the present survey was specifically tailored for the purpose, being the result of an adaptation of forms used in occasion of similar experiences from other researchers' epidemiological surveys published both in Italy and abroad (Finkelhor, 1990; Finkelhor, 1994; Zerilli, 2002).

The questionnaire consisted of two main parts:

a. An introductory section, with the view to giving the respondents a reason for answering, explaining the purpose of the survey, providing the filling instructions, granting anonymity and privacy;
b. A main part devoted to the collection of sexual abusive experiences, if any, suffered in childhood, as well as of some social and demographical information and eventual activities of primary prevention the respondent took part in his infancy.

The main part is divided into different sections, the first being dedicated to the registration of basic demographic data, of information regarding interpersonal relationships, sexual behaviour and participation in preventive programs. The next five sections investigate the different kinds of sexual abuse, which in the following analysis fall into the two categories of severe and slight/moderate incidents (see Table 1). For each kind of incident, the respondents were asked questions regarding the age the abuse was suffered, the frequency (serial or one-time only) of occurrence, the identity of the perpetrator, the disclosure to someone, whether help was asked for and provided and finally some contextual details such as secret coerciveness, lustful compliments or other similar nuisances.

Table 1

	Forms of abuse surveyed	Classification
1	Exposure to pornographic material	
2	Being touched in private parts	Slight/moderate
3	Coercion to touch the perpetrator's private parts	
4	Coercion to masturbation	
5	Coercion to penetration (anal and/or vaginal) and coercion to oral-genital contact	Severe

b) Organization

The survey went through various steps:

STEP I: Survey instrument drafting and master study on 5% of the recruited respondents (sub-sample of approx. 200 students) aimed at a preliminary check-up of the questionnaire, to verify if it could be easily understood and filled in. (January–February 2002)

STEP II: Survey planning, with recruitment of the 200 5th-year-classes to be involved, settlement of the working protocol and improvement of questionnaires giving out and collecting procedure. In selecting the participant classes, efforts were made to build up a school sample representative of all different types of courses as well as of their location on the wide city territory (January – March 2002).

STEP III: Giving out, gathering up and sending the filled questionnaires back to the research staff, with data entering and cross-validating into "Epi Info", a word processing, data base and statistics program. (March 2002 – April 2002)

c) Sample Selecting Procedure

For the present survey, it was established to interview of-age students attending the V-year classes of Milan high schools. Due to the nature of the survey, respondents involved had to be of age, capable therefore of voluntarily deciding their participation without any further permission (restraining the survey to parents' permission, for example, as headmasters had required in case of students under age, would have undoubtedly resulted in the exclusion of all those victims exposed to interfamilial sexual abuse). The directors of the schools involved were duly informed, and demanded to give their assent to the development of the research as indicated on the protocol specifically drawn up for the purpose.

d) Questionnaire Giving-Out Method

The questionnaires were distributed to respondents in each school involved and inside each class, in the presence of properly trained professionals not belonging to the school staff. They were presented, explained and handed over to the students by a non-resident operator on a usual lesson morning. Once filled in, the questionnaires were recollected the following morning by the same operator, placed into a closed envelope which, sealed, was finally sent to the researchers for data processing and analysing. Furthermore, the operators went to the schools for two more days to collect those questionnaires not given back on the first recollecting day for the most different reasons (absence from school, questionnaire forgetting or loosing, etc.).

Students were thus ensured that their questionnaires were not recognizable, and that episodes eventually reported were absolutely guarded in an atmosphere of strict severity and anonymity protection. It was chosen to recollect the questionnaires the following day, and not to have them filled in directly in class, in order to grant all respondents the compilation in full loneliness, in a selected place at the desired time. Recollection was carried out under the supervision of a researcher.

It is a matter of fact that this surveying method encouraged the students' participation. A girl wrote the following comment on her questionnaire after filling it in:

> To tell the truth, I generally think this kind of tests perfectly useless. But this one is different, perhaps for the method it was carried out (in private, without time limits). I have been totally sincere and I have found out that this subject is still painful to me; it hurts to talk about it, and perhaps you will say it is regular, that real harm is in silence.

RESULTS

1. Description of the Investigated Population

The filled-in questionnaires collected and entered into the word processing, database and statistics program were 2935, corresponding to 88.6% of the sample of students selected as respondents (3313), 46 high schools and 212 V-year classes altogether.

Of the 2935 forms delivered back, 2839 (up to 85.7% of the sample students) were considered as valid, the validity standard being an answer given to at least one of the questions concerning the abuse. The valid questionnaires made up, were not otherwise indicated, the denominator of analysis calculated ratios.

The division by sex indicated a high female prevalence on males within the sample of the present survey (respectively 56.4% vs. 43.5%, while 0.1% of the respondents did not give any information about the sex).

The majority of participants ranged between 18 and 19 years of age, corresponding to 81.8% of the interviewed students. A relevant percentage reported to be 20 years of age (12.1%), and 3.7% ranged from 21 to 29. No age was reported on 2.5% of the questionnaires. Participants averaged 18.8 years of age, slightly higher with males (18.8) as compared to females (18.7). As far as the kind of school attended is concerned, most respondents reported to be from a technical institute (34.7%), 22.6 % from Liceo specializing in scientific studies, 18.4% from vocational schools, 11.1% from Liceo specializing in classic studies, the remaining 13.3% attending other kind of schools (language, art subjects, pedagogic).

2. Global Evaluation of the Abuse Prevalence.

a) Total Prevalence Rate (Fig. 1)

Considering all kinds of abuse investigated, 415 cases were numbered corresponding to 14.6% of the whole sample of students, of which 97 reported by boys (7.9%) and 318 by girls (19.9%). The number of actual cases might be even higher (436, corresponding to 15.4% - boys 8.8%; girls 20.4%) if, as previously done in other similar surveys, are counted among victims not only those disclosing it, but also those hiding themselves behind the sentence "I'd rather not giving any answer" when interviewed on one of the five kinds of abuse investigated in the current survey.

Many cases of exposure to episodes of coerced sexual contact reported by the participants fell under the first three categories of abuse, exposure to pornographic material, being touched in private parts or being forced to touch the perpetrator's private parts. Of these forms of abuse, categorized by the authors of the current study into "slight/moderate" on the model of other epidemiological surveys of the literature on the topic, 350 cases were reported, corresponding to 84.3% of all detected accidents.

14.6% of participants (415 cases) reported experiencing at least one of the five forms of sexual abuse in their infancy:

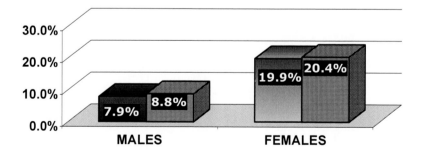

Figure 1: prevalence rate of cases of sexual abused surveyed

According to the classification of the current research, in other 45 cases (10.8% of all cases of abuse surveyed), the respondents endorsed experiencing, two different kinds of abuse, one or more "slight/moderate" form of sexually abusive experience, and one or more "severe" form of sexually abusive experience.

Finally, 20 respondents (4.8% of all cases of abuse surveyed) endorsed experiencing one or more "severe" form of sexually abusive experience, and no episodes of "slight/moderate" forms of abuse.

The absolute frequency rate of sexual victimization (14.6%) was then composed of 12.3% of victims exposed to "slight/moderate" forms of abuse and of 2.3% of victims exposed to "severe" forms of abuse.

b) Prevalence Rate of Slight and Severe Forms of Abuse in Male and Female Respondents.

Of the interviewed girls, 16.5% reported suffering a slight and 3.4% a severe sexual abuse, while of the interviewed boys, percentages were respectively 7% and 0.8%. These numbers, too, might be higher if added of those undisclosed episodes hidden behind the sentence "I'd rather prefer not answering". If this were the case, the total percentage would be up to 12.7% or slightly victimized and to 2.5% for severely victimized respondents. Considering the detected numbers, then, the chance of exposure to a slight form of sexual abuse is 2.4 times higher for girls than for boys, and the chance of exposure to a severe form of abuse is 4.2 times higher for girls.

c) Age of the First Exposure to Sexual Victimization (Fig. 2)

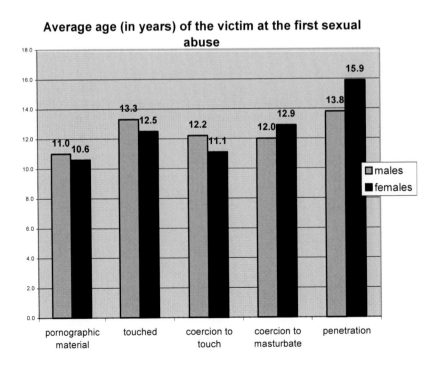

Figure 2: average age (in years) of the victim at the first sexual abuse

The average age of exposure to the first coerced sexual contact rises as the severity of the abuse increases.

Of the reported cases of exposure to pornographic material coerced by an older person, the first incident averaged 11 years of age for boys and 10.6 years of age for girls.

Of those reporting being forcedly touched in their private parts by an older person, the first incident averaged 13.3 years for boys and 12.5 years for girls.

Of those reporting being forced into touching an older person in his private parts, the first incident averaged 12.2 years for boys and 11.1 years for girls.

Of those being forced into masturbating an older person, the first incident averaged 13.8 years of age for boys and 12.9 years of age for girls.

Of those reporting being forced into an oral-genital contact or penetration by an older person, the first incident averaged 13.3 years of age for boys and 15.2 years of age for girls.

In case of slight forms of abuse, the average age of the first exposure is higher for boys rather than girls; on the contrary, it is higher for girls in case of the two severe forms of abuse investigated by the current research.

d) Relationship to the Perpetrator (Fig. 3)

The perpetrator is quite often well known by his victim; the fact is more evident whit girls who experienced the most severe forms of sexual abuse. In fig. 3 it is illustrated, for each kind of sexual abuse dealt with in the current study, the percentage of cases of sexually abusive experience suffered by victims who knew their perpetrator, as compared to all cases included in each sub-section of the analysed forms of sexual coercion. The same datum is also given subdivided according to the sex of the victim.

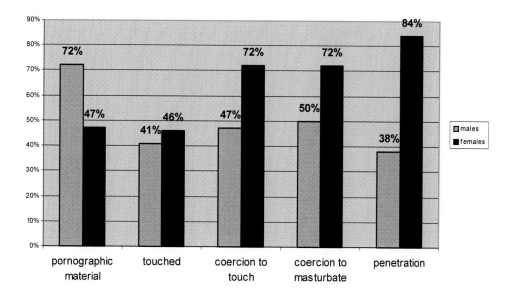

Figure 3: percentage of victims who knew their perpetrator

e) Factors Associated with Victimization Experience

The respondents having any brother or sister faced higher risks of being sexually abused rather than only sons or daughters, since 12.7% of interviewed students with at least one brother or sister reported cases of slight abuse, if compared with 11.1% of sole son/daughter respondents; 2.5% brothers or sisters reported cases of severe abuse if compared with 1.7% of sole sons/daughters.

A more elevated prevalence of episodes of sexual abuse was noted among those respondents who did not live with both parents and, specifically, of the 377 respondents living with one parent only, 17.8% reported an experience of slight sexual assault, while 4% an experience of severe sexual assault; on the other hand, the percentage rates being respectively 11.4% and 2.1% for those students living with both parents.

The number of victims appeared finally higher among students with separated or divorced parents (slightly abused respondents 18.9%, severely abused respondents 3.8%) than among those living with both parents together (slightly abused respondents 11.5%, severely abused respondents 2.1%)

Suffering a coerced sexual contact negatively alters the opinion of the victim's interrelationships, considered as "little satisfying" or "unsatisfying" by 7.5% of those respondents who did not suffer any form of abuse, by 13.1% of those respondents who experienced a slight form of abuse and by 10.8% of those who experienced a severe form of abuse.

Among victimized students, moreover, is lower the number of those who have already had a lasting affair (21.5% of severely abused respondents, 20.3% of slightly severed respondents and 25.8% of those who did not suffer any form of abuse), while, on the other hand, is higher the number of those reporting a complete sexual intercourse (73.8% of severely abused respondents, 65.7% of slightly abused respondents and 58.6% of respondents who did not suffer any form of abuse) or at least a partial one (82.4% of severely abused respondents, 64.2% of slightly abused respondents and 49.1% of non-abused respondents).

The reported average age of the first sexual intercourse is lower for those who experienced a severe form of abuse (15.4 years of age) if compared with those who experienced a slight form of abuse (15.8 years of age) or with non-abused respondents (16.2 years of age). On the contrary, the partner average age is higher among severely abused (19.4 years of age) or slightly abused respondents (18.1 years of age); higher is also the percentage of those defining the first sexual experience "unsatisfying" or "little satisfying", respectively 31.2% of severely abused and 32.6% of slightly abused respondents. For those respondents not experiencing any form of sexual coercion, the partner averaged 17.8 years of age; 23.1% of them considered their first sexual experience "unsatisfying" or "little satisfying".

In the end, those who suffered a coerced sexual experience remembered more often to have listened to educators explaining what a sexual abuse is (56.9% of severely abused respondents, 52.6% of slightly abused respondents if compared to 48.2% of non-abused respondents) and how to defend oneself against it (58.5% of severely abused respondents and 54.3% of slightly abused respondents if compared to 51.2% of non-abused respondents).

DISCUSSION

a) An Obscured Problem

It is clearly understood from the data revealed by the current research that sexual abuse on children is an actual and widespread problem, poorly represented in official statistics. The comparison between official numbers and those detected by interviewing the sample of 18-year-old respondents of the current study evidenced that, due to a minimum overlap, actual numbers are undoubtedly underestimated with levels of children victimization that far exceed those officially reported. As shown by the collected data, among the students of each class there is at least one victim of sexual abuse or assault; in each school are hiding victims of severe forms of sexual abuse never disclosed to anyone, who silently endured their sufferance and to whom no one has ever offered his help or care. The numbers detected overlapped those of most other epidemiological surveys of the literature on the topic, which means that the problem is as much spread in Milan as it is in other Western countries previously investigated.

b) Perpetrators are Well Known by Their Victims

The current study pointed out, furthermore, that sexual victimization on children is essentially perpetrated by persons closely related to the victim and his family. Globally, the detected numbers confirmed that only 10.6% of abuse accidents are perpetrated by a family member. As for the rest, the perpetrator belonged to the so-called "enlarged family" in 33.7% of reported cases and to the educational sphere in 4.8% of reported cases.

The reading of the current data gives a new perspective to the common comprehension of the problem of children victimization, as made by information taken from official statistics. The latter relate, in fact, an excess of number of incest cases, one of the less reported form of sexual abusive experienced by the respondents of the current survey. A new perspective is also gained on episodes of child sexual coercion perpetrated by persons belonging to the enlarged circle of interrelationships the child and his family live within.

It is therefore of no use and meaning to warn children against this or that adult person; in the same way it does not make any sense to enquiry on the main features of a paedophile, and on the way to recognize him.

c) The Importance of Helping the Victim to Disclose His Secret

The data surveyed by the current research showed how the average age of the victim rises with the increasing of the form of abuse suffered. As a consequence, the most severe forms of sexually abusive experiences are suffered by victims already emerged from childhood, in their pre-adolescence or youth. These teen-aged victims, as compared with children, can have resort to a mental frame with higher competences. They are namely capable of a deeper comprehension and identification of the traumatic experience suffered, but, notwithstanding this fact, they chose the path of silence. This reveals how strong can be the "secret alliance" between the perpetrator and his victim, an alliance which, considering what reported by the participants to the current research, can be broken only in case the victim realizes to be entrapped in a cage and to ask for help is the only way to get out. Victims are probably silent about the sexual abuse suffered because they feel strongly on them the "stigma" of the violence experienced. It is the typical implicit attitude of a person who, after experiencing a sexual coercion, feels partially guilty for the incident happened to him.

What the survivors really need is not forgetting, but rather working out and getting over the traumatic event. The more victims will be reassured by the presence of health care providers sensitive to the problem and not assuming denial or censure attitudes, the more this will be possible. This is particularly true in case of victims of extremely severe forms of sexual coercion, since the more severe the form of abuse is, in fact, the more it is experienced by the victim as a taboo which cannot be disclosed to others, and for which no help can be asked at all.

Quite often the survivor is well aware of the problem in its full seriousness, but he feels that he must face the traumatic event by himself, being convinced that nobody will be able to understand or really help. From this point of view, the survivor tends to consider a taboo not only the abuse suffered, but even his asking for help which, instead, might assist him in recovering health and self-reliance, self-esteem and respect so seriously compromised by the traumatic incident.

The taboo dimension appears in its full evidence with victimized boys. By analysing the average latency timing between the experience of sexual abuse and its disclosing or asking for help by those who were able to do it, boys are more likely to delay disclosure rather then girls. Moreover, the percentage of male survivors disclosing the abuse suffered to some recipient is constantly the lowest for all kinds of abuse analysed by the current research. Confirmation to this fact that abused boys are less likely to disclose episodes of both physical and sexual abuse, is given by scientific literature on the topic (M. Schwartz M., 1994).

It is then fundamental to help those male survivors who experienced coerced sexual contacts to disclose what has happened to them, to overcome their fear and " stigma" that they could be judged as weak or homosexual individuals, in opposition to the social/cultural stereotyped model of powerful and strong man, always in control of every situation, and, mainly, those events of sexual nature.

It is reported in literature that male victims, above all those who did not disclose the traumatic experience, show a much more elevated prevalence index as regards self-mutilation (R.Di Clemente, L.E.Ponton, D.Hartley, 1991), substance abuse, dejection and low self-esteem (D.L. Hussey, G.Strom, M.I.Singer, 1992).

Efforts must be made to encourage among victims favourable disclosure conditions even a long time after the traumatic experience. Moreover, the victims of the most severe forms of abuse as well as male-victims must be the recipients of dedicated messages within group preventive actions and public sensitisation campaigns, so as they could be at ease in disclosing their problem and trusting in counselling/care-providing on the part of helping professionals.

d)Enhancing Primary Preventive Actions is Mostly Needed

Of the various and most different aspects of child sexual victimization surveyed, the most problematic and unexpected finding of the current research resulted being the abuse perpetrated within horizontal relationships, among "peers". This form of abuse is actually very recurring in experiences and testimonies reported by the interviewed students. Deep ignorance, emotional incompetence and scarce sexual education are still quite common features of sexual and affective relationships between teens, thus making violent actions or sexual coercion possible even in situations apparently not classifiable as sexual abuses on a child.

And yet, the reported experiences confirm the fact that coercion might often occur even in sexual intercourses between peers. This problem must be a very significant warning for the whole adult society, since it indicates how often teens are totally incompetent to the control of their emotional sphere and to the recognition of the feelings they live inside their deeper and more intimate dimension. Preventive actions based on educating subjects, who might thus gain stronger self-control in sexual episodes of abusive nature, to identify the value and the function of their emotions seems to be the sort of "sexual education" mostly needed by those victims exposed at high risk factors of health, psychological and social kind.

It will not be possible to carry into effect any sexual abuse preventive campaign in our society without a strong action of primary prevention that has its chief aim in adequate emotional education. Sexual abuse will be eliminated only when grown-up people and children will be capable of a critical evaluation of their emotions, thus controlling and suitably filtering them within their interrelationships, an inborn competence for mankind often done away with by the social and cultural background each child is grown up in. The family, along with all educative sites attended by children, should strongly support and encourage programs aimed at enhancing emotional intelligence. In this way only, children will be able of self-controlling at-risk situations and, if on the victim's side, of trusting to and relying on qualified grown-up people.

REFERENCES

Barthauer L.M., Leventhal J.M. (1999) Prevalence and effects of child sexual abuse in a poor, rural community in El Salvador: a retrospective study in women after 12 years of civil war. *Child Abuse and Neglect*, 23: 1117-1126

Di Clemente R., L.E.Ponton L.E., D.Hartley D. "Prevalence and correlates of Cutting Behavior: Risk for HIV Transmission" *Journal of the American Academy of Child and Adolescent Psychiatry* 30, 5 (1991): 735-40

Epstain (2000) Memories of childhood trauma: who reports forgetting and why? *Dissertation Abstract Mar*; vol 60 (8-B), 4219.

Finkelhor D. (1984) *Child Sexual Abuse: New Theory and Research*. New York:The Free Press

Finkelhor D. (1990) *Ch. Ab. Neglect* 14:19-28

Finkelhor D. (1992) *Child Sexual Abuse in Maxcy-Roseneau-Last Public Health & Preventive Medicine,* 13th Edition USA:Prentice-Hall International Inc

Finkelhor D. (1994) The international epidemiology of child sexual abuse. *Child Abuse and Neglect,* 18: 409-417

Fontanarosa, P.B. (1995). "The unrelenting epidemic of violence in America." *Journal of the American Medical Association,* 273(22), 1,760-1,762.

Hussey D.L., Strom G., Singer M.I. "Male Victims of Sexual Abuse" *Child and Adolescent Social Work Journal* 9, 6 (1992): 491-503

Jones L.M., Finkelhor D, Kopiec K (2001) Why is sexual abuse declining. A survey of State child protection administration. *Child Abuse and Neglect,* 25(9), 1139-1158

Jones L.M., Finkelhor D (2003) Putting together evidence on declining trends in sexual abuse: a complex puzzle. *Child Abuse and Neglect,* 27(2), 133-135

Pellai A. (2002) Focus monotematico: La prevenzione primaria dell'abuso sessuale all'infanzia: perché e come intervenire". *Maltrattamento e abuso all'infanzia,* 4: 7-71

Russel D. (1983) The incidence and Prevalence of Intrafamilial and Extrafamilial Sexual Abuse of Female Children. *Child Abuse and Neglect:* 7, 133-146

Sandler J., Fanagy P. (1997) *Recovered memories of abuse: true or false?* Kornac books, London

Terr L. (1996) *Il pozzo della memoria,* Garzanti, Milano

Trocmè N., Fallon B., MacLaurin B., Copp B. (2002) *The changing face of child welfare investigations in Ontario: Ontario incidence studies of reported child abuse and neglect* (OIS 1993/98) Toronto, ON: Centre of Excellence for Child Welfare, Faculty of Social Work, University of Toronto

Zerilli M., Rigoni S., Caldana L., Magrin C., Schon L., Valentini R. (2002) Maltrattamento e ab. *All'infanzia* 4:73-104

In: New Developments in Child Abuse Research
Editor: Stanley M. Sturt, pp. 129-142

ISBN 1-59454-980-X
© 2006 Nova Science Publishers, Inc.

Chapter 8

SEXUAL VIOLENCE AGAINST GIRLS IN SITUATIONS OF ARMED CONFLICT

Myriam S. Denov[1]

Department of Criminology, University of Ottawa
25 University Street, Ottawa, Ontario
K1N 6N5, Canada

ABSTRACT

Despite its occurrence throughout history, sexual violence within the context of armed conflict has long been dismissed and minimized by historians, scholars, and military and political leaders. While often regarded as a private crime or stemming from the 'unfortunate' behaviour of renegade soldiers, literature over the past decade has revealed the widespread and systematic nature of wartime sexual violence. Drawing on examples from the former Yugoslavia, Rwanda, and Sierra Leone, this paper examines the phenomenon of wartime sexual violence against girls. In particular, it addresses the prevalence and patterns of wartime sexual violence, its meaning, purpose, and importantly, its long-term effects. Also explored are the historical and contemporary international responses to the phenomenon. The paper highlights the ways in which sexual violence is used as a strategy of conflict, acting as a weapon of war where ultimately, girls continue to be victims of a devastating form of child abuse.

INTRODUCTION

Although the focus of armed conflict is frequently on the actions and activities of soldiers and fighting forces, each year a rising number of civilians, particularly women and children, are forced to cope with the experience of armed conflict. According to Eriksson and Wallensteen (2004), in 2003, a total of 29 armed conflicts were active in 22 countries around

[1] Tel: 613-562-5800 (3973), Fax: 613-562-5304, e-mail: *mdenov@uottawa.ca*

the world. Meanwhile, the proportion of civilian casualties in armed conflicts has been steadily increasing. Statistics reveal that in World War I approximately 10% of the casualties were civilians; by World War II this had increased to 50%. Currently, however, over 80% of war victims are civilians (Cairns, 2005). According to the United Nations, in the last decade two million children have been killed in situations of armed conflict and six million have been injured (Globe and Mail, 2005). Despite their ongoing exposure to armed conflict, until quite recently, civilian experiences of war, particularly those of girls[2], have been largely ignored.

Females of all ages increasingly bear the burden of armed conflict and are affected by war both directly and indirectly (Gardam and Charlesworth, 2000; Giles and Hyndman, 2004, Handrahan, 2004). The direct effects include victimization through acts of murder, terrorism, torture, and rape, while the indirect effects include displacement, loss of home or property, family separation and disintegration, poverty, and illness (Fox, 2004; Higate and Henry, 2004). There has been mounting evidence suggesting that girls experience armed conflict differently than boys (Denov and Maclure, in press; McKay, 1998). This is because armed conflict often exacerbates the gender inequalities that exist in different forms and to varying degrees in all societies, and that make girls particularly vulnerable when conflict erupts. The predominance of sexual violence[3] against females during war provides a powerful example of this phenomenon. Women and girls have been ongoing targets for sexual violence during conflict because of their ethnicity but mainly because of their gender, and their bodies are used as figurative and literal sites of combat (Twargiramariya and Turshen, 1998). These crimes of sexual violence have been characterized by extreme brutality and are frequently preceded or followed by other egregious human rights abuses against the victim, her family and her community (Human Rights Watch [HRW], 2003). Despite significant sexual victimization against females during conflict, it is only within the last decade that it has begun to receive in-depth study and attention. Moreover, methods of investigating and documenting such human rights abuses against females have been inadequate and have frequently obscured their suffering. As an example, in 1994, the UN 'fact-finding mission' in Rwanda did not detect systematic sexual violence against women until nine months after the genocide when women began to give birth in unprecedented numbers (Gardam and Charlesworth, 2000).

Turshen (2000) has argued that rape during armed conflict can be viewed as distinct from what she refers to as 'common rape' (outside of the context of armed conflict) given that wartime rape is often perpetrated in a context of institutional policies and decisions. Moreover, wartime sexual violence against females can be seen as social and historical processes that are carried out collectively, giving them important collective meaning (Seifert, 1996). It is thus essential to explore this meaning and its implications, particularly for girls.

It is clear that the experience and after-effects of wartime sexual violence may have similar implications for both women and girls. However, in the case of girls, armed conflict is often more debilitating and dangerous due to the vulnerability exacerbated by the

---

[2] For this paper, the definition of a girl child will coincide with the definition set out in the 1989 Convention on the Rights of the Child. According to the Convention, a child is defined as "every human being below the age of eighteen years" (Art. 1).

[3] In this paper, sexual violence is the overarching term used to describe 'any violence, physical or psychological, carried out through sexual means or by targeting sexuality' (United Nations, 1998). Sexual violence includes rape and attempted rape, and such acts as forcing a person to strip naked in public, forcing two victims to perform sexual acts on one another or to harm one another in a sexual manner, mutilating a person's genitals or a female's breasts, and sexual slavery (Human Rights Watch, 2003).

combination of their gender, age and physical disadvantage (Fox, 2004: 477). Moreover, there as been a dearth of literature on the unique experiences of girls within situations of armed conflict. As such, this chapter will explore the phenomenon of wartime sexual violence specifically against girls[4]. The chapter addresses the historical significance and prevalence of sexual violence during armed conflict including its patterns, and perpetrators. It then outlines the functions of wartime sexual violence, revealing its use and application as a method of waging war. Drawing upon on the voices and experiences of girls, the chapter also highlights the many long-term effects of wartime sexual violence. In the final section, the historical and contemporary responses of the international community to wartime sexual violence are discussed. While contemporary armed conflicts have been replete with evidence and accounts of widespread sexual violence, the paper will draw largely upon examples from the former Yugoslavia, Rwanda, and Sierra Leone. In doing so, it will highlight the ways in which sexual violence is used as an effective strategy of conflict – as a weapon of war, where ultimately, girls have been victims of a horrific form of child abuse.

1. WARTIME SEXUAL VIOLENCE: A PHENOMENON IGNORED

During armed conflict, sexual violence can occur in a variety of settings: in the community, in camps for displaced persons, and during flights to safety. Regardless of the setting, during armed conflict, rapes tend to be characterized by multiple perpetrators (gang rapes), involve sexual torture, as well as the element of a 'spectacle' whereby the rape occurs in the presence of the victim's family, the local population or other victims (Omanyondo Ohambe et al., 2005). Adolescent girls may be particularly targeted for rape because they are thought to be less likely to be infected with the HIV/AIDS virus or other sexually transmitted diseases (McKay, 1998). Moreover, in societies where a high value is placed on virginity, young girls thought to be virgins may be targeted, with the aim of making them less eligible for marriage (HRW, 2003).

Historically, sexual violence has been routinely directed against females[5] during armed conflict (Brownmiller, 1975; Seifert, 1994, 1996) and was prevalent in the wars of the ancient Greeks, Romans and Hebrews as well as in the Trojan War (Brownmiller, 1975; Niarchos, 1995). Mass sexual violence has been documented during World War I, World War II, the Vietnam war and, over the last few decades, in the conflicts in El Salvador, Guatemala, Liberia, Kuwait, Rwanda, the former Yugoslavia, the Democratic Republic of Congo, and Sudan, to name but a few (Omanyondo Ohambe et al., 2005; Amnesty International, 2004; Niarchos, 1995). Despite its occurrence throughout history, the problem has frequently been ignored by historians and journalists, and has been minimized and dismissed by military and political leaders as a 'private crime' or the 'unfortunate behaviour' of renegade soldiers (Seifert, 1996). For example, in the context of the war in the former Yugoslavia, humanitarian organizations had apparently been informed about 'rape camps' where females were repeatedly raped, impregnated, and held prisoners until it was too late to have an abortion. Allegedly, the Red Cross and the UN had long possessed such information without objecting

---

[4] However, where pertinent, the experiences of women will also be highlighted.

[5] It is important to note that during armed conflict, males are also victims of sexual violence (see Zarkov, 2001; Women's Commission, 2002:40). This paper, however, is focusing solely on sexual violence against girls.

especially strenuously or bringing it to public attention. As late as October 1992, the UNHCR asserted that 'there is no indication of systemic rapes; it is a matter of wandering gangs' (Seifert, 1994).

Perhaps more disturbingly, sexual violence has been accepted because it is so commonplace; the numbers of sexually victimized females during recent conflicts have been staggering. For example, during the Rwandan genocide, females were subjected to sexual violence on a massive scale, perpetrated by members of the Hutu militia groups known collectively as the *Interahamwe*, by other civilians, and by soldiers of the Rwandan Armed Forces (Forces Armées Rwandaises). Reportedly, more than 250,000 women and girls were raped[6] (Twagiramariya and Turshen, 1998). In 1999, the Association of Widows of the Genocide, Agahozo conducted a study on the kinds of violence suffered by Rwandan women. This study, based on a sample of 1,125 women living in the prefectures of Kigali, Butare and Kibundo revealed that 74.5% had experienced sexual violence including individual or gang rape, incidents of forced incest (the rape of one's own child or parent), the cutting of genitalia, the insertion of cutting or piercing objects in the vagina, and rape by one or more men infected with the AIDS virus (HRW, 1996).

During the war in the former Yugoslavia it has been estimated that between 10,000 and 60,000 of women and girls were raped (Ashford and Huet-Vaughn, 1997). While Muslim females from Bosnia and Herzegovina were the main targets of rape, Croatian, and Serbian females were also targeted by the perpetrators whether they were Serbian soldiers, paramilitary groups, local police, or civilians (Niarchos, 1995).

Similarly, sexual violence has remained Sierra Leone's silent war crime. Although sexual violence was committed on a much larger scale than the highly visible amputations for which Sierra Leone became notorious, until recently, little attention was paid to sexual violence either nationally or internationally (HRW, 2003). Throughout the civil war in Sierra Leone from 1991-2002, thousands of women and girls of all ages, ethnic groups, and socio-economic classes were subjected to widespread and systematic sexual violence (individual and gang rape, and rape with objects), mostly by rebel forces. In 2002, Physicians for Human Rights (PHR) conducted a survey of female heads of households in communities of displaced persons. PHR calculated that as many as 215,000 to 257,000 Sierra Leonean women and girls may have been subjected to sexual violence during the conflict period. Moreover, throughout much of the conflict, young females were systematically abducted by warring factions (mainly rebel forces) and forced to assume the roles of combatants, commanders' 'wives', slave labour, or a combination of these roles (Denov and Maclure, in press). Many of these abducted girls were repeatedly raped throughout their captivity. Kept among the rebel forces for long periods of time, many girls gave birth to children fathered by the rebels. While the war was declared over in 2002, an unknown number of women and girls still remain with their rebel 'husbands' (HRW, 2003).

---

[6] Like all statistics regarding sexual violence, these figures should be interpreted with caution. In some cases, as a result of victim under-reporting, these numbers are likely to underestimate the problem. In other cases, statistics regarding sexual violence may be exaggerated for political reasons (Tetrault, 1997).

2. THE PERPETRATORS OF WARTIME SEXUAL VIOLENCE

The main perpetrators of wartime sexual violence are male[7] and are typically of the armed forces or parties to a conflict whether governmental or other actors (Machel, 2000). Moreover, as this 16 year-old Sierra Leonean rape survivor notes, the perpetrators may come from every age group, including the very young:

> The [ten] rebels ordered my parents and the two other women to move away. Then they told me to undress. I was raped by the ten rebels, one after the other. They lined up, waiting for their turn and watched while I was being raped vaginally and in my anus. One of the child combatants was about twelve years. The three other child soldiers were about fifteen. The rebels threatened to kill me if I cried (HRW, 2003).

Those directly involved in the fighting do not appear to be the only perpetrators of wartime sexual violence. Other perpetrators have included partners, acquaintances, local police, and other civilians (Machel, 2000). Moreover, there have been the ongoing allegations in several war torn countries that humanitarian aid workers have been implicated in wartime sexual violence. The United Nations High Commission on Refugees and Save the Children UK (2002) produced a joint report on the sexual exploitation of refugee women and children in West Africa. The report, which was based on focus-group discussions and individual interviews with 1,500 children and adults, documented allegations against 40 agencies and 67 individuals. It found sexual exploitation to be endemic in the displaced person camps and the exploiters were men in the community with power and money including camp leaders, casual labourers, and teachers. Perhaps the greatest moral outrage came from allegations against humanitarian workers. It was found that staff NGO's were the main customers of refugee prostitutes. Moreover, workers would reportedly withhold aid until sex was proffered. As these two refugee children explained:

> It's difficult to escape the trap of those [NGO] people; they use food as bait to get you to have sex with them (cited in Naik, 2002).
> An NGO worker made me pregnant but now he left me and is loving to another young girl (cited in Naik, 2002).

International peacekeepers have also been implicated in sexual violence against women and girls. In Sierra Leone, Human Rights Watch has documented many cases of sexual violence by peacekeepers for the United Nations Mission in Sierra Leone (UNAMSIL). This has included the rape of a twelve-year-old girl by a Guinean peacekeeping soldier in March 2001, and the gang rape of a woman by two Ukrainian peacekeepers in April 2002 (Human Rights Watch, 2003). Similar allegations have been reported against peacekeepers in the Democratic Republic of the Congo where six Nepali UN peacekeepers were recently sentenced to three months in jail after a general court martial found them guilty of sexual offences (Aljazeera, 2005). Machel (2000) has noted that the arrival of peacekeeping troops has been associated with a rapid rise in child prostitution. However, there appears to be reluctance on the part of the UN to investigate and take disciplinary measures against

---

[7] While males appear to be the main perpetrators of wartime sexual violence, it should be noted that sexual violence perpetrated by females has been reported in several armed conflicts (HRW, 2003: 41).

peacekeepers (Women's Commission, 2002). Nonetheless, testimonies from survivors corroborate that the problem exists. As one refugee child noted:

> When ma asked me to go to the stream to wash plates, a peacekeeper asked me to take my clothes off so that he can take a picture. When I asked him to give me money he told me, no money for children, only biscuit (cited in Naik, 2002).

3. 'RATIONAL' MADNESS: UNDERSTANDING SEXUAL VIOLENCE AS A STRATEGY OF WAR

Wartime violence of any sort, particularly violence inflicted on civilians, can easily be perceived by outsiders as senseless, chaotic and mindless. However, such portrayals obscure the reality that wartime violence against civilians, particularly sexual violence, is often a deliberate and organized part of official military policies. When examining sexual violence during conflict, it becomes evident that it is not simply an isolated incident or a sideline atrocity. Instead, it is a method of waging war - an extension of the battlefield and an integral tool for achieving military objectives. As Omanyondo Ohambe et al. (2005) found in their research on victims of sexual violence in the Democratic Republic of Congo, wartime rape is often planned and organized in advance. This section explores the 'functions' of wartime sexual violence, which include symbolic humiliation and terror, reasserting gendered power relations, and boosting the morale of soldiers.

3.1 Symbolic Humiliation and Terror

Wartime sexual violence is said to be used as a deliberate weapon of war to humiliate, demoralize, and weaken the identity and pride of the perceived enemy (Omanyondo Ohambe et al. 2005; Neill, 2000). The humiliation and terror that is inflicted is not only meant to degrade and dehumanize the individual girl or woman, but also to strip the humanity from the larger group from which she a part, and to instil a broader social degradation. In this sense, sexual violence during war can be considered a symbolic war - one waged on the physical bodies of those least able to protect themselves and least implicated in the war effort – girls and women.

Sexual violence is also used as a message of defeat - a form of communication whereby the message transmitted is that the men are not able to protect 'their' women and children, throwing into question both their masculinity and their competence (Seifert, 1994). Similarly, it is also said to send a message of defeat to the state - if a state is so weak as to allow women and children to be victimized, how can it successfully govern a population?

3.2 Reasserting Gendered Power Relations

Many scholars have argued that attempting to analyze wartime sexual violence without analyzing how it is a reflection of male and female relations is inherently deficient (Copelon,

1995). As Copelon (1995: 207) notes: 'emphasis on the gender dimension of rape in war is critical not only to surfacing women and girls as full subjects of sexual violence in war but also to recognizing the atrocity of rape in so-called times of peace.'

While authors may differ slightly in their approach, many agree that wartime sexual violence functions to assert and affirm gendered power relations. Seifert (1994) has maintained that rape and other forms of sexual violence are extreme acts of violence against females that would not be possible without hostility toward females. Accordingly, wartime sexual violence can be regarded as culturally rooted contempt for females that is lived out in times of crisis. Thus, females regardless of their ethnic, religious, or political belonging, become more susceptible to sexual violence in war than males (Skjelsbaek, 2001). This explanation accounts for why in the war in Bosnia-Herzegovina, Serb, Croat, and Bosnian females were raped, as well as both Hutu and Tutsi females during the genocide in Rwanda.

Skjelsbaek (2001) provides a complex account of wartime gendered power relations and, in turn, the meaning and function of rape. She argues that wartime sexual violence becomes a transaction of identities between the perpetrators and victims whereby females in war are targeted to masculinize the identity of the perpetrator, and to simultaneously feminize the identity of the victim. Moreover, the masculinized identities are situated in a hierarchical power relationship where masculinized identities are ascribed power and feminized identities are not.

3.3 Boosting the Morale of Soldiers

Another function of sexual violence during war is to boost the morale of soldiers (Omanyondo Ohambe et al., 2005). Historically, there has been a military commitment to the idea that soldiers deserve and need females for sexual gratification to enable them to continue to fight and kill (Brownmiller, 1975). Within this context, it has been argued that sexual violence is used to 'reward' soldiers for their efforts. For example, in Sierra Leone, after capturing a town or village, the rebel Revolutionary United Front (RUF) combatants rewarded themselves by looting and raping females. One of the RUF's military operations, aptly named 'Operation Pay Yourself', reflects the organized and deliberate nature of such activities. Sexual violence may also be used as a reward following active participation in combat (Maclure and Denov, in press). As this Sierra Leonean former boy soldier explained:

> If you carried out amputations and were very brave in combat you were offered promotion…[Once promoted] you got to choose the girl that you liked and wanted to be with. Girls were used as gifts. I had three wives (Maclure and Denov, in press: p. 20).

It is clear that sexual violence under such circumstances is not simply related to sexual gratification, but perhaps more importantly, to the search for power, authority and supremacy over those less powerful – particularly defenceless girls.

Evidently, a tangled web of political, ideological, psychological, and socio-cultural factors underlie these acts of extreme violence (Omanyondo Ohambe et al., 2005). Regardless of the multitude of underlying factors, sexual violence appears to be extremely effective as a weapon of war. Sexual violence destroys life, it produces unwanted life, it brings forth community upheaval, it damages cultural and religious beliefs, and it reaffirms the vulnerability of females in relation to males.

4. THE EFFECTS OF WARTIME SEXUAL VIOLENCE ON GIRLS

Sexual violence often continues to impact the physical and mental well-being of survivors long after the attack(s). Survivors of wartime sexual violence face overwhelming problems including severe physical and psychological health problems, social isolation and ostracism.

4.1 Physical and Psychological Health Problems

Doctors treating rape victims following armed conflict note that the most common medical problems are sexually transmitted diseases, such as syphilis, gonorrhea or vaginitis. Other medical problems include AIDS[8], vesico-vaginal fistula, and complications from self-induced or clandestine abortions. Doctors have also performed reconstructive surgery for those who were victims of sexual mutilation (HRW, 1996).

For females who become pregnant from rape, many experience severe medical problems as a result of complications from unassisted births. In Sierra Leone, there is evidence that some pregnant girls held captive by rebel soldiers underwent birthing practices which were reported to include jumping on the abdomens of expectant girls, or inserting objects into their vaginas to induce labour or, if the forces needed to move quickly, they were reported to tie the girls' legs together to delay birth (Mazurana and McKay, 2001). Such practices may lead to life-long gynecological complications (McKay, 1998).

It is important to note that in some countries affected by armed conflict, the lack of accessible of health facilities, transport, lack of money for transport, medical treatment and drugs has meant that the health status of survivors of sexual violence is often poor (PHR, 2002:45). Moreover, many girls avoid seeking medical treatment out of fear of being judged and rejected (McKay, 1998). As this survivor notes:

> I didn't want to tell anyone what happened...I was ashamed...I felt so bad because I wanted to save myself for someone special...when I think of them I feel so angry (HRW, 2003:53).

Indeed, there are devastating psychological after-effects of wartime sexual violence. Many victims experience anguish, flashbacks, persistent fears, difficulty re-establishing intimate relationships, a blunting of enjoyment in life, shame, and are unable to have normal sexual or childbearing experiences (Fisher, 1996). Girls forced to carry and bear the children of their aggressors may suffer serious mental, physical and spiritual harm (McKay, 1998). On

---

[8] While it is impossible to reach any firm conclusion about the transmission of AIDS as a result of rape or sexual violence (because of the difficulty of ascertaining when a given individual was exposed to the virus), it is certain that some girls and women are infected with the virus as a result of sexual violence (HRW, 1996). In Rwanda, thousands of pregnant girls and young women who were raped between April and July 1994 have tested positive for the HIV virus (HRW, 1996).

the whole, the psychosocial effects of wartime rape are difficult to resolve and, for the most part, have been ignored in post-conflict situations. As a physician treating Rwandan sexual violence survivors noted in 1996:

> It has been 2 years since the war, but these patients are very difficult to cure. Initially they come in with infections, vaginal infections, urinary-tract problems, problems that are sexually transmitted. You cure the direct illness, but psychologically they are not healed. They continue to come back complaining of cramps or pains, but there is nothing physically wrong with them. The[y] are profoundly marked psychologically. Medically they are healed but they continue to be sick. And there are no services that specifically deal with the problems that the[y] have (cited in HRW, 1996: 45).

4.2 Social Isolation and Ostracism

Sexual violence such as rape can carry severe social stigma. Many sexually victimized girls do not reveal their experiences publicly as they fear rejection by their family and the broader community. While some may fear retribution from their attackers for speaking out, others fear that they will never be able to marry if they disclose they were raped. In societies where females are valued primarily for their role as wives and mothers, the issue of marriageability is extremely important. For many girls, marriage is their best option to obtain economic security and protection. In such contexts, the social stigma surrounding rape has severe consequences. Girls who are cast out and stripped of their social standing may lose their access to an agricultural livelihood in rural societies, thus suffering enormous economic consequences. Such consequences are common knowledge and in the context of civil war, combatants may make deliberate use of this social information (Turshen, 2000).

Importantly, it is not only the individual rape victim who may suffer as a result of stigma and ostracism. In cases where girls have given birth to children of their aggressors, in some contexts these babies, who are often referred to as 'children of hate' or 'devil's children', may, in some cases, be rejected or vilified by their mother and the broader family and community (Carpenter, 2000).

5. INTERNATIONAL RESPONSES TO WARTIME SEXUAL VIOLENCE

International law has prohibited rape and other forms of sexual violence against females during armed conflict for over a century. International humanitarian law, also known as the laws of war, sets out protections for civilians, prisoners of war, and other non-combatants during international and civil armed conflicts. The four Geneva Conventions and their two Additional Protocols implicitly and explicitly condemn rape and other forms of sexual violence as serious violations of humanitarian law in both international and internal conflicts. Common Article 3 of the 1949 Geneva Convention expressly forbids: "…violence to life and person, in particular murders of all kinds, mutilation, cruel treatment and torture;…outrages upon personal dignity, in particular, humiliating and degrading treatment". In international armed conflicts, such crimes are grave breaches of the Geneva Conventions and are considered war crimes. Perpetrators can be held accountable for rape and other forms of sexual violence as war crimes, crimes against humanity, and as acts of genocide. International human rights law, which is applicable during armed conflict, also prohibits sexual violence and sexual slavery (Machel, 2000; HRW, 2003).

In spite of the prevalence of sexual violence during war, and its devastating impact on victims, according to the UN Special Rapporteur on violence against women, sexual violence 'remains the least condemned war crime' (UN, 1995). History has shown that sexual violence, particularly rape, has been insufficiently reported, condemned, and prosecuted as a war crime or a crime against humanity (Niarchos, 1995). Moreover, even with the presence of legal sanctions, crimes of rape have not necessarily translated into international legal action. Despite well-documented and publicized atrocities against women during World War I and World War II, the international military tribunals in both Nuremberg and the Far East (The Tokyo Tribunal[9]) never addressed rape explicitly under crimes against humanity or listed gender as one of the grounds of prosecution. Rather, the tribunals subsumed rape under the general category of 'ill treatment of the civilian population' (Brownmiller, 1975).

The conflicts in the former Yugoslavia and Rwanda have brought international attention to the issue of wartime sexual violence and following reports of widespread sexual atrocities, securing indictments for mass rapes became a political goal (Carpenter, 2000). Reports of mass rape were instrumental in the UN Security Council decisions to authorize the establishment of the International Criminal Tribunal for the former Yugoslavia (ICTY) in 1993 and the International Criminal Tribunal for Rwanda (ICTR) in 1994. Both tribunals, which have included rape in the specific list of crimes constituting crimes against humanity, and brought gender-based charges against the instigators of war crimes, represent a historic precedent in prosecuting sexual violence during armed conflict. The ICTY has implicit jurisdiction to prosecute crimes of sexual violence as grave breaches of international humanitarian law, and as violations of the laws and customs of war and genocide. The ICTR is empowered to prosecute rape as a serious violation of Common Article 3 of the Geneva Conventions and can prosecute crimes of sexual violence when they constitute torture or genocide.

Similarly, in recognition of the rampant sexual and gender-based violence that occurred throughout Sierra Leone's conflict, under the Special Court for Sierra Leone, acts of forced marriage are to be prosecuted as an 'inhumane act' – a crime against humanity – for the first time in the history of international law (Special Court for Sierra Leone, 2004). In fact, crimes against women and girls are the core charges for almost all of the 13 indictments issued by the Prosecutor's office, and include rape, sexual slavery, and mutilation (Denov, 2005). As the Chief Prosecutor explained:

> These additional charges of crimes against humanity reflect the fact that women and girls suffered greatly during the war, including through widespread forced marriage...The Office of the Prosecutor is committed to telling the world what happened in Sierra Leone during the war, and gender crimes have been at the core of our cases from the beginning. These new charges recognise another way that women and girls suffered during the conflict (Special Court for Sierra Leone, 2004).

---

[9] Although the Tokyo Tribunal was responsible for bringing international attention to atrocities, including sexual violence, the tribunal failed to prosecute members of the Japanese government and the military for the 200,000 'comfort women' forced into sexual slavery during the war (HRW, 2003).

The International Criminal Court[10] (ICC), which came into force in July 2002, has the potential to protect and promote the rights of women and girls, as it explicitly recognizes crimes of gender and sexual violence as war crimes and crimes against humanity. The Rome Statute of the ICC, adopted on 17 July, 1998 defines rape, sexual slavery, enforced prostitution, enforced sterilization, forced pregnancy and any other form of sexual violence as war crimes, whether committed in an international or non-international armed conflict (Rome Statute, Article 8 (2) (b) (xxii) and (e) (vi)). When such crimes are committed as part of a widespread or systematic attack against any civilian population, they are crimes against humanity (Rome Statute, 7 (1) (g)). Furthermore, the statute addresses the unique needs of victims by highlighting trauma counselling, rehabilitation, reparation, and compensation to victims of war crimes. It also calls for gender and child sensitive court procedures. While these are clearly important developments, Machel (2000) has noted that further efforts need to be made to assure a gender balance when nominating or promoting candidates for judicial and international bodies related to the peaceful settlement of disputes, including the ICTY, ICTR and the ICC. With regard to the ICC, there are currently eighteen judges who are permanent members of the Court. Of the eighteen judges, only seven are female. Moreover, Machel (2000) maintains that to ensure that the plight of victims of wartime sexual violence is sufficiently addressed, it is imperative that gender-specific training be provided for legal and medical program personnel, prosecutors, judges, and other professionals who are called upon to respond to crimes of sexual violence during conflict.

While the attention dedicated to the issue of wartime sexual violence within the ICTY, ICTR, the Special Court for Sierra Leone, and the ICC, illustrate the positive advancements that have been made, it is important to note, however, that there have been relatively few indictments for wartime sexual violence as compared to the thousands of offences committed. While the problem of impunity has plagued the crime of wartime sexual violence, the lack of prosecutions may also be related to victims being unwilling to testify at trial. Many survivors simply want to try to forget about the sexual violence and other human rights abuses they have been subjected to and get on with their lives in the aftermath of conflict. Other reasons include victims' shame and reluctance to present themselves in court, fear of reprisal from their perpetrators and/or community, and a lack of faith in the criminal justice system (Gardam and Charlesworth, 2000). Moreover, many survivors are unaware of their rights, which may be particularly problematic in contexts with high illiteracy rates, and where girls' status is low. The few indictments and the problems experienced by victims underscore the importance of overcoming impunity for gender-specific violence.

CONCLUSION

Child abuse takes many forms and touches the lives of children in a vast array of contexts, regions, and circumstances. While the issue of wartime sexual violence against girls is a horrific form of child abuse, until recently, little attention has been dedicated to the

---

[10] The International Criminal Court (ICC) is a permanent court capable of investigating and trying individuals of the most serious violations of international humanitarian and human rights law, namely war crimes, crimes against humanity and genocide. The court, created on the basis of the Rome Statute, officially came into force on 1 July 2002.

problem or to its long-term implications. The marginalization, suppression and normalization of sexual violence during armed conflict have worked to obscure the unique experiences and realities of war-affected girls. Furthermore, as this form of child abuse often occurs in regions of the world whereby, because of ongoing hostilities, documenting the problem and holding perpetrators accountable continues to be a challenge.

Given the profound physical, psychological, cultural, economic, and social implications of wartime sexual violence, the pursuit of reconciliation and societal reconstruction in the aftermath of conflict is enormously difficult. Although substantial humanitarian assistance in post-conflict societies has been aimed at helping to improve the welfare of war-affected children through improved health care, education, skills training, trauma counselling, and income-generating schemes, the foundations of structural violence, patriarchal authority, and the marginalization of the young (particularly girls) may be deeply rooted in the social fabric. As such, the satisfaction of the psycho-social needs of girl victims of sexual violence may be fraught with uncertainty and complexity. Clearly, the process of societal reconstruction in post-war contexts must be more responsive to girl victim's distinctive experiences and needs. In particular, social renewal, policy-making and programming must be expressly attuned to gender differentiation and to the ongoing potential for gender-based victimization and marginalization, both during and following armed conflict.

Although there have been recent positive strides made to recognize the experiences, trauma, and legal implications of wartime sexual violence, it is clear that the issue demands greater international incident reporting and monitoring. Moreover, greater action against the many individuals (whether soldiers, civilians, humanitarian workers, peacekeepers), factions, and governments responsible are necessary to bring a measure of accountability by ending impunity, and by allowing victims and their families to know that 'justice' has been attained. Importantly, attention is also needed to develop ways to prevent violations of international humanitarian law and other abuses, including sexual violence, during conflict.

Throughout the world, political rhetoric has increasingly emphasized the need to protect children from abuse and to ultimately put children first. However, within post-conflict societies where wartime abuses against children may have been rampant, the needs and best interests of children, particularly girls, may be inadequately addressed or actively undermined by mainstream models that fail to recognize the gender-specific human rights abuses and violations. Significant political will and adequate resources must follow an alleged commitment to children, particularly girls, if it is meant to represent real action, and not simply a reiteration of ongoing political rhetoric.

REFERENCES

Aljazeera (2005) *UN peacekeepers jailed for sex abuse*. Retrieved September 2, 2005 at: http://english.aljazeera.net/NR/exeres/8485B038-46BC-4D73-B7F3.

Amnesty International (2004) *No impunity for rape – a crime against humanity and a war crime*. Author.

Ashford, M.W., and Huet-Vaughn, Y. (1997). The impact of war on women. In Levy, B., and Sidel, V. (Eds). *War and public health*. New York: Oxford University Press.

Brownmiller, S. (1975) *Against our will: Men, women and rape*. New York: Simon and Shuster.

Cairns, E. (2005) Healing, reconciliation and the prevention of violence. *Journal of Social and Clinical Psychology*, 24, 3:335-337.

Carpenter, R. (2000). Surfacing children: limitations of genocidal rape discourse. *Human Rights Quarterly*, 22, 428-477.

Copelon, R. (1995). Gendered war crimes: Reconceptualizing rape in time of war. In Peteres, J. and Wolper, A. (eds) *Women's rights human rights*. New York: Routledge.

Denov, M. and Maclure, R. (in press) Engaging the Voices of Girls in the Aftermath of Sierra Leone's Conflict: Experiences and Perspectives in a Culture of Violence. *Anthropologica*, 48, 1.

Denov, M. (2005) Wartime sexual violence: Assessing a human security response to war-affected girls in Sierra Leone. Unpublished manuscript.

Eriksson, M. and Wallensteen, P. (2004) Armed conflict, 1989-2003. *Journal of Peace Research*, 41, 5, 625-636.

Fisher, F. (1996). Occupation of the womb: Forced impregnation as genocide. *Duke Law Journal*, 46: 91-133.

Fox, M. (2004) Girl Soldiers: Human Security and Gendered Identity. *Security Dialogue*, 35(4):465-479.

Gardam, J., and Charlesworth, H. (2000). Protection of women in armed conflict. *Human Rights Quarterly*, 22, 148-166.

Giles, W. and Hyndman, J. (eds.) (2004) *Sites of Violence: Gender and Conflict Zones*. Berkeley: University of California Press.

Globe and Mail (2005) UN moves to halt use of child soldiers. Retrieved July 27, 2005. http://www.theglobeandmail.com/servlet/story/RTGAM.20050727.wchildren0727/BNPrint/International/#

Handrahan, L. (2004) Conflict, Gender, Ethnicity and Post-Conflict Reconstruction. *Security Dialogue*. 35(4):429-445.

Higate, P. and Henry, M. (2004) Engendering (In)security in Peace Support Operations. *Security Dialogue*. 35(4):481-498.

Human Rights Watch (1996). *Shattered lives: Sexual violence during the Rwandan genocide and its aftermath*.

Human Rights Watch (2003). *We'll kill you if you cry: Sexual violence in the Sierra Leone conflict*. Volume 15, 1 (A).

Machel, G. (2000). *The Impact of Armed Conflict on Children*. Report of the Expert of the Secretary-General, submitted pursuant to General Assembly Resolution, 26 August.

Maclure, R. and Denov, M. (in press) 'I Didn't Want to Die So I Joined Them': Structuration and the Process of Becoming Boy Soldiers in Sierra Leone. *Journal of Terrorism and Political Violence.*

Mazurana, D. and McKay, D. (2001). Child soldiers: What about the girls? *Bulletin of the Atomic Scientists*, 57, 5: 30-35.

McKay, S. (1998) The effects of armed conflict on girls and women. *Peace and Conflict*, 4 (4): 381-392.

Naik, A. (2002). Protecting children from the protectors: Lessons from West Africa. *Forced Migration Review*, 15, 16-19.

Neill, K.G. (2000). Duty, honor, rape: sexual assault against women during war. *Journal of International Women's Studies, 2(1)*, [online].

Niarchos, C.N. (1995). Women, war, and rape: challenges facing the international tribunal for the former Yugoslavia. *Human Rights Quarterly*, 17, 649-690.

Omanyondo Ohambe, M., Berckmans Bahananga Muhigwa, J., Mulyumba Wa Mamba, B. (2005) *Women's Bodies as a Battleground: Sexual Violence Against Women and Girls During the War in the Democratic Republic of Congo South Kivu (1996-2003)*. International Alert.

Physicians for Human Rights (2002). *War-related sexual violence in Sierra Leone: A population-based assessment*. Boston: Physicians for Human Rights.

Seifert, R. (1994). War and rape: A preliminary analysis. In Stiglmayer, A. (ed.) *Mass rape: the war against women in Bosnia-Herzegovina*. Lincoln : University of Nebraska Press.

Seifert, R. (1996). The second front: the logic of sexual violence in wars. *Women's Studies International Forum,* 19, 1/2, 35-43.

Sideris, T. (2002). Problems of identity, solidarity and reconciliation. In Meintjes, S., Pillay, A. and Turshen, M. (eds.) *The aftermath: Women in post-conflict transformation*. New York: Zed Books.

Skjelsbaek, I. (2001). Sexual violence and war: Mapping out a complex relationship. *European Journal of International Relations*, 7, 2: 211-237.

Special Court for Sierra Leone – Office of the Prosecutor (2004) '*Prosecutor welcomes arraignment of RUF and AFRC indictees on charges related to forced marriage'*. Press Release 17 May.

Tetrault, M. (1997). Justice for all: Wartime rape and women's human rights. *Global Governance*, 3, 197-212.

Thorpe, C. (2002) *Statement at the UN Special Session on Children*. New York: UN.

Turshen, M. (2000). The political economy of violence against women during armed conflict in Uganda. *Social Research*, 67(3), 803-824.

Twagiramariya, C. and Turshen, M. (1998). 'Favours' to give and 'consenting' victims: The sexual politics of survival in Rwanda. In Turshen and Twagiramariya (eds.) *What women do in wartime: Gender and conflict in Africa*. London: Zed Books.

United Nations (1995). *Preliminary report submitted by the Special Rapporteur on violence against women*, E/CN.4/1995/42. p. 64.

United Nations (1998). *Contemporary Forms of Slavery: Systematic Rape, Sexual Slavery and Slavery-like Practices during Armed Conflict*, Final Report submitted by Ms. Gay J. McDougall, Special Rapporteur (New York: United Nations. E/CN.4/Sub. 2/1998/13, pp. 7-8.

UNHCR and Save the Children-UK (2002). *Sexual Violence and Exploitation: The Experience of Refugee Children in Guinea, Liberia and Sierra Leone*. [available on-line at: *www.unhcr.ch/cgi-bin/texis/vtx/home/opendoc*.pdf?id=3c7cf89a4andtbl=PARTNERS]

Women's Commission on Refugee Women and Children (2002). *Precious Resources: Adolescents in the reconstruction of Sierra Leone*. New York.

Zarkov, D. (2001). The body of the other man: Sexual violence and the construction of masculinity, sexuality and ethnicity in Croatian media. In Moser, C. and Clark, F. (eds.) *Victims, perpetrators or actors? Gender, armed conflict and political violence*. New York: Zed books.

INDEX

Q

R

S

T